THE IMPACT OF THE SIX-DAY WAR

The Impact of the Six-Day War

A Twenty-Year Assessment

Edited by
Stephen J. Roth
Director
Institute of Jewish Affairs

Editorial Consultants

Shlomo Avineri
Professor of Political Science
Hebrew University of Jerusalem

and

Itamar Rabinovich
Director of the Dayan Center
for Middle Eastern and African Studies
Tel Aviv University

MACMILLAN
PRESS

in association with the
INSTITUTE OF JEWISH AFFAIRS

First published 1988

Published by
THE MACMILLAN PRESS LTD
Houndmills, Basingstoke, Hampshire RG21 2XS
and London
Companies and representatives
throughout the world

Typeset by Wessex Typesetters
(Division of The Eastern Press Ltd)
Frome, Somerset

Printed in Great Britain by
Richard Clay Ltd, Bungay, Suffolk

British Library Cataloguing in Publication Data
The Impact of the Six-day war: a twenty
year assessment
1. Arab–Israeli War, 1967. International
political aspects, to 1987
I. Roth, S.J. II. Institute of Jewish
Affairs
956'.046
ISBN 0–333–47106–7

To the victims of the Six-Day War

Contents

Preface

The idea for this volume emerged from discussions with my colleagues in the Institute of Jewish Affairs. In our study of contemporary Jewish problems, we have consistently noticed the important changes which have occurred in and since 1967 – not only regarding Middle East issues but also the Jewish condition in the Diaspora, problems of anti-Semitism, the fate of Soviet Jewry and many other subjects. It became increasingly clear that many of these changes were connected with the Six-Day War. We therefore felt that, on the occasion of its twentieth anniversary, an assessment of the impact of the war should be undertaken.

I was fortunate in being able to enlist a number of distinguished contributors, each of them outstanding in their own field, and I want to thank them all for their contributions. The list includes, to my great pleasure, two Arabs. Some of their views may not be acceptable to many Jewish readers, but they are authentic and fairly representative. For that matter, many of the opinions of the Jewish contributors may not be shared by non-Jewish (or even Jewish) readers. The views they express, and their terminology (which in itself often reveals an ideological stance), are strictly their own. If, through the variety of these views, this volume stimulates further discussion of the issues, it will have achieved much of its purpose.

I also attempted to obtain a contribution from a leading Egyptian personality and from a Soviet scholar, in order to include a first-hand rendering of their respective perspectives. I regret that we could not obtain their co-operation.

The preparation of this volume was greately facilitated by the immediate willingness of two Israeli academics to act as editorial consultants: Professor Shlomo Avineri of the Hebrew University of Jerusalem and Professor Itamar Rabinovich of the University of Tel Aviv are distinguished experts on the politics of Israel and on the Middle East respectively. Their advice on the selection of contributors and their comments on the individual articles was tremendously helpful, and I wish to extend to them heartfelt expressions of my gratitude.

Two of my colleagues at the Institute of Jewish Affairs, Avriel Butovsky and Dr Barry Shenker, relieved me of most of the burden of sub-editing the texts, and made many perceptive comments on them. My thanks go to them for their assiduous labour.

Lastly I wish to thank my secretary, Mrs Claire Marks, for undertaking, among her numerous other duties, the typing of most of the manuscripts, as well as other colleagues at the Institute who helped in the preparation.

STEPHEN J. ROTH

Notes on the Contributors

Shlomo Avineri is Herbert Samuel Professor of Political Science at the Hebrew University of Jerusalem. From 1975 to 1977 he served as Director General of Israel's Ministry of Foreign Affairs. Among his many books are *Israel and the Palestinians* (1976) and *The Making of Modern Zionism: The Intellectual Origins of the Jewish State* (1981).

Haim Barkai is Professor of Economics and former Dean of Faculty of Social Sciences at the Hebrew University of Jerusalem, and Chairman of the Advisory Board of the Bank of Israel.

Amnon Cohen is Professor of History of the Muslim Peoples at the Hebrew University of Jerusalem, and Director of the Ben Zvi Institute for the Study of Eretz Israel. Former adviser on Arab Affairs in the West Bank Command. Author of a variety of books on Ottoman Palestine, as well as *Political Parties in the West Bank under the Hashemite Regime* (1973).

Abba Eban is Chairman of the Committee on Foreign Affairs and Defence of the Knesset, former Israeli Deputy Prime Minister, Minister of Foreign Affairs, Minister of Education and Culture, Ambassador to the United Nations and Ambassador to the United States.

Leonard Fein is a writer and teacher, and founding-editor of the magazine *Moment*. The subject of his article is dealt with at greater length in his recent book *Where Are We? The Inner Life of American Jews* (New York, 1988).

Itzhak Galnoor is Professor of Political Sciences at the Hebrew University of Jerusalem and a former Fellow of St Anthony's College, Oxford. He has written extensively on Israeli democracy, including *Steering the Polity: Communication and Politics in Israel* (1982).

General Shlomo Gazit is former Director General of the Jewish Agency for Israel. He served as the Co-ordinator of Israeli Government Operations in the administered territories (1967–74), and later served as Director of Military Intelligence (1974–79).

Zvi Gittelman is Professor of Political Science at the University of Michigan, Ann Arbor. He is author of numerous books of which the most recent is *A Century of Ambivalence: Jews in Russia and in the Soviet Union* (1988)

Atallah Mansour is a writer, journalist, veteran member of the editorial staff of *Ha'aretz*, and has written numerous political articles in magazines in various countries including the USA and the Soviet Union, as well as two novels and an autobiography. He was journalist in residence at Duke University, North Carolina and British Council scholar at Oxford University. He is the Editor of the weekly *Sennara*.

Ehud Olmert has been a member of the Israeli Knesset since 1973, representing Herut (Likud). He is a senior-ranking member of the Knesset's Foreign Relations Committee and a close confidant of Prime Minister Shamir. He is also a practising attorney in Jerusalem.

Itamar Rabinovich is Ettinger Professor of Contemporary Middle Eastern History at Tel Aviv University and Director of that university's Dayan Center of Middle Eastern and African Studies. He is the author, most recently, of *The War for Lebanon, 1970–1985* (1985).

Gideon Rafael is Visiting Professor at the Woodrow Wilson School of Princeton University. He is one of the founding members of the Israeli Foreign Ministry, was its Director General and served as Ambassador to a number of European countries and as Israel's permanent representative to the United Nations. He is the author of *Destination Peace: Three Decades of Israeli Foreign Policy* (1981).

Michael Rosenak is Morton and Barbara Mandel Assistant Professor of Jewish Education at the Hebrew University of Jerusalem. He is a former Director of the Melton Centre for Jewish Education in the Diaspora. His book *Commandments and Concerns: Jewish Religious Education in a Secular Society* was published in 1987. He contributed an article 'Theological Views of the State of Israel' in P. Mendes-Flohr and A. Cohen, *Contemporary Jewish Religious Thought* (1987).

Nathan Rotenstreich is Ahad Haam Professor of Philosophy and former Rector at the Hebrew University of Jerusalem. He is a founding member of the Israel Academy of Sciences and Humanities and past Chairman of its Humanities Section. He is also a former Vice-President of the *Institut International de Philosophie*, recipient of various honorary degrees and of the Israel Prize for the Humanities.

Stephen J. Roth is Director of the Institute of Jewish Affairs in London, former Chairman of the Foreign Affairs Committee of the Board of Deputies of British Jews (1979–85). He is an international lawyer and has contributed many articles to books and learned journals on contemporary Jewish problems.

Alvin Z. Rubinstein is Professor of Political Science at the University of Pennsylvania and Senior Fellow at the Foreign Policy Research Institute. He is the author of *Redstar on the Nile: The Soviet–Egyptian Influence Relationship since the June War* (1977).

Hanna Siniora is Editor-in-Chief of the Arab daily *Al Fajr* in East Jerusalem and one of the leading spokesmen of the Palestinians. He describes himself as 'an activist for peace'.

Steven Spiegel is Professor of Political Science at the University of California, Los Angeles. He has published widely on international politics and American foreign policy towards the Middle East. His latest book *The Other Arab–Israeli Conflict: Making America's Middle East Policy, from Truman to Reagan* (1985) received the 1986 National Jewish Book Award in the USA.

Harold M. Waller is Professor of Political Science at McGill University in Montreal where he has served as Chairman of the Department of Political Science. He has written extensively on Israeli politics and foreign policy.

Introduction
Stephen J. Roth

In 1988, the State of Israel reaches its fortieth anniversary. Almost half way through this span, the traumatic Six-Day War took place. Was it just one more war in the history of a troubled country and nation which, in its first twenty years, lived in a sea of hostility and has not achieved, even twenty years later, peace with all its neighbours? Or was the war a much more fundamental event which revolutionized the structure of Israel's politics and its relations with other countries, the Arab world, as well as world Jewry, and altered the original course of this new state?

The purpose of this volume is to try to seek some answers to these questions.

Twenty years may be too short a period for historians to make a sober retrospective assessment of the events of 1967. But the situation of 1967 did not remain static. The changes that occurred then had an impact that has lasted until today, and no terminal line where these changes may cease to influence events is in sight. In posing the question of the Six-Day War's revolutionary character, it is these repercussions which need assessing, rather than the war itself with all its surrounding circumstances. This is why we have invited not so much historians but rather political scientists and sociologists, as well as practitioners of statecraft, to analyze the trends and events of the subsequent twenty years and to identify, as far as this is possible, whether – and how far – they stem from the Six-Day War.

There are four main areas in which this enquiry appears particularly apposite. The first is Arab–Israeli relations and, through this, the wider Middle East scene. The second, closely related to the first, is the attitude of other nations – primarily the superpowers – to Israel and the Arab–Israeli conflict. The third and fourth areas are more introspective but equally important: the Six-Day War's impact on Israeli politics and society, and on world Jewry and Zionism.

A summation of the conclusions of our eighteen contributors is left to the reader. However, certain signposts can already be highlighted in this introduction.

There is no doubt that the war of 1967 in itself – if one can at all look at such an event in isolation – had something of a special character. Although only in existence for nineteen years, the State of Israel was already used to wars. Its creation had to be asserted in a War of Independence in 1948, and before completing its first decade, it was engaged in the Sinai Campaign of 1956. In between, Israel was permanently exposed to the incursions of hostile marauders from the neighbouring countries (which actually led to the 1956 war). If the 1967 victory is judged by what some religious Jews interpreted as a *miracle*, 1948 was an equal – or perhaps even greater – miracle; because then the Israeli population, just making its declaration of independence, had no army worth speaking of and only few weapons. If the *size* and *speed* of the 1967 victory is taken as a test, the Sinai campaign was no less stupendous a feat. Yet 1967 was different for two other reasons. The first was the genuine fear of extinction prior to the Six-Day War which gripped many in Israel (and among world Jewry) in those days and weeks when the United Nations troops were removed, at Nasser's behest, from the Sinai Peninsula and the Arabs threatened to destroy Israel and drive all Jews into the sea. For Jews worldwide, it poignantly revived all the memories of the Holocaust. I recall from the welter of newspaper comment in those harrowing days, a letter in the British press from a group of eminent writers which started with the words: 'Israel is a state the size of Wales: it is girding itself to prevent another Auschwitz'. There was no exaggeration in this succinct description of the precariousness of the situation and the perception of the danger. The second reason for the apocalyptic character of the Six-Day War was the unwillingness of any nation or international body to break Egypt's blockade of the Straits of Tiran which threatened to strangle Israel. Israel saw itself as utterly alone and here, too, the parallel with the abandonment of Jewry during the Nazi genocide was all too obvious.

Extinction was also feared in 1948, but it was thought less of a realistic danger, given the fact that the invading Arab armies were then far less strong, and mainly because Israel had the support of the United Nations, the Western countries – with the exception of Great Britain – and most effectively of the Soviet bloc which supplied arms to relieve the beleaguered Israelis. There was thus no isolation then, and even less so in the 1956 war, conducted with the support of Great Britain and France.

But, despite these cataclysmic features, the Six-Day War in itself might have had a lasting revolutionary effect only on the third and fourth areas of our investigation – Israeli society and world Jewry. For a people downtrodden for 2000 years, the pride and joy of a great victory had enormous significance. Among the Jews of the world it produced a paroxysm of solidarity with Israel and, among many, it evoked hitherto only latent bonds with their Jewishness. In Israel, it led to the discovery – emotionally as well as rationally – of a true ally, the only one they had – the Jewish people.

The other undoubted effects of the Six-Day War derive, however, mainly from its aftermath. To elucidate this point, let us assume for a moment that King Hussein had heeded the insistent pleas of Israeli Prime Minister Levi Eshkol in the first hours of the fighting not to join Egypt and Syria in the war. Israel would still have occupied the Sinai Peninsula in a rapid six-day campaign, it would have repelled the Syrian troops and taken the Golan Heights, but the West Bank with its 845 000 Arab inhabitants, including the Old City of Jerusalem, would have remained in Jordanian hands. Some territories – Sinai, Gaza and Golan – would have come under Israeli occupation, but only a much smaller Arab population, mainly in the Gaza Strip. Thus, for the Arabs, the outcome of such a more limited war would have meant far fewer additional Arabs under Jewish rule; and, for the Jews, no sizeable territories of biblical *Eretz Israel* (the Land of Israel) reconquered. A war would still have taken place with a dramatic Israeli victory, but these two crucial elements – which had deep emotional significance to Jews and Arabs alike, and which consequently have influenced Jewish and Arab thinking ever since – would have been absent.

That does not mean that without the conquest of the West Bank the Arab–Israeli problem would have disappeared; that conflict existed, after all, from the outset and became manifestly violent as long ago as 1920. Nor does it mean that without the new problems created by the territories' 'occupation' or 'liberation' (everybody can choose his or her preferred terminology), peace would have been more easily attainable; on the contrary, there is a widespread belief that only by holding valuable territories and offering them in exchange for peace, can a settlement be hoped for. Perhaps even the conquest of the West Bank would not have changed matters materially if it had been followed by a quick settlement. What exacerbated the conflict after the Six-Day War was the continued Israeli rule, by now lasting for over twenty years, over the West Bank and its large Arab population. It added not just one more element to Arab–Israeli relations, but a qualitatively different one – and therein lies the revolutionary character not of the war itself, but of its prolonged consequences.

These qualitative differences emerge very clearly from the analyses contained in this volume. For the Arabs in the West Bank who, under nineteen years of Jordanian rule (1948–67), accepted their non-independent status and who even approved of Jordanian rule of a territory which (according to the UN partition resolution of 1947) should have been a separate Arab state, the occupation of the West Bank gave an impetus – even more than the creation of Israel itself – to the development of a Palestinian identity and of Palestinian aspirations. Many of the Israeli Arabs – i.e., those living inside Israel's pre-1967 borders – also gradually changed their self-perception from living as a minority in a – for them – alien Jewish state, into being part of a Palestinian nation; thus many became 'Palestinianized' to a certain degree. The views of the Arabs in Israel and in the West Bank respectively are expressed in this volume by prominent members of their own communities. The Jews, who set out on their state-building venture with the noblest ideals of democracy and humanitarian principles, suddenly found themselves in the position of occupiers, a position which, even with the most benign occupation, is inherently anti-democratic and anti-humanitarian, and doubly so when the occupation has to cope with the active hostility of the occupied population. Any occupation harms the morale of occupier and occupied alike; nor could Israel escape either from its prolonged – if unwanted – role as a conquering nation gnawing at its basically healthy body. The occupation completely changed the tenor and the context of the political debate in Israel. Everything now had to be discussed in the context of war and peace, and of what to do with the territories. Festering frustration at not being able to solve the problem produced extremes on both sides. Increasing clashes with a recalcitrant population under Israeli rule inevitably led to resentment which created among Israeli Jews – fortunately only in limited circles – a hitherto unknown excessive nationalism and intolerance.

The changed geopolitical scene was bound to influence the attitude of other nations toward the Arab–Israeli conflict, first of all that of the superpowers, but even of smaller states. Between 1949 and 1967, most of the outside world considered that the problem of Palestine had been solved *de facto* by partition, and that sooner or later this could be turned into a *de jure* situation. 1967 provoked new approaches. The United Nations, which had originally signed the birth certificate of the State of Israel, now became the forum where attempts to delegitimize Israel were concentrated. World Jewry, elated by a Jewish victory and invigorated by a novel identity through its link with the Jewish state, experienced a new wave of anti-Jewishness, this time in the form of anti-Zionism, which was directly related to the changed situation in the Middle East. Anti-Zionism, of course, existed before, but it could be viewed as a reasonably tolerable intellectual negation of an ideology which offered a particular interpretation of Jewish history and a practical proposition to change its course by self-determination and independence. After the Six-Day War anti-Zionism deteriorated into a complete distortion of the meaning of Zionism, and assumed virulent and often violent forms which are deeply hurtful to Jewish dignity and even to Jewish interests. Zionism itself has been going through an ideological self-appraisal. It is arguable whether Zionism was ever sufficiently prepared to face the Arab problem; it certainly was not, and could not be, prepared to face Arabs in a situation of military occupation.

All these changes can rightly be termed 'revolutionary', and all have their direct roots in the Six-Day War. Revolutionary upheavals of this nature deserve expert analysis and thoughtful evaluation. It is hoped that this volume will provide it.

The manuscript of this volume was completed well before the beginning of the uprisings in the Gaza Strip and the West Bank on 9 December 1987. The facts and impact of these significant developments could therefore not be taken into account in the various articles.

Part I

The Arab–Israeli Conflict

1 Twenty Years in Retrospect: 1967–87

Gideon Rafael

The Six-Day War did not strike with the suddenness of a bolt from the blue. For weeks, the clouds of war had been gathering. In fact, the sky covering the Israeli–Arab area had never been bright since the invading armies from seven Arab countries tried to strangle Israel at its rebirth in 1948. Even when defeated, unrelenting hostility, although outlawed by the United Nations, continued to darken the Arab–Israeli horizon.

On 5 June 1967 hostility erupted into full-scale war for the third time in twenty years. Slow as the build-up to the war had been, as swiftly came its end. Six days after the first shots were exchanged, Israeli forces reached the Suez Canal, and were entrenched in Kuneitra on the Golan Heights.

The suddenness of victory stunned Israel's enemies and elated its friends. But neither was prepared to deal with the political aftermath of the war. The Israeli government, however, acted with alacrity nine days after the end of the fighting. The Government of National Unity, led by Levi Eshkol and counting among its members Menachem Begin, formulated its peace proposals. Two days later they were submitted by Foreign Minister Abba Eban to Secretary of State Dean Rusk.

The peace plan subordinated Israel's territorial claims to the postulates of permanent peace and security. It was based on the international boundaries which had existed between British-administered Palestine, Egypt and Syria, respectively. In the context of a peace treaty, Israel envisaged only such changes which security requirements in the South and the unimpaired free flow of the Jordan headwaters in the North necessitated. It contained provisions for the demilitarization of the evacuated areas and confirmed the government's willingness to consider a special status for the protection of, and access to, the holy places of all faiths in Jerusalem.

On the future dispositions in the West Bank and Gaza Strip, the cabinet decided to pronounce at a later stage since the coalition partners had as yet been unable to reach consent. They were torn

3

between two conceptions. The Labour Party and its allies sought to reach an agreement with King Hussein restoring Jordanian rule over most of the West Bank, taking into account territorial changes required for Israel's security. Herut (Begin's party) and its partners advocated a close association between the West Bank and Israel, leading, eventually, to its incorporation into Greater Israel.

CONFLICTING OBJECTIVES

Secretary of State Rusk, impressed by the realism and moderation of the proposals, transmitted them to the principal Arab capitals for consideration. Bouncing off the wall of Arab hostility, they did not even succeed in denting it. Vanquished in the field of battle the Arab governments hoped – with the help of their Soviet allies and Third World supporters – to snatch political victory from the jaws of military defeat. For them, the United Nations with its anti-Western voting blocs offered the ideal battleground. The Arab states, frustrated by the United States's powerful position in the Security Council, transferred their fight to the General Assembly, where they pursued their three main objectives:

(a) The immediate, unconditional and total withdrawal of Israel's forces from all the territories occupied by them in the course of the fighting
(b) the condemnation of Israel as aggressor
(c) full compensation for all war damages.

Israel confronted the Arab claims with its own three principal aims:

(a) to prevent the adoption of any resolution calling for the withdrawal of armed forces prior to the establishment of peace
(b) to oppose any reconstruction of the collapsed armistice regime, insisting on its replacement by a lasting contractual peace freely and directly negotiated between the parties
(c) to cooperate closely with the United States, to avoid the reactivation of that fatal American–Russian squeeze which in the wake of the Sinai–Suez campaign in 1956 had cracked the position of America's friends and allies and enabled its foes to regain their strength.

While none of the Arab demands was endorsed by the United Nations, Israel's main objective became embodied in Resolution 242 (adopted by the Security Council on 22 November 1967) and later in its companion Resolution 338 of 22 October 1973, ending the Yom Kippur War with an injunction on the parties to enter immediately into direct negotiations.

The two resolutions, taken together, established the guidelines for a peaceful settlement of the conflict. They called for:

(a) the establishment of a just and lasting peace between Israel and the Arab states
(b) the withdrawal of Israeli forces to secure and recognized boundaries to take place within the terms of a freely negotiated peace treaty
(c) the peace to be negotiated directly between the parties under suitable auspices
(d) a United Nations Special Representative to render his good offices
(e) assurance of the unrestricted freedom of navigation through all international waterways in the area
(f) the necessity for a just solution to the refugee problem.

The two Security Council Resolutions, postulating these six essentials of peace, have remained to this day the only accepted – though differently interpreted – common denominator for the peaceful settlement of the Arab–Israeli conflict. They constitute the master key designed to unlock the deadlock that has lasted for nearly four decades.

Decisive political and military events divide the two decades which have passed since the Six-Day War into two periods of similar duration: the first extending from the adoption of Resolution 242 in November 1967 to President Sadat's audacious peace initiative in November 1977, exactly ten years later; and the second lasting until 1987, marked by the conclusion of the Egyptian–Israeli peace treaty and the war in Lebanon.

The political stalemate persisted in defiance of numerous diplomatic efforts; these included the mission of United Nations Special Representative, Ambassador Gunnar Jarring, and marks the first decade. The deadlock prompted Egypt to try to break it by military action – first by Nasser's war of attrition, lasting until August 1970, and then, three years later, by Sadat's attack on the day of Yom Kippur 1973.

The strict interdictions of the Arab League summit conference in August 1967, the celebrated 'three nos of Khartoum' – no negotiations, no recognition and no peace with Israel – continued to dominate the diplomatic scene of the Arab–Israeli conflict until the Yom Kippur War.

UNDER ISRAELI RULE

While the diplomatic process between the Arab states and Israel was stalled, the Israeli administration of the West Bank and Gaza Strip, with its jurisdiction over more than 1 million Palestinians, did not allow standstill or passivity. Whatever Israel's ultimate intentions in regard to the final status of the West Bank and Gaza Strip were, during the first decade, while Labour was in power, it intended to return their major part to Arab rule. In the absence of a peaceful settlement, however, Israel was left with the task of governing the territories. Its military and civilian authorities, inexperienced and unaccustomed to their new role as an occupying power, groped with a variety of improvizations designed to reassure a fearful and hostile population. They had to ensure the continuation of normal civilian activities, regulate the uninterrupted flow of trade and traffic between the West Bank and Jordan, maintain law and order, and protect the safety of the armed forces and the security of Israel. It was a tall order, requiring for its implementation a well-measured mix of ingenuity, firmness, flexibility and minimal intervention in the day-to-day affairs of the local population.

The Palestinians, who had expected the worst from the 'Israeli occupier', recovered relatively quickly from the shock of the collapse of Jordanian rule. However, when they realized in the course of time that the prospects of an early return to Arab rule were receding, their impatience, discontent and self-assertion grew. With the waning of the attachment to Jordan, the influence of Arafat's PLO increased steadily, reaching a high point when the Arab summit conference at Rabat in 1974 proclaimed the PLO as the sole legitimate representative of the Palestinian people.

Frustration, fanned by PLO instigation, resulted in the sporadic outbreak of disorders and terrorist activity, prompting the Israeli military authorities to enact at times rather stern counter-measures. The more the Arab states entrenched themselves in their rejection of negotiations with Israel, notwithstanding the fact that King Hussein maintained a running, but inconclusive secret dialogue with high-ranking representatives of Israel, the national consciousness of the Palestinians solidified into a determined national will of self-determination – to be realized either within the framework of a Jordanian–Palestinian confederation or of an independent sovereign state.

INTERNATIONAL REACTIONS

The Six-Day War had, of course, international repercussions extending far beyond the immediate area of the Arab–Israeli conflict. It affected not only Israel's standing in the world and the pattern of its international relations, but no less the relationships of the superpowers and their positions in the Middle East.

The demonstration of Israel's military ability impressed the Arab governments and public in at least two ways. On the one hand, it deepened their resentment against the Jewish state in their midst, and on the other it initiated a process of rational assessment, concluding that in the foreseeable future the Arab states were not in a position to overcome Israel by military means. Both trends existed side by side during the first decade, with ideological rejection prevailing over pragmatic accommodation to the actual realities.

In Third World countries, feelings about Israel's victory were also mixed. They ranged from respect and even admiration for Israel's resilience, to solidarity with the Arabs, defeated and humiliated by a country closely associated with the Western world. The bloc of the so-called 'non-aligned states' had never practised a policy of strict neutrality. In most international conflicts the majority of them demonstrated their non-alignment by acting against the Western world and lining up in support of the Soviet bloc. These two sentiments – solidarity with their non-aligned Arab friends and sympathy for Soviet policies – prompted a number of Third World countries, predominantly in Africa, to sever diplomatic relations with Israel. Still, this was only the beginning of a process which, after the Yom Kippur War, led to a mass defection. Israel's African friends were now motivated not so much by sympathy with the Arab people as with the lure of rich remuneration from the oil-rich states basking in their new wealth.

However hurtful the default of the non-aligned states was, its political implications were insignificant in comparison with the step the Soviet Union took against Israel. On 10 June, the last day of the Six-Day War, Moscow announced the rupture of its relations with Israel. All states of the Soviet bloc, with the laudable exception of Romania and the regrettable addition of Yugoslavia, acted in unison. Notwithstanding the diplomatic vacuum and the vehement Soviet propaganda campaign against Israel, encouraging and siding with the latter's worst enemies, Moscow never interrupted completely its contacts with the Israeli government.

The foreign ministers of the two countries continued to meet over the years at the annual sessions of the United Nations General Assembly for serious but fruitless exchanges of views. Moreover, Israel agreed to participate in the Arab–Israeli peace conference in Geneva in 1973 under joint Soviet–US auspices. Even so, at the nadir of Soviet–Israeli relations – caused not only by massive Soviet arms deliveries to the Arab states at war with Israel, but also by the steadily increasing repression of Soviet Jewry and the toleration of a spreading anti-Jewish hate campaign – in the 1970s the Soviet government permitted the emigration of nearly 270 000 Jews, 164 000 of them settling in Israel.

The balance of gain and loss shows that Moscow derived hardly any benefits, if any at all, from its support of the Arab side. After President Sadat expelled the Soviet corps of military advisers in 1972, the Soviet Union concentrated its efforts on establishing bridgeheads in South Yemen and Somalia, astride the maritime oil lanes in the Red Sea. In the northern part of the region it made heavy political and material investments, establishing an impressive military presence in Syria; in North Africa it poured, at considerable profit, huge quantities of armaments into Lybia without gaining a stable strategic foothold in the Mediterranean basin. Intervening on the side of Ethiopia, Moscow lost its stronghold in Somalia.

Not even Soviet support of Egypt and Syria in the Yom Kippur War helped advance its overall position in the Middle East. Only by cooperating with the United States in terminating the fighting – when the fortunes of war had turned against Egypt and when the threat of a confrontation alarmed the superpowers – could the Soviet Union gain its cosponsorship of the Geneva Peace Conference in December 1973. However, its entirely one-sided political identification with the Arabs precluded any positive Soviet contribution to the peace process. At the end of the first decade the Soviet Union was completely excluded from the ongoing peace negotiations between Egypt and Israel conducted under United States' auspices.

Gideon Rafael

9

The Six-Day War affected the United States' position in the Middle East in a positive and a negative way. Egypt, Syria, Iraq and other Arab states cut their diplomatic ties with Washington, alleging that it had actively intervened in the war on the side of Israel. Apart from propaganda fiction these insinuations were apparently based on President Johnson's decision to move units of the Sixth Fleet 300 miles east, when the Soviet Union threatened to intervene actively on the side of the Syrians. The quick American reaction cautioned the Soviet Union, encouraged Israel, dispirited Syria and its allies, and produced an immediate halt in the fighting.

Despite the rupture of relations, Washington sustained an ongoing diplomatic dialogue with Cairo and Damascus – not to speak of Amman, which had retained its formal links – where United States' influence increased considerably after 1967. Egypt and Syria resumed their relations with the United States after the Yom Kippur War and Iraq followed suit a few years later, constrained by the exigencies of its war with Iran.

Israel's impressive military performance and America's steadfast material and political succour, the deepening awareness of Israel's key position in the Middle East, the conspicuous expression in word and deed of Jewish elation at Israel's deliverance from its enemies, converged into a formidable flow of friendship, fertilizing and solidifying the relationship between the United States and Israel. It was put to its severest test during the war of 1973. Israel, unprepared for the sudden Egyptian–Syrian onslaught, incurred serious initial losses, compelling it to ask the United States for an immediate massive airlift of military supplies. Washington's effective response helped turn the tide. At the end of nearly three weeks of fighting the Israel army had advanced to a point 100 kilometres distant from Cairo, while its artillery was in range of the outskirts of Damascus. Although Soviet threats played an important part in halting the further advance of the Israeli forces and in saving the encircled Egyptian Third Army from capitulation, it was Washington's influence with Jerusalem that brought about the termination of the fighting and the ensuing agreements on the separation of the hostile armies in the Suez Canal area and the Golan Heights. These agreements, concluded in 1974 and 1975, formed the foundation stones for the erection of the Egyptian–Israeli edifice of peace.

Israel's position in Western Europe in the wake of the Six-Day War underwent two contrary developments. It improved in Germany and the Benelux countries, which rejoiced in Israel's victorious emergence from the ordeal, as well as in Britain, which was impressed by the decisiveness of its military performance; it deteriorated sharply in de Gaulle's France. This was not only the result of de Gaulle's personal pique because his stern warning to Israel – *ne faites pas la guerre* – had been ignored, but was also largely caused by the shift in France's Near East policy after its withdrawal from Algeria, Tunisia and Morocco. The 'alliance' with Israel, as de Gaulle had praised the relationship existing between the two countries until 1967, had ceased to be a strategic asset for France, which concentrated after the settlement of the Algerian War on furthering its political influence and commercial interests in the Arab world.

The most far-reaching effect of the French–Israeli estrangement was caused by the arms embargo, imposed by France a few days before the outbreak of the Six-Day War. The cessation of arms deliveries, contracted a long time before, by Israel's principal supplier provoked a deep shock in Israel. The conclusions which it drew from this grim experience of abandonment were twofold: to spare no effort to induce the United States' government to replace France as its main source of arms supplies, and to extend its own arms industry, until then still rather limited, to new dimensions of mass production of nearly all the conventional types of military materiel and to expand its research facilities and development of sophisticated weapons. Israeli arms output became renowned for its quality and battle-tested reliability. Equipped to supply the country with the huge quantities of armaments required in modern warfare, it had to find outlets for its surplus production in times of relative calm.

This is normal practice for all arms manufacturing countries. Competition is high, but ethics are low. The Western states abide by a number of export licensing criteria, though unfortunately not always applied with the necessary scrutiny and strictness, it is no longer a secret that – under the cover of official discretion – quite a few shady deals have taken place. In this regard, Israel's record is no worse or better than that of its best friends and worst enemies. The revelations in 1987 regarding arms shipments to Khomeini's Iran by the United States and Israel – the so-called 'Irangate affair' – was just one, although most regrettable, example. It is an irony of fate that the French arms embargo, enacted in 1967 – which provided on the one hand the impetus for Israel to expand its arms production and on the other for the United States to become Israel's principal supplier of armaments – spawned as a by-product the dubious joint US–Israeli–Iranian arms deal, creating serious strains and dislocations all around.

Apart from its bilateral relations with the West European countries Israel succeeded over the years in establishing close ties with the European Community. They were formalized in a number of agreements mainly in the field of trade. Until the Yom Kippur War the Arab states – apart from those in North Africa – had not shown any particular interest in a rapprochement with the European Community. This changed after the Yom Kippur War, not so much because of its outcome but rather as the result of the oil embargo imposed by the Arab states against the members of the European Community and other states.

In the ensuing European 'oil panic', European governments separately and the Community jointly approached the leading Arab states in a desperate effort to alleviate their plight. The Arab producers, shrewdly recognizing the disarray of the Europeans, decided to make good use of their distress for the advancement of their political objectives in the Arab–Israeli conflict. In particular, the PLO astutely hitched its wagon to the Arab oil train. European governments, wishing to gain the good graces of the Arab oil producers, paid not only any price – extortionist as it might be – for their oil, but also a political premium to the PLO. Pronouncements of the European Community, such as the Venice Declaration, repeated to this day, enhanced the position of the PLO, and hampering instead of promoting the peace process.

In an effort to counter its relations with Israel, based on long-standing political affinity and compelling economic reality, the European Community established a framework of cooperation with the states of the Arab League. Unable to reconcile Arab political objectives with European economic interests, it failed to become an effective instrument of cooperation. Israel, however, succeeded in strengthening its ties with the European Community because their economic interests coincided. In 1975, they signed an agreement ensuring Israel's preferential access to the Common Market and the extension of cooperation between the two parties. In 1986, the volume of their mutual trade had reached US $7.1 billion, of which US $4.9 billion were European exports to Israel and US $2.2 billion Israeli sales to the Community. Over the last ten years the European Community's trade surplus with Israel amounted to US $12 billion.

DIPLOMATIC MOVES

By the end of the first decade after the Six-Day War, peace still eluded Israel, despite its astounding victories in 1967 and 1973. The shock of the Yom Kippur War with its inordinate losses in men and materiel sobered the mood of the Israeli people, and dampened its exaggerated belief in Israel's omnipotence. The two major wars Israel had fought in the span of seven years heavily drained its economic resources. Its economic growth slowed markedly, while external and internal indebtedness grew.

At the beginning of the second decade, Israel experienced a domestic upheaval of unthought-of dimensions and consequences. Labour, which had been the dominant party in all spheres of Israeli life since the inception of the state (and even long before it), lost the Knesset elections in 1977. The Likud party, led by Menachem Begin, Labour's implacable and perennial adversary, replaced it. Even before the Israeli public and world opinion had fully realized the impact and implications of the change, an event took place which altered fundamentally the nature of Arab–Israeli relations. When President Sadat of Egypt set foot on Israeli soil, the political scene of the Middle East was transformed. Sadat arrived neither as conqueror, as his predecessor Nasser had dreamed, nor as leader of a vanquished country, offering capitulation. He came as the head of the most important Arab state offering peace.

Sadat's bold leap over the abyss which had separated the two countries for three decades derived not from a sudden impulse but from careful preparation. Before landing in Israel, he had thoroughly tested the ground. In the wake of the Yom Kippur War, he had concluded two interim agreements with Israel, both involving partial military withdrawals in Sinai. Only after his special envoy had held a promising secret meeting with foreign minister Moshe Dayan, did President Anwar el-Sadat decide on his stunning peace initiative. Fifteen months later, after tedious negotiations, his mission was crowned by the signing of the treaty of peace between Egypt and Israel in the presence of President Carter.

Both sides meticulously observed their obligations under the treaty. They opened embassies, concluded a wide range of agreements designed to normalize their relations, carried out troop withdrawals on schedule and demilitarized the evacuated zones. By 25 April 1982, Israel had withdrawn all of its forces from Egyptian territory as stipulated in the treaty. The final stage, involving the evacuation of the Yamit enclave with its flourishing communities wrested from the sands of the desert, caused considerable disturbance in Israel. The camp of nationalistic and religious extremists was virtually up in arms, trying in vain to prevent the evacuation by force. Their failure and frustration spurred the emergence of a Jewish terrorist underground carrying out murderous assaults against Arab personalities and institutions in the West Bank.

THE LEBANON WAR

The Begin government, flustered by restiveness among its own supporters, decided to cool the overheated tempers by directing national attention from the southern to the northern part of the country, harassed for many years by PLO terrorist attacks launched from Southern Lebanon. Until the establishment of an informal cease-fire in July 1981, attained through the good offices of the United States, PLO artillery and rocket launchers had sporadically shelled towns and villages in Upper Galilee. While terror gangs raided the country, PLO headquarters in Beirut organized the highjacking of airliners, attacks against Israeli diplomats abroad, killings of worshippers in synagogues and the massacre of Israeli athletes at the Munich Olympics: a rollcall of terror unequalled in its diversity, perversity and cruelty.

The shots fired by Arab terrorists in London in June 1982, maiming the Ambassador of Israel, triggered Israel's military intervention in Lebanon, which became its longest and most frustrating war. The declared purpose of this long-prepared military intervention was to out an end, once and for all, to the terrorist operations. But, as the course of events revealed, its objectives were unfortunately much more ambitious. The planners of the operation were motivated by a maze of military concerns, by political goals far beyond the elimination of the actual PLO menace and by personal ambitions and ideological illusions as deceptive as the labyrinthine ways of Levantine politics.

The longer the war lasted, the more it extended beyond its original proclaimed objectives and the more victims it claimed, the stronger the people in Israel doubted its military justification and political sense. When the IDF became involved in heavy fighting with Syrian troops deployed in Eastern Lebanon, even normally docile members of the government began to wonder about the war aims and voiced warnings, faintly echoing the public outcry. The sharp divisons generated by the war in Lebanon provoked a national debate which touched the soul of the nation.

The massacre in the Palestinian refugee camps of Sabra and Shatila in September 1982, committed by Christian Lebanese Phalangist forces, was a tragedy which aroused the ire of the Israeli public. When it became known that Israelis in the highest position of government and command and officers on the spot had failed to stop the murderous rampage, an outcry of anguish and protest reverberated throughout the land. Under the pressure of mass protest the government set up a judicial enquiry which absolved the IDF from any participation in the killings in the camps, but charged political and military leaders with indirect responsibility, having neglected as the occupying power their responsibility in the maintenance of law and order.

The war caused deep apprehension not only in Israel, but also among its friends in the world. While the United States initially had watched the military initiative with an attitude of benign detachment, the expression of its concern and dismay grew in proportion to the scale of the fighting. The dissemination of gruesome media reports, some vastly exaggerated and inaccurate, the threatening voices from Moscow and fierce protests from the Arab capitals moved Washington to adopt a sterner and more active attitude. From now on, it took an active and persistent interest in the Lebanese situation, aimed at the termination of the fighting, the evacuation of Arafat's headquarters together with his armed men, the withdrawal of all foreign forces from Lebanon and the stabilization of the internal situation in this unhappy land. To realize these objectives Washington invested a major political effort backed up by a limited military presence in Beirut and off the Lebanese coast. It helped secure the evacuation of the PLO, and four years later the withdrawal of the Israeli forces from nine-tenths of the territory they had occupied. It failed, however, to impress upon the Syrian government the need to withdraw its forces from Lebanon, nor was American influence sufficient to ensure the implementation of the wide-ranging agreement negotiated directly and signed on 17 May 1983 between the governments of Israel and Lebanon. The accord collapsed under the pressure of Damascus which proved to be more persuasive than Washington's clout.

On 1 September 1982, one day after Arafat and his men had taken to the boats which rescued them from surrender, but while Lebanon was still seized by interminable turmoil, President Reagan outlined publicly a well thought-out plan for the overall settlement of the

Arab–Israeli conflict. It was a well conceived, but ill-timed initiative. It came too soon, and it aimed too high. Too soon, because the unsolved Lebanese crisis was still the central concern of the parties. The Syrian army and PLO units still occupied the Northern and Eastern parts of Lebanon and Israeli forces were deployed up to Beirut. It aimed too high, because it outlined in detail the expected outcome of the negotiations, instead of limiting itself to proposals for their initiation and conduct.

The Arab heads of state countered the Reagan initiative with their own plan, adopted at a summit meeting in Fez. It recognized neither the legitimacy of Israel, nor declared explicitly an Arab willingness to conclude peace with the Jewish state. It demanded the establishment of a Palestinian state, with Jerusalem as its capital and the PLO as its government.

Not only the Arab heads of state but also Prime Minister Begin rejected the Reagan plan out of hand. Like all his predecessors his government aspired to peace, but with the difference that Begin would accept only those proposals which did not jeopardize his principal goal – that is, the incorporation of Samaria, Judea and Gaza into the State of Israel. But precisely on this count the Reagan plan was diametrically opposed to Begin's aspirations. Its realization would thwart Begin's and Sharon's undeclared war aim – to remove, through the destruction of the PLO in Lebanon, the obstruction to the extension of Israeli sovereignty over the entire land of Israel.

The time lost in the drawn out and eventually fruitless negotiations between Lebanon and Israel became Syria's gain. It used it energetically to recover quickly, with the help of its Soviet ally, from the consequences of its military defeat in June 1982. The Soviet government replaced Syria's losses of armaments with better equipment and strengthened its air defence by the installation of longer range missiles, operated by special Soviet crews. Politically Assad manifested his regained self-confidence by warnings to King Hussein and Arafat to cease their discussions on their eventual participation in peace negotiations. At the same time, the limited military presence of the United States failed to restore calm to Lebanon and bolster its government.

Whatever the effect of the war on others for Israel it was a decisive turning point. It had been, as Prime Minister Begin had proclaimed, a 'war of choice' designed not only to make the Northern region of the country safe from depradation, but to restore the confidence in the preparedness and prowess of the IDF, shaken as Begin believed, by the shock of the Yom Kippur War. Sharon's war aims, as already pointed out, were even more grandiose. The 'war of choice', announced as a three-day quick march, dragged on for four years, ending with Israel's unconditional withdrawal. Sharon's 'New Order' vanished like a mirage in the desert. The Palestinian problem, which the architects of the military intervention had sought to solve once and forever by victory in Lebanon gained in weight and centrality in the wake of the war.

The international reactions to Israel's military operations in Lebanon were largely negative. The unaccustomed view of Israeli troops operating in a foreign country, occupying the capital of an Arab state, its airforce bombing heavily (though selectively) targets in urban centres, the sight of devastation and misery televized throughout the world tarnished Israel's human image. Amplified by a reckless propaganda campaign the tragedies of the war furthered existing anti-Israeli trends, noticeably among the younger generation in Europe, influenced by the 'New Left', and produced a more open and assertive expression of hidden anti-Semitism on the part of their elders.

What was the effect of the war on the relations between Israel and the Arab states? The rejectionist camp intensified its hostility, albeit without extending meaningful military support to the hard-pressed PLO. The fighting in Lebanon increased the growing Arab perception that their conflict with Israel could not be solved in the foreseeable future by military force. This conviction, however, was not sufficient to induce them, like Egypt, to enter into negotiations with Israel on a settlement by peaceful means.

Undoubtedly, Israel's involvement in Lebanon retarded the growth of the burgeoning peace with Egypt. Despite the strains and stresses to which the peace had been subjected – among them the deadlock in the talks on autonomy for the Palestinians; the dispute on the Taba enclave; Egypt's reluctance to infuse substance into the normalization process; its endeavour to regain its prominent place in the Arab world; and last but not least its reaction to Israel's military intervention in Lebanon – both countries continued to realize that their relations of peace, even limited in content, constituted a major asset for their own security, and the stability of the entire area. Twenty years after the Six-Day War Egypt had fully recovered all the territories it had lost in the fighting and formed with Israel a zone of tranquillity and peace stretching from the headwaters of the Jordan to the upper reaches of the Nile. At a meeting held in Alexandria in

September 1986, President Mubarak and Prime Minister Shimon Peres signed an agreement to solve the Taba problem by arbitration. In consequence, Egypt renominated its Ambassador to Israel who had been absent since the tragic events in the Sabra and Shatilla camps. Furthermore the two leaders discussed ways and means of securing the participation of Jordan and the Palestinians in the peace process within the framework of an international conference under the auspices of the five permanent members of the Security Council. PLO obstructionism, coupled with Jordanian evasiveness and Syrian rejectionism, increased King Hussein's hesitation about climbing down from the fence on which he had been perched since 1967. Not that the King had shunned secret contacts with leading members of the Israeli government, producing practical informal arrangements of cooperation between the two countries, but he failed to muster the courage to make the decisive step to participate in official negotiations on the future of the West Bank and Gaza as envisaged in the Camp David accord or any other freely agreed framework.

Since the signing of the Taba agreement the 'cold peace' – as Egypt preferred to describe its relations with Israel – began to warm up. The definition depicted more a current mood than a precise assessment of the substance. Even during the 'chilly period', Israel's Embassy operated normally. In Cairo, its Academic Centre continued to organize meetings between Egyptian and Israeli academics. Israeli tourists, with the exception of one tragic shooting incident caused by an aberrant Egyptian soldier, enjoyed the warm welcome of ordinary citizens and officials. Airline and bus companies continued to run daily connections between the two countries and Israeli ships passed freely through the Suez Canal. It is not unreasonable to expect that the improvement of the relations beginning at the end of 1986 will have its effect on the so far rather restricted Egyptian trade and tourism with Israel. The cultural relations between the two countries, virtually at a standstill, will probably regain momentum. The salient fact remains that the peace has struck roots in both countries. Its fruits may not yet be as abundant and tasty as anticipated, but it proved its vitality in the face of threats and ostracism by the Arab states; it outlasted Israel's evacuation of Sinai; survived the assassination of President Anwar el-Sadat and the political demise of both its cosignatories, President Carter and Prime Minister Begin. The peace endured the deadlock of the Palestinian autonomy talks and weathered the storm of Israel's military intervention in Lebanon. It has proved to be a basic necessity for both Egypt and Israel.

DOMESTIC DEVELOPMENTS

In October 1984 Yitzhak Shamir succeeded Begin. The new Prime Minister, lacking the flair and the popular appeal of his predecessor in his more potent years, tried to follow in his oversized footsteps, obstinately soldiering on with his stranded policy. Incumbered by a factious party and unreliable coalition partners, Shamir's primary preoccupation was to avoid rocking the rickety coalition boat. Yet the waters of Israeli politics are rarely calm, and after a few months his government capsized. New elections became unavoidable.

In the light of the record of the Likud government, it was widely assumed that the voters were eager to decide whether they wished to live in an economic or social wasteland or in a productive society; whether they wanted Israel's destinies to be guided by illusionary policies or preferred sane rationality, moral rectitude, sound realism uplifted by the grandeur of Israel's spiritual heritage and the vision of Israel's honoured place among the nations.

But the voter failed to make the expected choice. He avoided a clear-cut decision. The elections resulted in a draw between the two principal contenders, the Likud and the Labour Alignment, preventing either of them from forming a government at the exclusion of the other. After the new 'National Unity Government' was formed under Prime Minister Shimon Peres in September 1984, it was faced with four central tasks: the rehabilitation of the economy, the extraction of Israel from the Lebanese quagmire; the revitalization of the relations with Egypt; and the activation of the peace process with Jordan and the Palestinians.

Peres's first priority was the termination of Israel's involvement in Lebanon; it took him eight months to reach that objective in June 1985, patiently negotiating his path through the political minefields. The Labour alignment was convinced that the improvement of Israel's relations with the neighbouring Arab states would enhance its position in the world and elicit not only much goodwill from its traditional friends but also their support for its pressing economic needs.

Relations with the United States centred in the second decade on vital and highly appreciated economic aid and military cooperation. Both had grown steadily and rapidly since the signing of the Camp David Accords. In the economic field, the two countries concluded a unique free trade zone agreement, the first in United States' commercial history. Notwithstanding the strain which the relations underwent on various occasions – for instance, when Israel instituted the extension of its law for the Golan Heights, bombed the Iraqi nuclear reactor and undertook certain military operations in the course of the fighting in Lebanon – the Reagan administration as a whole lent its unswerving military, political and economic support to the Government of National Unity. It manifested in word, vote and deed its intimate association with Israel as a reliable ally in a region where friendship with the United States was not a surplus commodity. Particularly in their joint struggle against terrorism, the United States found in Israel an experienced and determined partner.

While the Likud party advocated an all-out strategic cooperation with the United States against the expansionist politics of its principal adversary, the Soviet Union, the Labour alignment followed a more cautious course. It opposed commitments extending beyond Israel's direct national security concerns, arising from the enmity of the Arab states and their supporters. In the political domain it aspired to the deepening of understanding and cooperation with the United States on the issues relating to the peace process. The United States' policy contained the same components, from President Johnson's five points on 18 June 1967 via the Rogers Plan in 1969 and Carter's Camp David Accords to the Reagan proposals of 1982. Respective governments of Israel have either rejected, ignored or argued with Washington about its proposals, but have never made a sustained effort to harmonize the positions of the two countries on the substance of the desired solution of the conflict.

When the Government of National Unity was formed, Prime Minister Peres realized that Israel's unbalanced foreign relations required a rearrangement of priorities and reactivation in a variety of areas. Wide empty spaces – stretching southwards from the Jordan border to the Indian subcontinent, and northeast from the Golan Heights to the Chinese wall – were completely devoid of any Israeli diplomatic presence. The Soviet Union and the other Warsaw Pact states had not always been diplomatically uninhabited territory on Israel's political map. Until 1967, when the Soviet Union and its East European allies broke off their diplomatic relations, Israel had enjoyed normal – and at times friendly – ties with all of them.

The process of Soviet–Israeli alienation, beginning in the early 1950s when Israel drew closer to the United States and the Soviet Union gradually aligned itself with the hostility of the Arab states, had culminated since the Six-Day War in a number of crises. They affected not only Israel but also relations between the superpowers. The Soviet military presence in Syria had created a particularly hazardous situation. The imbalance existing in the relations of the Soviet Union with the states in the Middle East increased not only the regional tensions – probably not to Moscow's dislike – but deprived it of any meaningful diplomatic influence on political developments in the Arab–Israeli conflict. The political antagonism prevailing between the Soviet Union and Israel was sharpened by the suppression of the legitimate aspirations of Soviet Jewry.

The Israeli government felt that the resumption of the dialogue between the Soviet Union and Israel was not only an indispensable requisite for the normalization of their relations, but no less a necessity for the reduction of dangerous tensions in the area. Such a dialogue, hoped Prime Minister Peres, might lay the ground for the Soviet Union to participate constructively in an international Arab–Israeli peace conference and alleviate the plight of Soviet Jewry. In the last two years an intensification of contacts between representatives of the Soviet Union and Israel has taken place, including a Soviet mission to Israel, but without producing a corresponding growth of comprehension.

NEED FOR REASSESSMENT

How does the balance sheet look twenty years after the end of the Six-Day War? Although Israeli rule over the West Bank and Gaza has now lasted longer than the previous Jordanian and Egyptian rule respectively, the Arab population does not show any sign of accommodation to or resignation about the continuation of the Israeli administration. But the strong arm of, and close surveillance by, the military authorities prevented for twenty years, though not always successfully, the degeneration of the discontent into open rebellion or a state of lasting civil disobedience.

Relations with the Palestinian inhabitants in the administered territories, approaching now the figure of 1.5 million, nearly 500 000 of them living in particularly precarious conditions of density and destitution in the Gaza Strip, constitutes today, and in the coming years, one of Israel's weightiest existential problems. It will aggravate if left drifting without direction. The nature of the Israeli–Palestinian relationship will determine the character of the Jewish state, the moral fibre of its people and the quality of its society. The twenty-year rule over an unwilling unassimilable restive people, different in faith, tradition, allegiance and aspiration, has not only hurt the occupied but scarred the occupier.

Others will elaborate on the internal implication of this problem, its external consequences are no less grave. In the last few years – and especially since the war in Lebanon – it has become axiomatic that the solution of the Palestinian problem is the key to the settlement of the Arab–Israeli conflict. Whether this is a correct assessment is questionable. It could be argued that the readiness of Israel's Arab neighbours to live in peace with the Jewish state and accept it as an integral part of the Middle Eastern community of nations are the prerequisites for a Palestinian solution. Be that as it may, the acuteness of this problem, and its growing aggravation, cannot be left to theoretical disputation, but create inescapable challenges necessitating urgent pragmatic answers.

In the elation of its swift and overwhelming victory in 1967 Israel's sense of proportion and values became flawed. It began to overestimate the effect of military power and underrate the strength of international political realities. It extended its control over new territories, exceeding three times its original size, but also acquired a heavy burden of demographic, political, moral, social and economic problems straining its limited capacities. Entering the fifth decade of its independence Israel will have to do much rethinking about its place in the world, its position in the Middle East, its scale of values and its relationship with and responsibility towards the Diaspora.

2 Israel's Dilemmas: An Opportunity Squandered

Abba Eban*

The Six-Day War is the formative event in Israel's history. Israelis still divide their experience between what happened before 5 June 1967, and what happened after. Twenty years later it is evident that the 1967 war is more often celebrated than understood.

It was, of course, a stupendous military victory. The drama of the triumph was enhanced by memory of the fear that had gripped Israeli hearts a few days before, as Arab armies in their hundreds of thousands moved toward us from north, south and east. A cold numerical calculation of divisions and tanks, of guns and aircraft in Israel and the Arab world told us that a great doom was sweeping towards us.

The sympathy that poured in from the outside world had the ironic effect of sharpening our apprehensions. Israelis reasoned with shrewd Jewish perversity that if people abroad were showing concern for them, they must be in deadly peril. As May came to an end, our people faced a single certainty. The choice was to live or perish – to defend the national existence or to lose it for all time.

It had taken only six days to reverse this condition. By the end of the second week of June, Israel had exchanged its peril for a position of unprecedented military domination in the Middle East.

Not a single Arab soldier or weapon was now in range of Israel's population centres. We held 26 467 square miles of territory previously in Arab hands. The armies of Egypt, Syria and Jordan were in disarray. Israel's flag flew over the Temple Mount. The contrast between the threats of Arab leaders on the eve of the war and the total disintegration of their power added humiliation to their defeat.

More unexpected than the military victory was the political success that followed. More unexpected because in the political arena the Arabs begin with an even greater initial advantage than on the battlefield. Reason and precedent supported their belief that their

* This article appeared in the Colour Supplement to the *Jewish Chronicle*, 26 June 1987.

command of international voting systems and their preponderance in money, oil and strategic space would force Israel to relinquish its gains without the compensation of a durable peace.

To their incredulous horror, they lost on what should have been their home ground. The United Nations ordered a cease-fire without Israel's prior withdrawal, rejected Soviet-Arab attempts to condemn Israel's self-defence and voted down all resolutions requiring withdrawal ahead of peace. 'You only got eight votes, Mr. Gromyko', exclaimed a Latin American representative as I led the victorious Israeli delegation out of the assembly hall.

So the 1967 diplomatic battle subsided with Israel's position in the West Bank and Gaza legitimised so long as the Arabs refused peace. Moreover, Israel now had concrete assets which it could either withhold or confer.

FRESH CAPACITIES

For the first time we had a viable capacity of negotiation. We now know for certain that Eygpt would not have made peace with Israel in 1979 if Sinai had not been in our hands.

To the advantages which the 1967 victory bestowed on Israel we must add the elevation of the nation's spirit. We had shown qualities which shine brightest in adversity. Israel had something to say to small and threatened countries everywhere.

The Israeli political victory owed much to the moderation and lucidity of the Eshkol government's posture. We had laid the foundations of American and British support by giving those countries a chance – which they did not seize – of challenging Nasser's blockade themselves. The 'waiting period' (*hamtana*) was a crucial element in our diplomatic success. It ensured that the major Western powers would not object to Israel's independent resistance when it came.

While the Six-Day War had been a military victory and had brought political advantage, it was to be followed by a psychological setback.

Successful war can prevent your enemy from destroying your life, your home, your freedom and your national independence. That is its crucial justification. But it is remarkable, once its defensive vocation is exhausted, how little it can do to create the harmonies, acknowledgements, and changes of attitude that are part of the elusive notion of peace.

The aim of modern war is not to destroy your enemy but to change his mind. There is room only for limited war; war in which you employ less than your total power in order to achieve less than the total destruction of your enemy. Israelis have become so accustomed to Arab obduracies that they make no provision for the possibility that Arab attitudes may change, despite the fact that to change Arab attitudes is the central purpose of Israel's defence and diplomatic effort.

The victory was seen not as one phase in a continuing evolution, subject to changes of fortune, but as a providential enactment which had put Israel beyond reach of danger. It was mistakenly assumed that since we did not need Arab consent to wage successful war, we might not need Arab consent to the conditions of a future peace.

This was an illusion. The victory was only in the military sphere; it was therefore superficial. Victory over Nasser would fade. The balance of power in the Arab–Israeli area had not been substantially altered. We had captured no Arab capital, brought down no Arab regimes, imposed no new political culture on the neighbouring world. The Soviet Union swiftly replenished the lost Arab weaponry. The Arabs had retained their capacity of refusal.

Israel, to be sure, had confirmed its power of 'deterrence'. We could prevent our enemies from doing what they wished. But we had no power of 'compellence' – the power to force your opponent to take a positive action that you would like him to take. As one author has written: 'the power to knock a man down does not give you the power to force him to play the piano'.

The first official Israeli reaction to the victory was sober and controlled. It was also audacious. The Eshkol government dramatically proved that it preferred peace to territorial gain. On 19 June 1967, we had informed the Egyptian and Syrian governments through the United States that Israel would be willing to conclude peace treaties with each of them on the basis of the international boundaries.

This would have involved the renunciation of Israeli gains in Sinai and Golan. At the same time, the Israeli government, ignoring Moshe Dayan's ill-considered advice to wait for a telephone call from Hussein, initiated direct talks with Jordan on the basis of the Allon Plan which would have restored most of the West Bank and Gaza to Jordanian rule, subject to demilitarisation and moderate boundary improvements. I recall how leading members of the Lyndon Johnson administration to whom I conveyed these proposals were astounded by their generosity.

But within a few weeks, the Arab governments meeting in

Khartoum published their virulent document of rejection. They would not make peace with Israel; they would not recognize Israel; they would not negotiate with Israel; and they would not bargain about boundaries or territories. The Arab leadership has never lost a chance of missing an opportunity. It was the first time in the history of war that the victor had sued for peace while the vanquished demanded unconditional surrender.

'Nothing except a battle lost can be half as melancholy as a battle won.' The words are those of Wellington who was a victorious soldier and then a prime minister. This would be an exaggeration of Israel's predicament. After all, whatever else Israel has missed, it has gained survival from the 1967 war and in terms of Jewish history this is no small matter.

Yet the 1967 war has left us with two heavy predicaments which are not yet in sight of resolution. The first affects the structure of our society which, as a result of the occupation regime in the West Bank and Gaza, makes Israel a quintessentially different sort of nation than it was twenty years ago. The second has to do with the intellectual and moral climate in which Israel lives. Here too, there are features which were far less salient before the 1967 war.

The idea that Israeli rule over 1 300 000 Palestinians in the occupied territories might become permanent by inertia or by intention scarcely occurred to thoughtful Israelis on the morrow of the war. A dozen years later, in 1975, Golda Meir could write in her autobiography: 'No sane Israeli ever assumed that all the territories were going to remain under Israeli rule. New borders would have to be drawn up between Israel and Jordan' (*My Life*, 310).

NEW GROUND

The appeal to sanity is not artificial. The annexationist idea has lost ground in the theoretical domain. Thus, the Labour party conferences in 1984 and 1986 unanimously adopted resolutions declaring that permanent Israeli rule 'would violate the nation's Zionist principles, undermine its moral foundations, contradict its democratic character and thwart any possibility of peace in the future'. This text went on to say that 'the settlements established in the heart of the Arab populated areas not only fail to serve Israel's security needs, but also constitute a security problem and a heavy economic and political burden'.

More than a million of the two million Israeli voters supported these and other anti-annexationist texts in the elections held in 1984. There does not exist a single country anywhere that resembles what Israel would look like if it were to exercise a permanent jurisdiction over a foreign population already constituting more than a third of the total number of people under Israeli rule. This disfranchised population neither gives nor owes any allegiance to our flag, our faith, our tongue, our name, our Jewish solidarities or our historic experience. And it is recognised by every government in the world (including that of Israel in the Camp David agreement) as a separate people endowed with a specific particularity within an Arab context.

If we were to hear that Holland was thinking of incorporating four million Germans against their will, or that the United States, for whatever reason, proposed to enforce permanent rule over 80 million rebellious Russians, we would assume that they were bent upon national suicide. Yet there are still some Israelis and some Diaspora Jews who speak and act as if the incorporation of the West Bank and Gaza were a viable option.

It is extraordinary to find so many Diaspora Jews indifferent to whether or not Israel is to be a land of double jurisdictions, or whether there is a Jewish duty to affirm the principle of consent and equality. The Palestinians in the West Bank and Gaza cannot vote or be elected to anything, have no juridical control over the government that rules their lives, have no appeal against the judgements of military courts, are not free to leave their land with assurance of the right to return, are not immune, as are their Jewish neighbours, from such penalties as expulsion or the blowing up of homes or administrative detention, have no flag to revere, and do not possess the same economic and social conditions as their immediate Jewish neighbours.

Their workers enter Israel daily to work at low wages and are forbidden to spend the night in the area of Israeli law. This is an unattractive symbolism in an unappealing situation. So long as there is no settlement we have a society in the administered territories in which a man's rights are defined not by any egalitarian principle, but by his ethnic identity.

The historic paradox is that the injunction *choq echad yihyeh lachem* (one law for everybody in a given jurisdiction) enters history as a revolutionary Hebrew idea. Moreover, the present duality of regimes in the West Bank and Gaza is precisely the condition from which the French and American Revolutions and British common law protected or saved the Jews during the centuries of enlightenment and emancipation.

The dilemma is inescapable. If we give the Palestinians their full weight in the Israeli parliament, we shall cease to be an intrinsically Jewish society with a power of majority decision; we would ultimately become a minority like the Lebanese Christians, who lost their majority by foolishly annexing areas of vast Muslim population a few decades ago.

On the other hand, if we maintain our rule without formal annexation, which is a more likely contingency, we shall be a society of first-class citizens (Jews) and third-class residents (Arabs) thus making a mockery of the human values and democratic ideals which gave Israel its moral quality and its universal resonance from the day of its birth.

History and literature are full of paradox in defining victory and defeat. By the very fact of their defeat the Palestinians have inflicted a deep structural injury on Israeli society. Israel was never more secure against external threat and never more vulnerable to domestic error. On the other hand, the objective conditions for peace would seem to have improved. If Israeli rule in the West Bank weighs at least as heavily on Israel as on the Palestinians there is a common interest in moving away from the present situation towards a lesser Israeli involvement in the fate and control of the West Bank and Gaza. It is this logic which has inspired Shimon Peres's effort to bring about an Israeli–Jordanian dialogue within an international context.

Unfortunately, the unsolved structural problem is not the only embarrassing legacy of the 1967 victory. The idea of exercising permanent rule over a foreign nation can only be defended by an ideology of self-worship and exclusiveness that are incompatible with the ethical legacy of prophetic Judaism and classical Zionism.

The national rhetoric since the 1967 war has shades of meaning and style which set the period apart from those that were familiar before the war. Here are some examples of statements by Israeli leaders during the ecstatic period between the Six-Day War and Yom Kippur 1973. They all come from the central sector of Israeli opinion, mostly from cabinet ministers and generals who are still in the higher grades of Israeli establishment:

'Israel is a great power and there is no place between Baghdad and Khartoum, including the area of Libya that our army could not capture' (September 1973).

'Golda has better boundaries than King David and King Solomon' (August 1973).

'Egypt has no military option' (July 1973).

'We must see ourselves as the permanent government in the territories and must plan and carry out whatever we want without leaving options open for peace' (Moshe Dayan, August 1971).

'Sharm al Sheikh without peace is better than peace without Sharm al Sheikh' (1971–3).

'The probability of an Egyptian attack is remote' (*Intelligence Report* 5 October 1973).

TRAGIC DEVELOPMENT

Some of this rhetoric has now reappeared cautiously as the memories of the Yom Kippur surprise fade away. In the meantime a new phenomenon has become increasingly ominous. One of the most tragic developments in Jewish history has been the replacement of the pragmatic, intensely peace-seeking ideology of the National Religious Party by a new young leadership with a sharper appetite for Arab populated territories than for Torah principles.

The parliamentary balance is now in the hands of groups who seek divine sanction for conquest, domination and in some Gush Emunim quarters, even for the organisation of 'transports' for expelling non-Jews from their homes.

Gush Emunim is a more disquieting factor than Kahanism since it springs from more central roots in religious Zionism. Its philosophy as laid down in 1974 and thereafter by its leaders such as the late Rabbi Zvi Yehuda Kook and Rabbi Aviner, tells us that 'there is no such thing as an Arab home or an Arab piece of land in Eretz Israel, since they invaded the land in the seventh century knowing that it belongs to the Jews, taking advantage of our temporary absence abroad. They are therefore illegal squatters.'

Sometimes the adherents of these views pass from opinion to action, such as those who tried to blow up the Muslim holy places in Jerusalem on the grounds that the Temple must be restored on its original site.

In defending members of the Jewish underground who had murdered Arab students and mutilated Arab mayors, Rabbi Yisrael Ariel invokes the Rambam: 'Whoever seeks in the *Yad Chazaka* of the Rambam the concept of "thou shalt not kill" or "sacred blood" as applicable to the killing of a non-Jew will seek in vain; he will not find it.'

The Rambam anniversary gave rise to a spate of quotations on the 'great Eagle's' commentaries laying down that 'when Israel's hand is powerful against the gentiles' no idolator (*oved avoda zara*) shall be allowed to dwell in Jerusalem.

Scorning historic relativism and preaching an anachronistic view of history in which they assume that the great thinkers of the past would write in the same strain today, the learned zealots succeed in presenting even the most enlightened rabbinic authorities as vengeful chauvinists.

Dr Mordecai Nissan, a lecturer to foreign students in the Hebrew University of Jerusalem (!) writes in a Zionist Organization periodical (*Kivvunim*, August 1984) that since the Jews are an aristocratic element in humanity, defined as 'a light unto the nations', they are exclusively entitled to have a political role in Eretz Israel. The 'son of the handmaiden (*ben hashifcha*) does not belong to the tribe of Abraham' and is therefore disqualified.

These fanatical and unscholarly ideas are not new. They have always had their place on the outer fringes of Zionism, but they had nothing like their present volume or extent before the 1967 war. I see no chance of reducing this virulence in the intellectual and religious life of the country unless the rule over a disfranchised foreign nation is replaced by the kind of pragmatic approach which Shimon Peres is trying – vainly so far – to restore to Israeli diplomacy. The present condition is hurting Israel even more than it injures the Palestinians.

It is in the name of self-interest rather than of altruism that we must look at the Six-Day War. The war was an opportunity, not a solution. We cannot dictate the conduct of our foes, but we can at least keep the sanctuaries of reason intact and turn the sacrifice and daring of our defenders to sane account.

3 Israel's Dilemmas: No Simple Short Cuts
Ehud Olmert

The twenty years since the Six-Day War have completely changed the nature, form and self-image of the State of Israel. In 1967, Israel still lacked confidence in its ability to survive the constant threat from the surrounding Arab countries. The most dramatic example of the gap between the state's objective strength and its poor self-image is the famous 'waiting period' that preceded the war itself.

The Six-Day War surprised Israel almost as much as did the Yom Kippur War six years later. But its circumstances – and, most importantly, its consequences – were entirely different. For several weeks – from the time that Egyptian military forces first moved into the Sinai Desert to the moment when actual fighting broke out – many sectors of the Israeli population were stricken with depression and anxiety, fearing the catastrophe that might bring the state to its end. The waiting period before the actual fighting was more a result of doubt, lack of confidence and uncertainty on the part of the Israeli leadership, than of any calculated initiative designed to prepare world opinion for the Israeli military blow. These fears were the result of continual military threats – since 1948 – which undermined Israel's belief in its ability to withstand them.

From this point of view, the Six-Day War was a turning point. The war changed Israel's comprehension of security. The Arab threat continued, the real or imaginary fear of catastrophe was still overwhelming, but a strong feeling that there were now wider and more stable parameters for existence could be detected. The Six-Day War removed from Israeli consciousness any sense of its own temporary nature and enhanced its confidence, almost to the point of arrogance and unwarranted disdain towards the enemy.

The Six-Day War also changed Israel's regional and international position. It now became a dominant factor not only in the Middle East but also in the broad international arena. Strategic considerations at superpower levels suddenly intermingled with events that had Israel as their focus. Israel began to play a part on the world stage, not just as 'yet another state' but as a member of the international community with rights and a status that could not be ignored. From a historical perspective, the outcome of the Six-Day War initiated the process that gradually led to a fundamental change in the relations between Israel and the Arab countries. The war and its achievements created an infrastructure of power without which some Arab countries would not have felt that there was no choice but to come to terms with Israel's existence. It was this that finally led to the peace treaty with Egypt and the recognition by other Arab countries (such as Jordan) of the desirability of finding a political arrangement with Israel.

Nonetheless, even though we may enumerate the effects of the Six-Day War, we cannot escape the conclusion that fundamentally it did not remove a single one of Israel's problems from the national agenda. In certain respects, the war even sharpened these problems, giving them a deeper and more comprehensive dimension than they had previously possessed. It raised the profile of the dispute between Israel and the Palestinians and, at the same time, brought to the surface fundamental questions within Israeli society about the desired identity of the state, the relationship between the Jewish and non-Jewish components and, in particular, the basic aims towards which Israeli society should aspire, its order of priorities and the much-sought-after mutual relations with world Jewry.

Twenty years after the Six-Day War no formula to resolve the problem of Judea, Samaria and Gaza has been devised which reflects a national consensus and could serve as an agreed platform for all major political forces in Israel. The war also heightened adherence to the concept of *Eretz Yisrael ha-shelemah* (Greater Israel), which clashes with the traditional Labour Party approach that had always aspired to ensure the continued existence of Israel on the basis of a territorial compromise. This confrontation, which peaked in the argument for and against the Partition Resolution of 1947, appeared to have ended with the Declaration of Independence and the signing of the Armistice Agreements of 1949. The outcome of the Six-Day War renewed the debate, made it more bitter and created two large camps of equal size within Israel.

AN OLD ZIONIST CONCEPT

Though the *Eretz Yisrael ha-shelemah* concept was born in the wake of the war, its origins lay in the beginning of the Zionist movement.

The man who represented this position more than anyone else was Zeev Jabotinsky, the founder of the Revisionist movement in the World Zionist Organization (WZO), who later resigned from the WZO and, to this day, is considered to be the spiritual father of the Herut movement, one of the leading political movements in Israel in the last generation. Jabotinsky viewed the Balfour Declaration of November 1917 as the granting of a binding international confirmation of the perception that the rights of the Jewish people in all parts of Palestine, to the west as well as to the east of the Jordan, were inalienable.

In 1922, Great Britain determined that the realistic basis for confirmation of the Mandate over Palestine should include only those parts of Palestine to the west of the River Jordan. Chaim Weizmann, subsequently the first President of the State of Israel, supported the British policy, which meant willingly giving up areas of Palestine east of the Jordan.

In 1925, Jabotinsky declared: 'The aim of Zionism is to turn Palestine (including East Trans-Jordan) gradually into a Jewish commonwealth, that is a self-governing commonwealth with a permanent Jewish majority. Any other interpretation of Zionism, particularly the 1922 White Paper, is declared invalid.' The platform of the Revisionist Party states: 'Trans-Jordan has to be included in the area of Jewish settlement. All sections of the mandate have to apply equally to Trans-Jordan' (The Zionist Revisionist Conference, 10 May 1925).

At the 1931 Zionist Congress Jabotinsky proposed that 'the aim of Zionism as expressed in terms of "State of Jews", "national home" or "a declaredly safe haven" meant creating a Jewish majority in the population of Palestine on both banks of the Jordan'. But Jabotinsky's proposals were rejected by the Zionist Congress, and he and his followers resigned from the Zionist Organization.

In 1936, Britain appointed a commission to examine the possibility of a settlement of the Palestine problem. Jabotinsky, who was at that time forbidden to enter Palestine, stated before the Peel Commission in London: 'When I use the term "Palestine", it applies to both banks of the Jordan River'.

The Peel Commission did not accept Jabotinsky's position, and recommended that two sovereign states be established in British-ruled West Palestine. On this, Jabotinsky retorted: 'Nothing of the kind'. He considered it a nightmare that should be ignored.

Jabotinsky's great pupil, Menachem Begin, who headed the *Irgun*

Tsva'i Leumi and subsequently led the Herut movement from its inception until 1983, adhered to the basic position of his teacher and master that the State of Israel had to realize the historical right of the Jewish people to live throughout the Land of Israel. He was, therefore, one of the opponents of partition in 1947, even though it created convenient political conditions for the establishment of the State of Israel.

In innumerable debates and in confrontations with Israel's first Prime Minister, David Ben Gurion, Begin formulated his position with respect to the desirable borders for Israel in unequivocal terms: 'Our homeland is the whole of the Land of Israel, yes, on both banks of the Jordan. Rabat Ammon as Nablus, the Gilad as Samaria . . . and it is now under alien rule, but why was the government in such a hurry to recognise it? What justification is there for the impure and impurifying desert king to sit on the Temple Mount?' (Knesset proceedings, 7 November 1949).

In short: Menachem Begin, or Jabotinsky, the Herut movement or the Revisionist movement that preceded it, viewed any waiver over the demand for sovereignty in the Land of Israel as a sort of withdrawal or deviation from one of the most substantive bases of the Zionist perception.

From 1948 to 1967 the shadow of self-flagellation concerning missed opportunities hung over the debate over the Land of Israel; amongst the right an ideological conviction developed that, should opportunities occur in the future, they would not again be wasted. However, the accepted feeling was that the War of Independence and the establishment of the state within the 1949 borders had closed off the State of Israel's territorial options for many a year and that, anyway, the issue was not relevant to the real problems besetting the state at that time.

REVIVAL OF THE TERRITORIAL ISSUE

The Six-Day War changed all that in an instant, and brought the territorial issue back to the centre of national debate. But this issue cannot be disengaged from the complex fabric of problems that accumulated, the longer Israel's presence in Judea, Samaria and Gaza continued.

The Israeli presence in the Areas provided Israel with a security belt, and those who are convinced that Israel should withdraw from these areas cannot contest its value and importance. At the same time, however, it brought the Jewish population into confrontation with a large Palestinian population and presented the Jewish public with a complex moral dilemma. How could legitimate national requirements and vital security interests, together with Jewish historical rights, be reconciled with the moral difficulties of a military government being forced on the Palestinian population? How was one to cope with the problem of increasing terror? How could one balance the advantages of cheap Arab labour from Judea, Samaria and Gaza and Israeli's increasing dependence on it, with the tremendous disadvantages inherent therein for the work ethic of the Jewish population?

These pressures have, over the past twenty years, turned Israel into a country entirely different from what it was at the time of the war. From a small, self-enclosed society, preoccupied with fears and still-fresh memories of the Holocaust, Israeli society adopted the typical standards of the rich Western countries with a high standard of living and the typical characteristics of a consumer culture, without even one of its gravest problems having been permanently resolved.

The Six-Day War gave rise to the first Government of National Unity in Israel. For the first time in his life, Begin was a member of the government; and now, for the first time, he had to face the duty of bearing responsibility for government policy in circumstances which made possible the realization of an important part of the great historic vision for which he and his movement had fought for many years. This issue became the main objective of Menachem Begin's work in the government.

His deputy in the Herut movement leadership, the late Arye Ben Eliezer, said shortly after the war: 'Israel has to remain in Western Palestine'. He proposed that the problem of the Arab refugees be solved and made the continued presence of Arabs in *Eretz Israel* conditional on their not subverting the existence of Israel (Knesset proceedings, 31 July 1967). Menachem Begin said: 'I have proposed and propose that housing development for Jewish residents be established in all the liberated towns of Eretz Israel – in Jericho, Hebron, Bethlehem, Ramallah, Nablus, Jenin, Tulkarm, Qalgiliya, Ariel, Rafiah and the rest' (Knesset Proceedings, 11 June 1969).

This approach contradicted the traditional line of the Labour Party majority in the government and the Knesset. Its approach, formulated by Yigal Allon, favoured Israeli withdrawal from extensive areas of Judea, Samaria and Gaza – mainly those that were densely populated with the creation of a security belt, held by the IDF, in which Jewish settlements would be established.

Menachem Begin's attitude was based on two central postulates: the natural right of the Jewish people to the land of Israel and its right to security and peace. Ideological arguments and a pragmatic analysis led Begin to conclude that support for retention of the territories and consolidation of the Israeli presence in them by setting up many rural and urban settlements.

Opposing Begin was the practical approach, lacking any ideological–historical dimension, of the leaders of the Labour Party, who favoured compromise. Labour was the dominant factor in the government and in any case dictated its policy. The Herut movement proferred the option of realizing the historical right, but spoke out for this from the inferior position of a minority opposition party. Thus the years between 1967 and 1977 were typical of the classic debate that had always taken place in the country's Jewish community.

1977 – A NEW SITUATION

But the outstanding difference between the new situation and that prior to establishment of the state was the fact that the Labour Party was gradually losing its strength and influence, while the Herut movement was gaining – until it finally came to power in 1977.

International conditions had also changed radically. While the Labour Party ruled, Israel enjoyed unprecedented room for manoeuvre. Now, the weakness of the Arab countries, the internal splits between them and above all their unwillingness to disclose even minimal flexibility, meant that any possibility for negotiating a political settlement was out of the question and the political situation remained frozen.

The peace between Israel and Egypt, because of its momentousness, did indeed change an important dimension in the relations between Israel and Arab countries, but it did not liberate the State of Israel from the distress of the increasingly complex conflict with the Palestinian people.

In the absence of any real outside pressure (mainly because of a lack of sufficient flexibility on the part of Arab countries who were not wise enough to provide a suitable reason for international pressure on Israel), the central problem moved from the conflict between

Israel and the Arab countries to that of the relations between Jews and Palestinians.

Since 1977, the internal Israeli debate over this issue intensified against the background of the government's policy of expanding Jewish settlement in Judea and Samaria. This was designed to block any possibility of pressure for Israel to withdraw from those areas. As a result, these areas were enriched by scores of thousands of Jewish inhabitants, and the internal dispute in Israel became increasingly embittered. The more people realized that options were being closed and that there was no simple formula for resolution of the conflict with the Palestinians, so the distress stemming from increased interaction with them was aggravated.

Twenty years after the Six-Day War, we are asking virtually the same questions as those we asked immediately after the war, but with increased tiredness, less enthusiasm and greater recognition that the political options have narrowed to a choice between (almost) complete withdrawal from the territories (in the hope of proper security arrangements) and continued presence and involvement in them, leading to their full integration into the State of Israel.

I believe that the option of total withdrawal is undesirable for Israel, and could expose her to grave existential dangers. This approach does not evidence insensitivity to the serious distress created by continued possession of Judea, Samaria and Gaza. But it does recognize the immanent geopolitical and ethnic instability of the region, and the fear that this reality will undermine any political arrangement and lead to the sort of anarchy that characterizes the terrorist-replete country of Lebanon that has suffered from civil war for more than a decade.

For Israel to undertake a complete withdrawal would be a simplistic solution, despite its attractions. Disengagement from an inimical Arab population, the lack of desire to face confrontations with the population that would be inherent in continued rule over it, and the feeling that Israeli society suffers from a complex moral problem because of the confrontation with this population – these considerations contribute to the attraction of that solution.

However, the inherent risks could be such that they would cost the State of Israel its very existence. The claim that is heard in Israel from those favouring withdrawal – namely, that the state has sufficient strength to enable it to defend its citizens within even less convenient borders, similar to those that were in force up to 1967 – ignores the possibility that most of the population of Israel would be exposed to the phenomenon of terrorism in the wake of withdrawal.

True, Israel does have a trained air force and defence systems that ensure its security from overall military attack, although clearly the 1967 borders enable such an attack to be frustrated only at the heaviest cost for the sensitive human fabric of Israel. However, I have no doubt that those old borders cannot block Israel from exposure to daily terrorist actions that would make the life of its citizens intolerable. Total withdrawal would be tantamount to tempting extremist Palestinian elements to take control of Judea, Samaria and Gaza should Israel, heaven forbid, vacate them, to continue to undermine the stability of life in Israel. The Middle East really contains so many uncertainties that to volunteer for such a dangerous adventure, comprising as it does an intolerable risk, would be completely insensitive.

PATTERN FOR A SOLUTION

The question is: Is there some other solution that provides an adequate response at least to some of the traditional and practical problems that continued presence in Judea, Samaria and Gaza creates? The historic rights governing the answer cannot, to the best of my understanding, be queried, but the question cannot only be examined from that point of view. Belief in these rights is not subject to political argument. Were they and only they to dictate political positions, it would be superfluous to conduct any political debate and the outcome could be determined in advance. I believe that realization of Israel's historic rights to Israeli land has to be implemented in association with the existing data on the ground, cautiously, with restraint, and with a sense of political wisdom.

The Camp David Accords do indeed propose a model for such a solution, one which preserves the most important factor for Israel: continued presence in the areas of Judea, Samaria and Gaza, while yet circumventing part of the demographic problem that cannot be ignored. The genius of Camp David lies in its understanding that a reasonable solution must circumvent the historical problems – which are so loaded emotionally – and concentrate on those practical spheres which can be dealt with without arousing such bitter emotions. The importance of the framework determined in the Camp David

Accords lies not in exact implementation in all details and minutiae but in acceptance of the basic concept as a guide line.

The underlying principle should be to achieve a number of aims:

(a) To reduce to an unavoidable minimum the involvement of Jews in the life of the local population in Judea, Samaria and Gaza. Israel's defence requirements and historical rights do not necessitate individual supervision of almost every municipality, institution or public body in these areas. The greater the number of points of contact between Jews and Arab, the greater the friction and motivation for terrorism. The Israeli interest must be to minimise these contacts, with a continued Jewish presence in the territories.

   The operative significance of this approach must lead to a gradual removal of the military government from the towns of Judea, Samaria and Gaza. This must be an ongoing process, which should be initiated immediately.

(b) At the same time as the military government is removed from the towns of Judea, Samaria and Gaza, the Israeli army should be positioned in these territories at key strategic points, as determined by the Camp David Accords. The Israeli military presence in the Areas and along the Jordan River has to serve two purposes: defence against military infiltration of these areas and protection of the main roads against terrorist acts.

(c) The local leadership should be permitted to run its affairs with a maximum degree of independence from the Israeli government. Israel should seek a situation in which the local inhabitants themselves define exactly what form of rule they prefer, either establishment of governmental bodies representing the whole population, or through the municipalities and local councils. These bodies will obviously have to function on the assumption that they have no authority to conduct foreign relations other than through the government of Israel.

(d) With the removal of the military government from the towns and the placing of affairs in the hands of local bodies, a body that will deal with law enforcement within the towns will have to be set up. This body will function on a pattern to be defined exactly in advance, and it will be subject to the governmental bodies to be established in the territories.

(e) Jewish settlement in Judea, Samaria and Gaza will not be halted but it will be confined to areas where there is minimum chance for friction between Jews and Arabs. I believe that the axiom that it is vital to settle close to Arab conurbations, including the Jewish Quarter of Hebron, should be re-examined. The right of Jews to do so is not questioned, but the wisdom of exercising that right in certain areas, specifically when the outcome could be an increase in violence between Jews and Arabs, is. Other problems associated with control over water resources, for example, can be discussed between Israel and the local governmental bodies.

The pattern proposed here is based on an assumption that there is no chance in the foreseeable future for reaching an overall political settlement in formal and open negotiations between Israel and Jordan over the Palestinian problem and its territorial aspects.

UNILATERAL STEPS

Israel should implement these policies unilaterally. A considerable portion of this does not necessarily require the concurrence of the other party, but, should such consent be necessary, there is a better chance of achieving it informally than by way of formal, public and comprehensive negotiations.

In recent years, various formulas have been put forward, representing code-like names for political perceptions, for example, 'improving the quality of life in the areas of Judea, Samaria and Gaza', 'Jordanization of the territories' or 'unilateral autonomy'. Each of these formulas, with varying emphases, reflects a willingness to take the situation out of the current deep freeze and to initiate steps leading to a reduction of the burden that these territories form for us, without, however, ignoring matters that are vital for our defence and our future.

Were it possible to achieve a formal agreement on this it would, of course, be preferable. But the fact that such an agreement cannot necessarily be achieved must not serve as an excuse to disregard the obligation of working for their gradual and cumulative implementation.

Unilateral steps, initiated by the State of Israel, could be welcomed with quiet understanding by Jordan. That country, which finds it so difficult to disclose a willingness to enter into formal contacts with Israel, wisely and with restraint cooperates with Israel realistically on various common issues.

The difficulty in reaching an agreement is not derived from the lack of a proper framework for the actual holding of negotiations. The argument over the international conference idea is basically artificial. Neither Israel nor Jordan need the framework of the United Nations or superpower involvement in order to ascertain, at the highest level of leadership, what the flexible limits of each are regarding a possible settlement.

Twenty years of Israeli rule in Judea, Samaria and Gaza have developed mechanisms for direct contacts that have proved their effectiveness and credibility for both sides. Were an opening to be created for understanding as to the anticipated final result of such contacts, it would have been achieved long ago, without any conference or any superpower mediation. The fact that innumerable personal, direct contacts over twenty years have not produced any agreement only testifies to the fact that the difficulties in achieving it are not associated with negotiation techniques. An international conference, of the sort discussed in Israel in the past year, will not achieve what direct contacts could not, unless such conference is designed to be a lever for concentrated international pressure on Israel by the great powers. And the fear of such pressure is one of the main causes for the opposition to such a conference by the Likud leaders in Israel.

In the final resort, we are sentenced to continue living with the political problems and moral issues deriving from the Israeli–Palestinian conflict for many more years. There are no simple short cuts to a solution and there are no simplistic formulas that can outflank basic, substantive issues such as that of sovereignty in the territories, the status of Jerusalem, and so on.

After twenty years, during which Israel has sought a comprehensive formal settlement, one must draw the lesson from its absence and reduce the level of expectation, taking slow steps toward a change in the actual situation in the territories. Such steps, it is true, will not lead to an ideal solution (apparently there is simply no such thing) that, in one blow, will remove the pressure of these problems from our national agenda. But it does, for the first time, contain the opportunity to create a dynamic of reference that will assure Israel of compliance with two conditions that I consider vital for the future: the first is to guarantee Israel's continued presence in those areas of the Land of Israel integral to its historic heritage; and the second is minimizing the points of daily friction with the Arabs of the country and assuring them of a minimum of respectable human conditions, while running their own affairs.

4 The Politics of the Region

Itamar Rabinovich

In the voluminous literature devoted to current developments in the Middle East, it has been common to describe the Six-Day War as a watershed in the region's recent history. But was it? Much has happened in the Middle East during the intervening twenty years. Three Arab–Israeli wars (if the War of Attrition is counted as one) were fought and a peace treaty was signed between Egypt and Israel. Jamal Abdul-Nasser, Egypt's and the Arabs' messianic leader, died and his legacy has been seriously eroded. The energy crisis and the steep rise in oil prices brought legendary wealth to parts of the Arab world and turned the Arabs, for a number of years, into influential actors on the international scene. Soviet influence in the Middle East rose steeply in the immediate aftermath of the 1967 war but sank drastically after 1972 as the United States regained its hegemonic position in the region's core area. In the 1970s Islam – eclipsed, or so it seemed, in earlier decades by other ideas and forces – was again a dominant force in the region's political life. The Iranian monarchy was toppled by an Islamic revolution and the war between Iran and Iraq was added to the Arab–Israeli conflict and the Lebanese crisis as a persistent focus of tension and violence.

THE MAJOR ISSUES

It is obviously difficult to identify the precise impact of a single event within this rich history. The task can be simplified to some extent by a separate examination of the major issues. Thus, it is clear and not at all surprising that the war had a decisive influence on the course of the Arab–Israeli conflict. For one thing, it demonstrated Israel's military might and persuaded most of the Arab states and leaders that the notion of a military solution to the conflict had to be ruled out. In this respect, the Israeli victory of 1967 was far more persuasive than that of 1956. In 1967 Israel acted alone, did not attack by surprise and defeated several Arab states simultaneously. The

42

Tunisian president, Habib Bourguiba, had argued in 1965 that the vision of a simple military victory over Israel had to be abandoned. He was vilified and denounced at the time, but the events of 1967 gradually brought others round to a similar point of view.[1]

Israel's territorial gains in June 1967 introduced an element of flexibility into the Arab–Israeli conflict that had been significantly absent during the preceding eighteen years. Among the factors militating against all serious attempts to resolve the conflict had been the Arab insistence on significant Israeli territorial concessions. As the Arabs saw it, Israel's very existence was illegitimate and, in return for their willingness to extend recognition, Israel had to make far-reaching concessions that would have both a symbolic and a practical value. From the Israeli perspective, the 1949 borders were unsatisfactory and difficult to defend, and territorial concessions or the return of a large number of Arab refugees unthinkable.[2] Of the territories captured in June 1967, the Sinai Peninsula and the Golan Heights were originally seen by Israel as bargaining chips to be traded as part of a peace settlement.[3] This was not yet acceptable to the Arabs, but ten years later Egypt came close to accepting the Israeli outlook.[4]

But the June War had other, less than benign, consequences. The Arabs' humiliating defeat, Israel's conquest of and lingering stay in Egyptian and Syrian national territory, and its control of Muslim holy places and of the Palestinian population of the West Bank and Gaza Strip, all had an exacerbating effect on the Arab–Israeli conflict. In military terms – the order of battle of the Israel Defence Forces and its Arab rivals and the weapons systems used by them – June 1967 undoubtedly represents a turning point. This is illustrated clearly by the development of the Syrian armed forces. In 1967 the Syrian army consisted, according to the Military Balance of the International Institute of Strategic Studies in London, of two armoured brigades, two mechanized brigades, five infantry brigades, one parachute battalion and six artillery regiments. Its total strength was estimated at 50 000 men. The same source for 1986–7 describes an army estimated at 320 000, consisting of eight divisions (five armoured and three mechanized), six independent brigades, one special forces division and three missile brigades. Comparable developments took place in Syria's air force, navy and aerial defence.[5] To assess the full significance of these figures, it must be remembered that the quantitative leap was accompanied by a similar qualitative upgrading of weapon systems, and that the Israeli armed forces and those of the other major Arab protagonists underwent a similar development during the same period.

It is more difficult to measure the June War's impact on the Palestinian problem. The Palestinian component of the Arab–Israeli conflict was brought back to the fore in the early 1960s. The Palestine Liberation Organization (PLO) was established in its original form by the Arab states in 1964. The genuine Palestinian organizations – i.e., Fatah and the organizations emanating from the Arab Nationalist Movement – began their anti-Israeli activities in 1965. It is idle to speculate on the course of their evolution had the crisis of May 1967 not developed into a full-blown war. But the war, once it broke out, reopened and reshaped the Palestine question.

For one thing, Palestine west of the Jordan was again controlled by a single government. Israel could in theory decide to try and effect an historic compromise with the Palestinian Arabs in that territory, or could seek a solution of the problem through a settlement with Jordan. However, neither Israel nor the Arabs took a bold initiative or decision in this direction and in the meantime powerful forces developed on both sides that are still militating against an accommodation on, let alone a solution of, the Palestine issue.

In Israel there was a significant body of opinion which saw the capture of the West Bank and Gaza Strip not as an act of conquest but as an act of liberation. The claim to the whole territory of the Land of Israel was still upheld in the 1960s by parts of the Zionist spectrum, but was dormant and increasingly ritualistic. The events of 1967 awakened it, and gave it new life. In the following years, the call to hold on to the West Bank and Gaza for religious, ideological and security reasons grew more powerful. It led to the establishment of a specific political movement dedicated to this cause, *Gush Emunim*, and was also embodied within the political parties. It was soon reinforced by an actual body of settlers and by the development of economic and other ties between Israel proper and the administered territories.

But the war also propelled the PLO forward and turned it into an effective national movement. This was not only a consequence of Israel's capture and control of the West Bank and Gaza Strip with their Palestinian population. Rather, in the political conflict that followed the war the Arab side found it expedient to emphasize the Palestinian cause; the cases of the Sinai and the Golan Heights had their own merits, but they lacked the same emotional impact. The PLO, moreover, acquired an influence in Arab politics that was disproportionate to its actual power. This undoubtedly reflected its leadership's tactical skills, but was primarily a by-product of the failure in June 1967 of the Arab states, regimes and regular armies and, above all, the older revolutionary movements. The PLO, or the Palestinian revolution, became for a number of years the focus of Arab hopes for change and achievement.[6]

But for the majority of Israelis the PLO represented the Arab (and more specifically Palestinian) claim over the whole of historic Palestine. The PLO establishment may have accepted the idea of a Palestinian state in the West Bank and Gaza Strip in 1974 but that Israeli majority continued to view the claims embodied in the Palestinian National Covenant (of 1964 and 1968) as the significant and operative document, and the June 1974 decisions as a tactical manoeuvre. Since the Arab consensus formally defined the PLO as 'the sole legitimate representative of the Palestinian people', it became practically impossible for Israel to seek a solution to the Arab–Israeli conflict without addressing its Palestinian component, and in a fashion acceptable to the PLO. All attempts to ignore or circumvent the PLO have so far failed.

The Egyptian–Israeli peace treaty of 1979 thus demonstrated two contradictory consequences of the 1967 war. In the bilateral Israeli–Egyptian conflict the Six-Day War had resulted in short-term exacerbation, but in the longer term the Egyptian desire to regain the Sinai enabled the two parties to overcome numerous obstacles and trade territory for peace. On the other hand, Israeli hopes for a far-reaching amelioration of the Arab–Israeli conflict were disappointed by the war's other consequence: the Palestinian issue had become so salient that what had been known as the Arab–Israeli conflict was largely telescoped into an Israeli–Palestinian conflict.

SUPERPOWER RIVALRY

Allusion has already been made to the 1967 war's effects on the Soviet and American positions in the Middle East. The Soviet Union's successful advances in the Arab world during the 1955–67 period were greatly facilitated by two factors: clear-cut support for the Arab side to the Arab–Israeli conflict, particularly in the military sphere, and the absence of a colonial past in the region. Both factors were undermined during the years immediately following the war. The process unfolded in three stages.

In the war's immediate aftermath the Soviet Union's standing and prestige declined. Its two principal allies were defeated without any effective Soviet intervention. Soviet weapons systems, military doctrine and military training were all discredited, and the Soviets were openly accused by Nasser of having generated the May crisis which led to the June War.

These reverses were soon overshadowed by other developments. The Soviets helped to rebuild the Egyptian and Syrian armies and enabled the Arabs to launch the War of Attrition. Their support was contrasted with the considerable degree of agreement between Washington and Jerusalem. Soviet influence in Egypt and Syria increased while the US position in the Arab world was seen to be eroding. The fall of the Libyan monarchy in September 1969 was viewed as a harbinger of still greater losses for the West.

The expulsion of Soviet advisers from Egypt in July 1972 marked the transition to a third phase. The Egyptians came to the conclusion, five years after June 1967, that the Soviets were unable to help them regain the Sinai, that the US was the one power that could possibly achieve this for them, and that the course of events since 1967 – particularly the Soviet–Egyptian treaty of May 1971 – was costing Egypt its freedom. The Soviet Union may not have had a colonial past in the Arab world, but it was fast acquiring a colonial present.[7]

These changes in the superpowers' respective positions in the Middle East can and should be traced directly to the circumstances and outcome of the 1967 war. But an accurate assessment of the war's significance for Washington and Moscow must take into account the changes in the pattern of their rivalry which had occurred in the mid-1960s. Lyndon Johnson's particular approach to foreign policy, the stiffer competition in the Third World and the escalation of the conflicts between Moscow's Middle Eastern allies on the one hand and Washington's conservative Arab allies and Israel on the other turned the Middle East in the years 1964–7 into a major arena of direct and indirect Soviet–American conflict. The Soviet Union was using the Arab–Israeli conflict in an unprecedented way in order to consolidate its Arab support, while the US found itself in a direct and bitter confrontation with Nasser.[8] In this, as in other respects, the 1967 war grew out of the circumstances of the mid-1960s but served, due to its scope and impact, to alter – and in some cases to transform – these circumstances.

Events in the 1972–4 period fully vindicated Henry Kissinger's position in his debate with the architects of the Rogers Plan in 1969–

70. They had argued that, in order to check the erosion of American influence in the Arab world, the US should exert pressure on Israel to withdraw from the Sinai (and other territories captured in 1967) in return for something less than a full peace settlement. Kissinger's position was that such pressure should be used only in a fashion likely to benefit the US: the Rogers Plan, in his view, was bound to benefit the Soviets, who would be perceived as the Arabs' effective benefactors. The outcome of the 1973 war enabled Kissinger to implement a policy based on Israeli withdrawal from Arab territory in return for Arab political concessions. The US appeared in the 1970s as the only power capable of seeing such agreements through, and its own standing in the region rose accordingly.

ARAB POLITICS: A COMPLEX PICTURE

An examination of the June War's impact on Arab politics – more specifically on the domestic politics of the principal Arab States – yields a complex picture. The unprecedented defeat generated an unusually gloomy mood in the Arab world, which was expressed in a rich body of literature, *belles lettres* and social and political commentary. The despair, cynicism, self-deprecation and self-flagellation, so characteristic of this period, were most eloquently rendered by the poetry of the Syrian Nizar al-Qabbani and by the novels and stories of, among many others, Naguib Mahfuz and Suleiman Fayyad in Egypt, Zakariyya Tamer and Abdul Rahman al-Ujeyli in Syria and Abdul Rahman Majid al-Rubay'i in Iraq.[9]

In his poignant poem 'On the Margins of the Defeat's Notebook', Nizar al-Qabbani wrote: 'In short/we wore civilization's skin/but the spirit belongs to the age of ignorance/with flute and whistle/a victory is not won/our improvization cost us/fifty thousand new tents'. It is easy to see how this frame of mind gave rise to what seemed the dominant school in the social and political commentary of the late 1960s – a radical, secularist, often Marxist, call for a total transformation of Arab society and politics.[10]

These writers devoted less time and space to the obvious criticism of traditional and conservative regimes than to the devastation of the regimes known as 'progressive' or 'revolutionary' – the Nasserist regime in Egypt and the Ba'th regime in Syria. The Syrian philosopher Sadeq al-Azm, the Lebanese sociologist Nadim al-Bitar and the poet Adonis were among the most distinctive representatives of this outlook. Politically, it manifested itself in the radical Palestinian organizations of the Marxist school of George Habash.

This school may have been the most prolific, but it was far from monopolizing the intellectual scene. A populist revolutionary Islamic school and a conservative one drew their own conclusions from the defeat of 1967 – and, as it turned out, their outlooks were more effectively represented in the realm of power politics than those of their secularist and Marxist counterparts. In that realm, a number of factors combined to prevent the reckoning and the radical transformation that many expected. One was the psychological mechanism which, in an hour of crisis, serves to reinforce the public's adherence to a familiar and experienced leadership, despite its glaring failure. The genuine reaction in Egypt and other parts of the Arab world to Nasser's resignation speech was the best illustration of this factor at work.

The regimes of the day also displayed impressive resilience and ingenuity in their struggle to survive. Nasser purged his deputy, General Amer and his faction and turned them into culprits and scapegoats. In Syria, Salim Hatoum, who returned from his exile in Jordan, was executed by the regime and used in order to create a Syrian version of the 'stab in the back' theory. The conservative Arab regimes headed by the Saudi royal house soon came to the conclusion that it was in their interest to extend a helping hand to the weakened Nasser; he no longer threatened them and in co-operation with him the radical tide could be effectively stemmed. As Fouad Ajami puts it:

> Several factors were to bring about an alliance between the traditional states and the Egyptian regime: the radicalism of the new revolutionaries . . . the emotional appeal of the slogan of 'a war of national liberation' and the dangers to a totally discredited Arab system of states of a military outcome that had dishonoured all the regimes and ridiculed all those in power.[11]

The Jordanian crisis in the summer of 1970 was a culmination of these developments. The Hashemite regime asserted itself against the radical Palestinian challenge and quashed the Palestinian organizations. Nasser, himself at loggerheads with the Palestinians, did not support King Hussein but instead assumed a neutral posture by becoming a mediator in the conflict. In Syria the crisis forced a decision between Salah Jadid's radical faction and Hafez al-Asad's pragmatic one, and brought the latter to power in Damascus.

Nasser's death and succession by Anwar Sadat and Asad's rise to power led to similar results – in Cairo and Damascus the regimes defeated in June 1967 were altered from within. In Egypt the changes were far-reaching – Sadat over time reversed Nasser's policies on most major issues. A different man acting in entirely different conditions, Asad introduced more limited changes. In any event, in neither country were these changes, advocated by the radical critics in the aftermath of the June war, introduced.

It was in Jordan that the political system's resilience was demonstrated in the most remarkable fashion. In 1949 King Abdallah had transformed his kingdom by incorporating East Jerusalem and the West Bank. In 1967, these were detached and have remained so for what is now a twenty-year period. And yet the Hashemite regime not only survived the 1967 defeat and the subsequent crises but has also retained its essential features throughout the transformations. As one historian of Jordan wrote in 1974:

> the socio-political characteristics of Jordan in 1973 were essentially the same as those of Jordan in 1967 prior to the Six Day War. One may state even more sweepingly that with respect to these characteristics Jordan has remained essentially unchanged throughout its existence as a state from its establishment shortly after WWII as Transjordan to this very day.[12]

The same cannot be said with regard to Israel and the West Bank. The 1967 war's impact on both is described in detail elsewhere in this volume, but it is important to mention even in passing the far-reaching changes they underwent as an important part of the larger regional picture.

THE COMBINED EFFECT OF OTHER FACTORS

Any attempt to measure the role of the June War in the shaping of the current Middle Eastern scene encounters an important methodological problem. That scene has been shaped by several processes. Some of these processes, as we saw above, were directly affected by the war's outcome. Other cardinal developments – the 'oil revolution', the Iranian Revolution and the war between Iran and Iraq – were clearly the result of other forces at work. But much of what has happened in the region was the outcome of a lengthy chain of events or a convergence of developments to which the June War has made at least a partial contribution.

The development of inter-Arab relations is an excellent case in point. The inter-Arab system has been transformed during the past two decades: the ideology of pan-Arabism declined, Egypt's centrality and predominance were diminished, new competing centres of influence rose (and in some cases declined again), old lines of division and alliance were replaced by new ones and the Arab system of states became ever more fragmented.[13]

In some of these developments the influence of June 1967 is easily discernible. Abdul-Nasser's stature was tarnished by his military defeat, while his reliance on the conservative Arab states enhanced their position, and his successor's determination to regain the Sinai and to disengage from the conflict with Israel led to Egypt's formal ousting from the Arab League.

But a closer examination reveals that the decline of Nasser, Nasserism and pan-Arabist ideology had begun well before 1967 and that the failure of the Egyptian–Syrian union, Egypt's abortive intervention in the Yemen and Nasserism's domestic shortcomings and failures were important contributors to the same set of developments. Likewise, the decline in Egypt's centrality must also be seen as a consequence of its impoverishment, the accumulation of great wealth in oil-producing Arab states and the crystallization of relatively powerful regimes in Syria and Iraq.

Islam's 'return' as a powerful political and ideological force in the mid- and late 1970s, and the radicalization of Islamic politics in the late 1970s is another example of the complexity of the forces at work; but they also provide an excellent illustration of the combined effect of the events of 1967 and 1973–4 on the Middle East. As we have already seen, the defeat and humiliation of 1967 gave rise, among other currents, to a radical populist Islamic school. It blamed the defeat on the Arabs' deviation from Islam's way and advocated a full return to Islam as the system of belief upon which every society must be predicated. The events of 1973–4 gave Arabs and Muslims a sense of power that was all the more intoxicating against the background of recent humiliations. But it did not take long to realize that the new sense of power was largely illusory. The humiliating effects of 1967 were long-lasting; the elation of 1973–4 was short-lived and left a bitter after-taste.

Like so many other wars, then, the Six-Day War served as a catalyst for and an accelerator of numerous changes. Its impact is all the more impressive given its brevity and in comparison with other, longer, Arab–Israeli or Middle Eastern wars. The difficulty has been mentioned above of separating the consequences of June 1967 from those of October 1973. Future historians armed with a better perspective may, indeed, telescope these two wars and the intervening War of Attrition into a single conflict. It should also be borne in mind that new material is bound to come out that is most likely to alter our understanding of the May 1967 crisis, the June 1967 war and their impact on the region.

Notes

1. For an elaboration of these themes see several of the essays included in I. Rabinovich and H. Shaked (eds), *From June to October* (New Brunswick, N.J., 1978).
2. For a useful survey and overview of the various efforts to resolve the Arab–Israeli conflict, see Saadia Touval, *The Peace Brokers* (Princeton, N.J., 1932) 214–33. The opening of British, American and Israeli archives for the first half of the 1950s has, as several imminent publications will show, shed new light on these efforts.
3. On 19 June 1967, the Israeli Cabinet decided to seek peace treaties with Egypt and Syria based on the international borders between Israel and these two Arab states. For details see Moshe Dayan, *Milestones* (Hebrew version, Jerusalem and Tel Aviv, 1976) 490–1.
4. For an authoritative account of the Israeli–Egyptian peace process and the transformation of Egypt's position, see William B. Quandt, *Camp David* (Washington D.C., 1986) passim.
5. International Institute for Strategic Studies, *The Military Balance 1967–8*, 40–1 and *1986–7*, 108–9.
6. See William B. Quandt, Fouad Jabber and Ann Mosley Lesech, *The Politics of Palestinian Nationalism* (Berkeley, Cal., 1973) and G. Ben-Dor (ed.), *The Palestinians and the Middle East Conflict* (Ramat Gan, Israel, 1978) particularly the editor's own contribution.
7. For the best and most comprehensive study of the Soviet–Egyptian relationship see Alvin Z. Rubinstein, *Red Star on the Nile: The Soviet–Egyptian Influence Relationship Since the June War* (Princeton, N.J., 1977) and his contribution to this volume (Chapter 9). For a different perspective – that of an Egyptian journalist and politician sympathetic to the Soviet Union – see Mohamed Heikal, *The Sphinx and the Commissar* (New York, 1978).
8. See Steven L. Spiegel, *The Other Arab–Israeli Conflict* (Chicago, 1985) 118–30, and his contribution to this volume (Chapter 8); also Nadav Safran, *Israel, the Embattled Ally* (Cambridge, Mass., 1978) 381–8.

9. Shimon Ballas, *Arab Literature in the Shadow of War* (Tel Aviv, 1978) (Hebrew).
10. Several of these writings are included in the Hebrew-language anthology, Y. Harkabi, *Arab Lessons from their Defeat* (Tel Aviv, 1970) (Hebrew). More recently, they were analyzed in an unusually perceptive way in Fouad Ajami's *The Arab Predicament* (Cambridge, 1981).
11. Harkabi, *Arab Lessons from the Past*, 72.
12. Uriel Dann, 'The Jordanian Entity in Changing Circumstances, 1967–73', in Rabinovich and Shaked (eds) *From June to October*, 231–41.
13. See P. J. Vatikiotis, 'Inter-Arab Relations' and 'Regional Politics', in Vatikiotis, *Arab and Regional Politics in the Middle East* (London and New York, 1984) 27–134.

5 Policies in the Administered Territories
Shlomo Gazit

The twenty years that have elapsed since the Six-Day War are too short a time for the purpose of historical analysis or conclusive evaluation; nor is this my purpose. A short summary of the main lines of Israeli policy in the conquered territories is a more appropriate perspective from which to present Israel's contemporary situation.

Israel's policy in the administered territories was initially successful. Although the Israel Defence Forces (IDF) entered the Six-Day War unprepared for the role of military administration in the territories to be conquered, it was blessed with a great deal of luck. Combat in the West Bank area, which lasted only 72 hours, was conducted without inflicting physical damage and loss of life on the local Arab population. The physical infrastructure and the local economy, principally an underdeveloped agricultural economy, were unharmed and could resume functioning on the morrow. Another source of Israeli good fortune was the remarkable talent for improvization shown by the commanders in the field and by the civilians drafted from high-ranking government positions to serve as staff officers for the civil administration. Naturally, endless problems arose, but immediate solutions were always found. The third element of good fortune came in the form of Moshe Dayan, Israel's Minister of Defence at the time.

Moshe Dayan was never prone to dissipate his efforts over the full range of his field of responsibility. He always chose one or two fields on which to focus and which he deemed worthy of his personal dedication and enterprise. In 1967, and throughout the entire period during which he served as Minister of Defence (some seven years), Dayan regarded Israel's policy in the territories as an issue of primary importance. Immediately following the Six-Day War, Dayan enjoyed an incredible reputation. Overnight, he became a living legend, admired by almost everyone in Israel. Most, if not all, of his colleagues within the government envied him his success and feared him. Nevertheless, they respected him and were almost always unwilling to enter into a confrontation with him.

Dayan knew nothing of the doctrine of military administration. But he had a clear opinion that the 'professional' military administration personnel (i.e., those who had, since 1948, stood at the head of the military government network in Israel proper, administering the population centres of the Arab minority) were unfit for the new task, and he refrained completely from engaging them in the new network. Dayan relied heavily on his own sense of intimate acquaintance with the Arab people. Policy in the territories developed in an empirical fashion, based on the cardinal premise that Israel would have to learn to live with the Arab people.

CONSISTENT POLICY

Examination of the current situation in the territories reveals that Israel's principal policy objectives have been achieved. For twenty years Israel has administered the territories with a minimal onus; neither an overwhelming security problem, economic burden, nor (in everything pertaining to the local Arab population) an intolerable political liability. It is doubtful that in the days immediately following the Six-Day War there were many in Israel who entertained the possibility that, twenty years later, Israel would still, in the absence of a political solution, be administering the territories. From the point of view of these who shaped and executed this policy, the achievement has eclipsed all expectations.

If one were to examine the form and structure of the administration, its basic policy guidelines and conventions, one would find that little has changed over twenty years. This is to no small extent surprising in view of the many changes that have taken place in Israel and the world since the Six-Day War. During this period, seven defence ministers and six chiefs-of-staff have served in Israel. In 1970, an internal conflict broke out in Jordan that threatened the very existence of the Hashemite Kingdom, a war that ended in 'Black September' and the elimination of the PLO as a political and military factor in Jordan. In 1973, the Yom Kippur War brought about significant transformations in Israel's self-image and reputation, its standing in the Arab world, and in the United States' involvement and function as an active factor on the scene. Another result of the Yom Kippur War was the oil embargo and the consequent rise in importance of the Arab oil-producing states. In 1975, civil war broke out in Lebanon, with the PLO and other Palestinian organizations playing leading roles. 1977 saw the 'upheaval' in Israel which transferred power from the Labour Alignment to the Likud. A few months later, Israel witnessed the dramatic visit of Anwar Sadat, President of Egypt. This visit paved the way for the Camp David Accords and the Israeli–Egyptian peace treaty. A short time later, the Shah of Iran was deposed; Muslim fundamentalist rule was established in Iran, spreading fanaticism and encouraging religious extremism in the entire area. At the beginning of the 1980s, autonomy discussions were held to determine the shape of the administration of the territories and the degree of independence to be granted their inhabitants. Finally, in 1982, Israeli forces moved into Lebanon, with concomitant repercussions regarding the Palestinians, Lebanon, Syria and Israel. The PLO lost its one and only base along Israel's borders; its military forces were dispersed all over the Middle East and, for the first time in twenty years, Arafat's leadership was contested. This opportunity was immediately exploited by Jordan to re-establish and strengthen its position among the West Bank population.

Surprisingly enough, these changes and convulsions in the Middle East have not only failed to effect any real change in policy guidelines, they have not (more surprisingly), even led to the opening of a discussion of this policy or a re-evaluation of its appropriateness to a reality that now has changed.

COLLATERAL FOR A SETTLEMENT

Immediately following the cessation of hostilities in the Six-Day War, Israel had a definite objective in mind: the victory achieved in this war must not be wasted. Israel and its neighbours could not return to the boundaries of 4 June 1967, and to a situation of chronic instability. The occupied territories were the collateral which Israel would agree to trade only in return for a true and comprehensive settlement of the Arab–Israeli conflict.

Even if there were those in Israel who hoped and believed that it would be possible at the time to expel the inhabitants of the territories, they were quickly disabused of this expectation. The first attempt at such expulsion took place during the fighting itself, when military commanders angrily destroyed several Arab villages in the Latrun enclave and the southern part of the Hebron district as well as some houses in the towns of Kalkilya and Tulkarm. But the inhabitants remained in the area, homeless refugees finding shelter in the shade of nearby trees. Not many days passed before the Minister of Defence proposed to the government that most of the villages that had been destroyed be immediately rehabilitated. This was also the case in the matter of evacuees; many inhabitants, especially families whose heads had been away from the territories during the war, had been afraid to remain under the IDF's rule and had fled to the East Bank. As the dust of war settled and it quickly became evident that the conqueror was not as terrible as he had seemed, these evacuees declared their willingness to return and most of those applying (excluding refugees from 1948) were permitted to do so. It was a distinctive expression of Moshe Dayan's character; he found no difficulty in reneging on policies and decisions he himself had made only several weeks before as soon as it became obvious that they had not succeeded.

Israel's policy in the territories had some positive outcomes too. First of these was the creation of norms for coexistence, for almost complete normalization, between Israel and the inhabitants of the territories themselves. Second, under the auspices of the inhabitants of these territories and their serving as a binding link, norms of coexistence and normalization were to take effect in relations between Israel and the Arab world beyond its borders.

This later aspect of Israel's policy, termed the 'open-bridges policy' has become the most important instrument in Israel's 'carrot and stick' security policy. The harshest punishment devised by Israel and one which does not contradict the rules of international law, is the abrogation or constriction of the right of movement over the bridges.

Two principles have underlain and still lie at the heart of Israeli policy. The first holds that a political solution will be achieved through negotiations between Israel and the leaders of the Arab states beyond Israel's border (Egypt, Jordan and Syria), whereas the inhabitants of the territories will be unable to play a part or carry much weight in the formulation of a future settlement. Therefore, any political organization or uncontrolled political activity within the territories is to be totally prohibited. Military administration and free and democratic political activity cannot coexist; this would be a contradiction in terms. Real unregulated political activity under the conditions of occupation could take only one conceivable direction – a nationalist movement directed against the imposed domination from the outside. As long as Israel refused to consider leaders within the territories as possible partners to future negotiations, any such activity would have necessarily led to confrontation, conflict and increased frustration

within the population. Another policy in the territories, more plausible under the circumstances, regarding political activity would have
been just as undesirable – political organization of Israeli-backed
figures, the kind that could breed only one result: Arab quislings in
the territories. (There have been a few exceptions to this principle,
but they have been fruitless and have only succeeded in further
emphasizing the basic policy of non-participation and absence of
political dialogue with local leaders.)

This first principle has been expressed in two ways. One has been
the total prohibition of political organization. The other has been the
rejection of any initiative or attempt on the part of the territories'
inhabitants to serve as a channel for negotiation or as middlemen
between Israel, Arab and Palestinian leadership outside the territories. It can be stated that this policy stands in contradiction to the
'open-bridges' policy which has permitted – and over time even
encouraged – free contact between the inhabitants of the territories
and the Arab world beyond the borders. One should mention,
however, one recent exception to this principle, and that is Israel's
agreement to having Palestinians from the West Bank, who are not
identified with the PLO, serve as members of a joint Jordanian–
Palestinian delegation to direct talks with Israel. This is in line with
Israel's understanding of the Camp David Accords.

The second principle is the policy of enabling the local population
to conduct their lives with a minimum of involvement or interference
on the part of the Israeli administration (though there have been
important developments regarding the development of local services
and the rise in the population's standard of living). There are those
who consider that this principle stands in stark contradiction to
another basic line of thought in Israel's policy, a line of thought that
has grown stronger over the years – *de facto* annexation, the creation
of a new reality in the area through Jewish settlement and even closer
integration between the territories and Israel. In this matter, it is
difficult to obtain a reliable and universally agreed picture. All sides
collaborate, not necessarily wittingly, in exaggerating the extent of
'Israelization', with the resultant media publicity. Supporters of this
policy are eager to vaunt their accomplishments; its opponents within
the Jewish community point out the 'disaster' it is bringing upon
Israel; and Arab propaganda repeatedly points out the 'terrible
danger' attendant upon Israel's presence in the territories.

THREE FUNDAMENTAL FEATURES

The three major features of Israel's resolve to remain uninvolved in important and sensitive areas were determined twenty years ago and still hold today.

The first of these has been the retention of Jordanian law. This law has remained in force regarding the local population, as long as it does not interfere with or contradict any vital Israeli interests (mainly in the field of fiscal and monetary legislation). This not only expresses Israel's non-interference in the population's affairs, it also, to no less a degree, differentiates between the status of the territories' inhabitants and of Israel's inhabitants respectively. As early as 27 June 1967, when the Knesset passed the law annexing East Jerusalem to Israel, the different status of the rest of the West Bank was emphasized and even strengthened as a result. And, to the contrary, the effective annexation of the Golan Heights, as a result of the desertion by the local Syrian population of the region, led to a totally different policy toward the few Druse inhabitants who remained. This can be taken as an indication of what might have also occurred in Judea and Samaria had the IDF found this region abandoned by its inhabitants. Placing Jewish inhabitants who have settled in the territories over the years under Israeli law has also emphasized this differentiation and strengthened the local Arab inhabitants' feeling of a link, from their viewpoint, with the situation as it stood before the 1967 war. It is quite remarkable that even in East Jerusalem, annexed to Israel from the very beginning and with a population of some 130 000 Arabs, there has been no pressure on the local Arab population to adopt Israeli citizenship.

The second feature involves religion. Israel has not interfered with or disturbed religious life in the territories (this is true regarding all religions in the area – Muslims and Christians alike). The majority of the Arab population is religious and strict in its observance of ritual. This observance has been neither damaged nor disturbed; in some ways, the population now enjoys greater freedom, compared to the situation that existed before the entry of Israel's forces. The media do tend to focus attention in the opposite direction, towards the Temple Mount in Jerusalem and the Tombs of the Patriarchs in Hebron – explosive spots in which an act of provocation could any day set loose a conflagration that will be extremely difficult to extinguish. But with the exception of these two locations, the religious life of the local inhabitants, Muslims and Christians alike, goes on undisturbed. Furthermore, even on the Temple Mount, no censorship is exercised over the weekly sermon at El Aksa (as was customary during the Jordanian administration).

The third feature lies in the realm of local education. In 1967, towards the beginning of the first school year under the auspices of Israel's administration, an attempt was made to subject the population to an Israeli teaching programme and curriculum. The administration quickly abandoned this intention, and since then the local educational network has continued to function in accordance with the Jordanian format. In this fashion, not only has the continuation of the link with Jordan and a traditional Arab teaching programme been maintained, but the administration has also demonstrated its disinclination to subject the local population to 'Israelization': the differentiation between the Arab citizens of Israel and the Arab population of the territories has been established. Once again, the Arab population of East Jerusalem (which is part of Israel) has been allowed to retain the Jordanian teaching curriculum.

These three features have given rise to an immediate result – the local administration has remained almost entirely in Arab hands. Israel's policy in the territories has had another distinctive feature – open borders and no restraints on transportation. Everyone has learned to live with this policy. Its opponents among both Jews and Arabs have disappeared. As an instrument for exercising control over the Arabs, the open-borders policy has succeeded immensely; an Arab – whether an inhabitant of the territories or from the outside – who sabotaged it in any way would be considered a traitor to one of the local population's cardinal interests and thus blamed for depriving it of the greatest privilege conferred under Israel's rule. And as far as Israel is concerned, opening the borders and bridges has acted as a safety valve for these past twenty years.

SECURITY ASPECTS

It was obvious to Israel that this policy could be maintained only if it was proven, beyond all doubt, that it did not pose a security threat. Time and time again, after spectacular terrorist actions, voices have been heard calling for the closing of the bridges and curtailing of freedom of movement on both sides of the 'Green Line' (the pre-1967 borders). Yet time and time again, when the advantages are weighed against the liabilities, even from the narrow security viewpoint, a decision to maintain the existing situation has been reached.

There is no doubt that twenty years of relative quiet in the territories is Israel's most important achievement. True, terrorist attacks have taken place, and still do: stones are thrown and demonstrations are held. But considering the long span of time during which Israel has had a hostile population under military rule, it can be noted with some satisfaction that the number of incidents of this nature remain small. After Israel's bitter experience in the south of Lebanon, it is not hard to imagine what might have happened in the territories had they become the scene of an extensive terrorist struggle. Furthermore, almost from the very beginning, security measures have been reduced and constrained and the security forces have lowered their profile. This success of Israel is especially noteworthy when we bear in mind that the inhabitants of the territories enjoy the right of free travel beyond the territories to any destination in the Arab world, and vice-versa: hundreds of thousands of Arabs from the outside exercise the same right of free travel in order to visit Judea and Samaria and Israel yearly. The small number of terrorist actions is also impressive in view of the phenomenon of some 100 000 Arabs from Judea, Samaria and the Gaza Strip who enter Israel daily in pursuit of their occupations.

From the security viewpoint, the most important development, as far as Israel is concerned, is that Jordan no longer serves as a firm base for terrorist operations, a base with direct access to Judea and Samaria. Since 1970, the terrorists have been deprived of a land route of penetration, and the concomitant ability to smuggle in weapons and ammunition – prerequisites for any terrorist activity. This was achieved only after a bloody civil war on the East Bank, but most of the credit should be ascribed to the IDF defensive network along the Jordan Valley. The calm in the territories has also contributed to the non-renewal of the terrorist operational base in Jordan. Today, there are hardly any penetrations or pursuits along the length of the Jordan Valley; no blockades, searches and pursuits in the territories themselves. Punitive measures – curfews accompanied by searches, roundup, screening and identification of suspects – have disappeared as well. Houses are seldom destroyed and deportations beyond the border are becoming rarer and rarer, despite the fact that such deportations have proved to be the most painful and effective form of punishment. This success along the Jordanian border stands in marked contrast to the Palestinian campaign and struggle in the south of Lebanon; today, this is the only front from which the Palestinians can operate against Israeli targets beyond the border, even if only in a most limited way.

This success has been achieved due to four principal factors. The first has been the prevention and suppression of attempts by terrorist organizations to smuggle arms and ammunition into the occupied territories. Without explosives, grenades, small arms and the like, it is extremely difficult to execute effective terrorist actions. Lately, Israelis have been witnessing a new phenomenon – terrorists striking at Israelis with knives. This is no doubt a result of the scarcity of arms and ammunition.

The second factor has been the variety of measures for control, inspection and security, accompanied by the highest degree of public alertness. A large number of terrorist attacks has been avoided by these preventive and deterrent measures, and many others through the detection by civilians of bombing devices placed in public areas before they were activated.

The third factor has been the amazing success of the Israeli intelligence and security services in uncovering attempts at organization in the region. Immediately after the war, on 20 June 1967, Yasser Arafat declared that he would 'transfer his headquarters into the conquered territory'. And he did try to make good on his declaration, operating in person out of the West Bank for a period of two months. But when it became clear that he could not remain in the territory without being exposed and arrested, he put on women's garb and quickly decamped. Since then, the terrorist struggle has not been conducted from within the territory.

The Israeli Government appointed the Landau Commission to investigate the methods and the procedures of interrogation by the Shin-Beth interrogators (the Israeli Internal General Security Service). In its report published on the 30 October 1987 the Commission exposed, for the first time, the existing routine of employing both psychological as well as limited physical pressure on Arab terrorist suspects. The Commission approved these measures as an unfortunate necessity in some cases, being the only way to produce prompt and accurate intelligence on terrorist organization, plans and operations. Such pressure does also serve in many cases as a means to extract confessions accepted by the court. This explains the high number of convicted Arab prisoners on the one hand, as well as the very limited number of administrative detainees; in January 1987 a total of some 3500 Arab sentenced prisoners compared to some 6800 in May 1985 prior to the massive release of sentenced prisoners in exchange for Israeli POWs in Lebanon.

Recent statistics show the following:

	1984	1985	1986	1987 (May)
Deportations	1	31	5	4
Administrative detainees	0	131	37	62
Houses demolished or sealed	4	55	45	28

The fourth and final factor has been the local population's acceptance of the principal message relayed to them by Moshe Dayan twenty years ago: the inhabitants of the territories must choose between a way of life that is normal in as many respects as possible – a way of life that permits them to remain in place undisturbed, with their income guaranteed and with a rise to be expected in their standard of living and services – and a policy of terror and rebellion against Israel. A policy of terror and rebellion would be unable to defeat Israel or effect the IDF's evacuation, but it would force the use of countermeasures that would make life insufferable.

But even the record of achievements cannot conceal the fact that the real problem has not yet been solved. Today, as in the past, no political solution for the 'problem of the territories' is in sight. All sides involved feel locked in an impasse almost impossible to circumvent. Twenty years ago, Israel made its decision not to decide, with the intent of holding on to the territories as a bargaining chip while leaving all political options open; it now seems those options have all been blocked. No implementable solution – one that can be achieved with understanding and goodwill and is acceptable to both sides – is in sight. This cul-de-sac situation is intolerable and cannot be maintained for any great length of time. Sooner or later, almost inevitably, a radical move accompanied by a general outburst will take place.

TWO CONFLICTING OPTIONS

Immediately after the war in 1967, two basic possibilities were taken into account, at least in theory. The first envisioned a political settlement that would eventually terminate Israel's military rule in the territory (or at least most of it). The other possibility was Israel's total annexation of the territory, advocated by those who held the view that, as a result of the war and the state of occupation, the great majority of the local Arab population would prefer to leave.

Perhaps because of the National Unity Government that was formed just before the Six-Day War (in which many opposed and irreconcilable views were represented), a 'no-decision' policy was adopted which led to the commencement of a two-pronged process. On the one hand, action was taken in the interest of a political accord that would put an end to Israel's administration of the territories (with the possibility of minor border adjustments). To this end, liberalization measures were enacted for the benefit of the conquered population, allowing it to maintain its close web of contacts with the Arab world. The *status quo* on the day of occupation in all matters regarding the administration of justice and the teaching programme in the schools was maintained. But the next step – political organization, its encouragement and the cultivation of a local partner to negotiation – was never taken. Such organization was consistantly banned.

On the other hand, steps were initiated with the intent of bringing about the total annexation of the territory. A large-scale process of settlement began (especially after 1977), indiscriminately scattered over the entire area. A substantial infrastructure was laid: roads, waterlines, electricity and communications. As a result, the physical link between Judea and Samaria and Israel has been strengthened. Israeli law is in effect within the Jewish enclaves in the territories. While this has been going on, the Arab population has remained in place and even grown (at the end of 1985, the Arab population of Judea and Samaria numbered 807 000 and the Arab population of the Gaza Strip 520 000, as opposed to 590 000 and 350 000 respectively after the Six-Day War). The Arab population's standard of living has risen, and the normal routine of life continues.

And so, despite the considerable effort invested in Jewish settlement of the region, the hoped-for change in the demographic constitution of Judea and Samaria has not been brought about. In 1986, the Jewish population of Judea and Samaria *and* the Gaza Strip numbered 62 000, which is just a little over 4 per cent of the Arab population in these two regions.

In this way, over the years, as the Jewish presence in the territories grew and the political impasse remained unresolved, the rage and frustration of the Arab population of Judea and Samaria intensified. If, at times, there has emerged a certain willingness – even if only on the part of some of the inhabitants – to 'pay the price' and agree to coexistence with Israel, it seems that this willingness has always been suppressed by the feelings of the majority and by intimidation on the part of extremist elements, both internal and external. Most of the inhabitants yearn for change, for freedom and independence, but they have come to the conclusion that the desired change can be brought about only by means of an external directive forced upon Israel, or through the strength of Arab arms.

When the devotees of the idea of Jewish settlement and annexation to Israel became aware of the fact that a rare opportunity had been missed in 1967, during the war itself, and that Israel would never again have the political ability to expel the Arabs from the territory, there were those of them who turned to the formation of a Jewish underground in the hope that spectacular and damaging Jewish terrorist actions would succeed in doing what no legitimate, responsible Israeli government could place on its agenda or even suggest. It is no wonder that the plan of action drawn up by the members of the underground included schemes of a totally insane character, such as the bombing of the Temple Mount in Jerusalem; only such a step could lead to the creation of an explosive situation in which the expulsion of the Arab inhabitants from the territory would be possible.

Another important development, unforeseen by anybody at the time twenty years ago (due, of course, to the fact that nobody believed this situation would remain in force for such a long period of time), will perhaps, indirectly, have a notable influence in the course of future events. It should be remembered that approximately two-thirds of Israel's 3.5 million Jewish inhabitants were born and grew up in what may be termed 'the reality of Israel's occupation of the territories'. Almost the entire corps of regular servicemen in the IDF today were born after the Six-Day War. Three-quarters of the 1.3 million inhabitants of the territories also belong to a generation that has known no previous reality. On both sides, there is little or no personal sensibility or first-hand experience of the background and circumstances which gave rise to the Six-Day War and the Israeli occupation. Those who base their political doctrine on the past will not be understood by this present generation. Those who wish to lead and offer solutions for the future must take this fact into account. The problem is that the entire present generation of leaders consists of those who had already reached maturity in 1967. Can this generation of leaders possibly really understand the thoughts, desires and positions of the great majority, born into a different reality?

Whereas the declared policy of Israel was that there should be no change in the status of the territories except within the framework of a comprehensive political settlement between Israel and her neighbours, it was clear from the outset that the present situation was unacceptable and that Israel should implement measures that would alleviate the growing pressure from within the area. The only possible direction, short of a political settlement, was to promote self-management for the local population.

The first step was to bolster the status and the responsibilities of the local mayors. But that was not enough. Parallel to the Israeli official position which was 'waiting for King Hussein's phone-call', and which refrained from any other political initiative, the Prime Minister, Levi Eshkol, ordered a study of possibilities for the establishment of self-government for the Arab residents in the West Bank.

Between April and July 1968, such a plan came very close to realization. Following lengthy talks between the Israeli administration and the local leadership, Mohamed al-Ja'abari came up with a proposal to be nominated as Governor of the West Bank. This was to be done by a decree of the Israeli Military Commander of the area. He wanted to be responsible for all civilian affairs (including local police force), while the IDF would retain responsibility for combatting terrorism and for funding the local administration's budget.

July 1968 saw this initiative come to an end. Amman received notice of the plan, and responded with strong threats; moreover local leaders would not accept the leadership of Ja'abari. This led the Mayor of Hebron to abandon his plan.

A year later, in April 1969, Ja'abari mooted his plan again. His approach this time was different, however, he tried to overcome the obstacles which had killed his initiative in 1968. The recommendation now was to have no negotiations, that the military commander should impose the new order. By such an act, the Israelis would enable the local leaders to face the Arab world and to explain their predicament – i.e., that it was in the interests of the local Arab population to co-operate with this new Israeli imposition. Ja'abari's proposal received no response from Jerusalem. The timing was most unfortunate, Mrs Golda Meir was sworn in as the new Prime Minister on 17 March

1969, and she was not ready yet to discuss such an important proposal.

About ten years later, another proposal emerged which never reached the stage of formal discussion, and was never put to the test. That was Moshe Dayan's plan, which followed both the peace agreement with Egypt and the failure of the bilateral talks to reach an agreement on the implementation of autonomy in the administered territories. Having learned the lessons of 1968, Dayan advocated that Israel should impose a 'unilateral autonomy', according to which both Israel and the IDF would disengage themselves from any responsibility for local Arab civil affairs. This proposal was never discussed by the cabinet. Strong forces within the country and the cabinet realized that such a plan would be the first step, and a most decisive one, which would end the aspirations of those who saw the future boundaries of Israel as coinciding with those of 'Greater Israel'. Dayan died in 1981. His plan and proposal, however, are still very much alive. More and more elements, representing the moderate line and extremely concerned with the demographic threat to the Jewish character of Israel, are repeatedly raising Dayan's plan.

Another plan and initiative is known as the 'Village Councils' experiment. President Sadat's visit to Jerusalem, and the peace talks that followed, encouraged the Arab opposition to establish the Committee for National Guidance (CNG). This committee was expected to spearhead the popular struggle against the Camp David Accords and to serve as a foundation to the future Palestinian independent state.

As long as Moshe Dayan and Ezer Weizman were ministers in Mr Begin's cabinet, they succeeded in holding out against the opposition to the CNG. Weizman has even recommended having a direct dialogue with members of the committee in the hope that such talks would promote the peace process. Once the two were no longer ministers, and even more so following the Knesset elections in May 1981, after which Ariel Sharon became Minister of Defence, the government adopted a new policy aimed at uprooting any PLO influence in the West Bank. This new policy is currently identified with Professor Menahem Milson, who served as the first head of the Civilian Administration (from 1981) in Judea and Samaria, while Ariel Sharon was Minister of Defence.

This policy had three main thrusts. The first was to break up and annihilate the pro-PLO political establishment in the area, by putting an end to the CNG and by the dismissal of all local mayors who tried to demonstrate some independence. On 11 March 1982, the CNG was declared illegal. Two weeks later, Ibrahim Tawill, Mayor of el-Birah and one of the leading figures in the CNG, was removed.

The second thrust was to encourage an alternative leadership, mainly relying on the rural population (the silent majority) in the area, which was, according to the originators of this policy, neither PLO nor pro-Jordanian. This led to the establishment of the 'Village Councils' with Mustafa Doudin heading the first council in the Hebron area, following which four others were established – in Ramallah, Bethlehem, Tul-Karem and Jenin.

It did not last long. Threats were made by the PLO against the active members of these councils (highlighted with the murder of Yussuf el Khatib, the head of the Ramallah Council, by PLO agents); Jordanian statements declared all members of the councils were traitors whose property would be confiscated and who would be subjected to other repressive administrative measures. These threats led to a quick disenchantment with this policy.

The third thrust was to replace the 'Military Government' by a 'Civilian Administration' with Professor Milson serving as its first head. This move was interpreted by the Arabs as the greatest threat and as the first Israeli step towards the complete annexation of the West Bank to Israel. It resulted in strong reactions and in clashes between local Arab demonstrators and the Israeli security forces. The demonstrations and clashes escalated, resulting in numerous casualties. These events generated strong condemnations in many parts of the world.

This latest attempt was ultimately stifled by the outbreak of the war in Lebanon and its consequences. Early in 1983 Ariel Sharon was removed from his post as Minister of Defence and some time afterwards Menachem Begin resigned as Prime Minister. This was the end, for all practical purposes, of this new political experiment.

Israel's policy in the territories continues, for better or worse, through the power of inertia. The policy shaped by Moshe Dayan in the first days following the Six-Day War has not been re-examined in the light of changing events and circumstances. Moreover, since the time of Moshe Dayan, who served as Defence Minister and to all intents and purposes as Minister responsible for the occupied territories, Israeli policy in the territories has had no 'guiding authority'. Today, there is no Israeli figure of national stature devoting all his power, energy and consideration to the territories. Even the General Staff of the IDF is unfamiliar with the subject; since all responsibility for both policy and administration rests with the

Minister of Defence and the government, there has been no need to call upon the General Staff, with its remarkable planning capabilities, to intervene. The decision not to decide, the lack of familiarity and lack of constructive thought regarding this crucial subject, the lack of a proprietary 'boss', and the contradictory nature of steps and actions undertaken – all of these have led to the impasse and frustration on the part of many on both sides. Someday, the government of Israel will have to make some difficult and painful decisions. The choice with which it will be faced might be agonizingly cruel, a choice between a decision leading to inevitable military conflict with the Arab world or a decision leading to an internal confrontation beside which the evacuation of Yamit in 1983 will seem like child's play.

The quandary that has arisen can be described as a 'Gordian knot'. Every passing day adds new strands to complicate the snarl. Under these conditions, perhaps only 'Alexander's sword' can cut through the tangled snarl and untie the knot. The Judea and Samaria regions are like a bone lodged in Israel's throat, a bone that Israel can neither spit out nor swallow.

6 The Shaping of Palestinian Nationalism

Amnon Cohen

It is wrong to assume that twenty years of Israeli occupation of the West Bank and Gaza Strip have created a 'Palestinian identity' and caused the emergence of a Palestinian national movement. It is true that this period has played a major role in crystallizing, at the emotional and theoretical levels, a sense of Palestinian identity and of national sentiment. However these phenomena existed well before the occupation; and the period under review has also served to indicate their limitations and drawbacks.

Moreover, no single, unified national bloc or 'front' has emerged; despite a broad common denominator, a survey of political trends among the Palestinians under Israeli control since 1967 reveals quite a variety of colours and shades. The quantitative element here is almost as important as the historical setting. Twenty years are relatively few with reference to the development of a national movement: we should bear in mind that the earliest expressions of Arab nationalism in this particular area are less than a century old. Moreover, these twenty years followed a similar period of time (1950–67) in which the very same population was part and parcel of the Hashemite Kingdom of Jordan. For the first time, they were granted independent political rights within the context of an Arab state (although many were dissatisfied with the extent of their actual participation and lack of equal opportunity). But the state they were then part of not only ruled over them by means of military occupation but was a monarchy run by the family that most Palestinian nationalists had despised and rejected throughout the British Mandate of the preceding thirty years. The Hashemites nevertheless granted formal equality to the Palestinians newly incorporated in their state and attempted to imbue their lives with a new sense of partnership. Judging by the political (and occasionally aggressive) opposition of certain Palestinian groups after April 1950, it is doubtful if they totally overcame their erstwhile antagonism. Under Israeli rule they were physically separated from the Hashemites; this enabled them to resume their former course of Palestinian, rather than Jordanian, development.

Having overcome the initial shock of their defeat by the Israeli Defence Forces, the immediate reaction of the Palestinians under Israeli control was to incite the local masses to fight. The first attempt to foment a popular uprising was in the Gaza Strip, which owed allegiance to no Arab regime. In autumn–winter 1967 an underground infrastructure for a national Palestinian Front was established there to lead the projected political and military struggle. When the major instigators were arrested early in 1968, this work was discontinued and the centre of political gravity shifted to the West Bank, its more natural setting. Yasser Arafat, who had infiltrated into the West Bank and was trying to build up a network of Palestinian militants prepared to wage a popular war of independence, was equally disillusioned. The few successful acts of sabotage perpetrated did not trigger any widespread nationalist activity and the militants were found and brought to justice. The understanding reached between the Israelis and the local school authorities that put an end to their ongoing strike added an important element of stability to everyday life. Although obviously antagonistic, the masses were impervious to efforts to activate them in an armed struggle – or even to civil unrest and insubordination.

THE DILEMMA OF IDENTITY

The situation in which the Palestinians found themselves as a result of the 1967 war had several political dimensions. Their immediate concern was how to cope – both individually and as a community – with the omnipotent Israeli presence. No less important was the question of identity: were they Jordanians, Palestinians, or something else? The physical severance of the West Bank from the rest of the Hashemite Kingdom did not rupture the elaborate network linking the two. Paradoxically, there were even some major fields in which it became mandatory to maintain the symbols of Jordanian sovereignty. The 'open-bridges' policy introduced by Israel enabled every Palestinian to move freely to and from the West Bank – unless barred by the Jordanians from exercising this right. The Palestinians used Jordanian passports, the Jordanian dinar, the Jordanian banking system – as well as many other facets of modern life – as ways of preserving and reinforcing their Arab identity, particularly as they had no parallel Palestinian facilities.

The various attributes of Jordanian identity were buttressed by the Hashemite crown's growing desire to re-establish itself in as many ways as possible in the West Bank (and to gain an ever-larger foothold in the Gaza Strip to support a potential claim there). The term officially used was 'the Hashemite family', which comprised two elements, one Jordanian, the other Palestinian. It expressed itself financially through the allocation of *sumud* ('steadfastness') funds to those individuals and institutions on the West Bank engaged in activities considered supportive of Hashemite interests.

Material and spiritual incentives of varying forms and intensity were initially introduced to counterbalance the growing Israeli presence. These became even more meaningful in the tug of war that developed between Jordan and the PLO (Palestine Liberation Organization). Although Israel repeatedly declared the PLO to be the arch-enemy, a plethora of institutions with a distinctly local character emerged in the administered territories; this accentuated the particularist – i.e., Palestinian – nature of the population. By definition – as well as in actual performance – this local character underscored the non-Jordanian nature of all these institutions. Israel permitted – sometimes encouraged – the publication of more than a dozen local newspapers and the establishment of five universities – all of these regularly heightened awareness among the young and the politically informed that they were distinct from the 'other' Jordanians. Many openly preached support of the PLO, as was the case with several mayors and other major political figures. Support for the PLO increased also as a result of its growing importance in Jordan, particularly in late 1969 and 1970. Palestinians returning from visits to Amman reported that the place seemed on the verge of a takeover by the PLO; it therefore became expedient, not only emotionally satisfying, to come out openly in support of its cause. Israel's expulsion of the most vociferous protagonists of the PLO, while temporarily limiting the volume of the Palestinian voice, added another attraction to their cause – that of self-sacrifice. Jordan, which had been active against Israel immediately after the Six-Day War (shelling Israeli positions, encouraging passive resistance by way of strikes, etc.) was steadily losing points to the PLO.

'Black September' 1970 marked a turning-point: King Hussein crushed the PLO, removing it first from his capital, then from other parts of his kingdom. In the context of the West Bank this meant more polarized feelings, an increased identification with the underdog. It also distinctly contributed to the already existing perception that the Jordanian establishment was anti-Palestinian and not just anti-PLO.

This growing awareness of Palestinian identity in the West Bank and the Gaza Strip did not drastically change daily life in the territories. Terrorist acts were perpetrated from time to time by small underground cells, and whenever those involved were brought to justice they declared themselves part of the PLO (in most cases Fatah mainstream, but occasionally other factions as well). Recurrent PLO attempts to mobilize the masses openly to defy Israeli rule – by organizing public demonstrations, general strikes or even refraining from going to work in Israel – all proved futile. On the other hand, major public figures increasingly expressed open support for the Palestinian cause: Rashad ash-Shawwa, the mayor of Gaza, Hamdi Kan'an the mayor of Nablus and, more militantly, Abd al-Jawwad Salih, the mayor of al-Bireh, and Hanna Nasir, the president of Bir Zeyt college (later university).

The position taken by some of these men was significantly different from earlier stands: Hanna Nasir's father Musa, founder of the college, had been an active member of the Jordanian Establishment, while Kan'an's pro-Palestinian declarations were a bitter reminder to the Jordanian authorities of the ground they were losing. Another political group, comprised of leaders who remained pro-Hashemite (such as Anwar al-Khatib and Anwar Nuseiba of Jerusalem, Kadri Tuqan or Hikmat al-Masri of Nablus, some prominent figures within the religious establishment), kept their communication lines with the Jordanians open. They continued to receive ideological and material inspiration from Jordan, but became less inclined to express their sentiments in public. Open threats from Beirut, sometimes reinforced by intimidation, were a further incentive to maintain a lower political profile. There was, however, a third group: those who could no longer adhere to the Jordanian line or opt for a Jordanian solution, but by the same token were fully aware of the futility of the PLO option, opposed as it was by both the Israelis and the Hashemites. This group included public figures such as Mohamed al-Ja'abari, the mayor of Hebron, formerly a staunch supporter of the King; Aziz Shihada, a Christian lawyer and Hamdi Taji al-Faruqi, a Muslim lawyer, both from Ramallah. They propagated the idea of a Palestinian entity to replace the Israeli occupation, one that would truly represent their goal of disengaging themselves from, on the one hand, Hashemite tutelage and, on the other, from attempts at imposing an equally undesirable PLO rule. Attractive as this programme seemed to outsiders, the concept had limited political relevance. Some of its protagonists were frightened off by the PLO, while others never attained any significant support outside of their immediate followers. Al-Ja'abari was the most outstanding of these men. He had maintained a consistent and authentic Palestinian view for many years, but remained on close terms with the Israelis in an attempt to turn his ideas into political reality. Even he, however, became aware of the diminishing appeal of this group and he declined all suggestions to stand for re-election to the municipality in 1976.

INCREASING 'PALESTINIANIZATION'

Israel's image of invulnerability was shattered by the 1973 war; the image of Jordan, which did very little during the war, remained as tarnished as it had been before. The general trend of Palestinianization in the West Bank resumed its thrust, becoming increasingly pro-PLO. The Rabat summit of autumn 1974 dealt Jordan's Palestinian interests a heavy blow: the PLO was unanimously confirmed by the Arab states as the sole and legitimate representative 'of the Palestinian people'. Both Arafat's address to the UN General Assembly in November 1974 and Resolution 3236 boosted the PLO's role as the respectable representative of the Palestinians; by the late 1970s it had been recognized by more than 100 states. These achievements, coupled with world-wide terrorist acts, further enhanced the Palestinians' self-image as well as their identification with the PLO. Although the King never relinquished his rights over the West Bank or his plans for eventually retrieving it, he abided by the Rabat resolution and implemented a 'hands-off' policy *vis-à-vis* his subjects under Israeli administration. This helped to weaken the pro-Hashemites among the Palestinians while the various manifestations of pro-PLO sentiment were further entrenched.

One of these was the PNF (Palestinian National Front), first established in Beirut in November 1972, then adopted by the eleventh PNC (Palestinian National Council) in January 1973. Yasser Arafat was less than accurate when he told *al-Ahram* (18 January 1974) that after the Algiers summit conference late in 1973 all the high commands of the West Bank and the Gaza Strip, the leaders of political parties and all the progressive national movements had convened and declared the establishment of the PNF. Neither the timing nor the location were correct, but his words nevertheless projected an image of the situation Arafat envisioned in the future. In the wake of the 1973 war an attempt was made to implant the idea in the occupied territories: an umbrella organization was set up with the avowed aim of uniting those Palestinians in the territories who supported the PLO and had engaged in subversive or military activity with those who now ascribed to the concept of 'armed struggle' (particularly the Communist Party).

This was the first significant attempt since 1967 to bring to the fore a nationwide leadership capable of conducting a unified, subversive, political Palestinian struggle, on a broader scale than the PLO. The PNF, however, never actually progressed beyond its formative stage. The 12th meeting of the PNC (June 1974) referred to the 'new and important dimensions' with which the PNF endowed the political and military struggle in the occupied territories; it also included several former PNF activists in its executive committee who had been deported from the West Bank. These were all understandable moves from the standpoint of public image, but they had very little relevance for Palestinian reality, which virtually ignored the PNF's existence.

There are three possible explanations for the failure of this attempt to build up a national leadership for the Palestinians under Israeli control. First, the PLO (primarily Fatah) element and the Communists – the projected bedfellows – discovered that some of their basic positions were irreconcilable. While the Fatah group suspected the Communists of scheming to take over the national movement and turn it into a Soviet satellite, the PNF took a more moderate stand and supported the idea of an international peace conference in Geneva. It was also willing to settle for a Palestinian state within the borders prescribed by the UN Partition Plan of 1947. A second possible reason for the failure may have been the preventive measures taken by the Israelis, who hoped to nip the incipient organization in the bud: several of its outstanding individuals were expelled, while others, under threat of expulsion, were detained. Third, the municipal elections of 1976 brought a new crop of mayors to power in the most important urban centres; supporting the PLO seemed to them more promising than any other organizational link. Finally, in later years, particularly after the conclusion of the Camp David Accords, the PLO itself drew closer to the Soviet Union, so that neither side deemed it essential to revive the virtually defunct PNF.

The PNF episode indicated, among other things, the quest for a leadership capable of coordinating and conducting the national struggle of the Palestinians living under Israeli occupation. Torn between pro-Hashemites and pro-PLO, split by loyalty to different local leaders whose interest in family and regional affairs was quite as strong as their ideological commitment, the Palestinians were suddenly confronted by the bitter surprise of the Camp David Accords. The Arab rejectionist front, which united diverse political rivals (including Hussein and Arafat) in an attempt to nullify a political settlement of the Middle East conflict, inspired an attempt to effect a similar front in the West Bank. Several political meetings which took place in Jerusalem and at the universities of Bethlehem, Bir Zeyt and Nablus were attended by a broad spectrum of political and religious leaders. Unanimous resolutions were adopted and signed, the media provided extensive coverage and the entire operation was orchestrated by the pro-PLO mayors. Twenty-two self-appointed political figures led the 'National Guidance Committee' that consisted of representatives of municipal councils, trade unions, voluntary organizations, the religious establishment, the local press, etc.

Encouraged by the enthusiastic reaction to their first meeting (1 October 1978), they decided to form follow-up committees in the various regions, to be headed by an executive body of six. Their main aim was to mobilize local public opinion for a political struggle against the possibility that the Camp David concepts might be implemented in the West Bank and the Gaza Strip. To attain their objective they combined threats, intimidation of anyone who dared think in terms of a settlement that included Jordan, and even murder (e.g., Shaykh Khuzindar in Gaza). In addition, the Baghdad Conference of January 1978 promised them financial support, which they received in part. The Palestinians regarded some of the mayors as PLO representatives, while these officials increasingly incited their people to adopt aggressive means of promoting their national aims. The Israeli reaction was somewhat belated, but it was harsh: a few mayors were expelled to Amman while the National Guidance Committee was outlawed in March 1982 and never reactivated. While it lasted, the Committee arrogated to itself the right to represent the entire local population, basing itself as it did on a broad Arab consensus – the rejection of the Camp David Accords. As it consisted predominantly of pro-PLO public figures, it was a clear indication of the growing trend in support of that political option.

THE HUSSEIN–ARAFAT EMBRACE

For most Palestinians the choice between a pro-Jordanian and a pro-PLO orientation had always been hard to make. The ever-increasing awareness of their special identity – no matter what its historical validity or practical implications at any given time – manifested itself in a variety of ways, leading toward greater identification with the PLO. Almost by definition this ruled out any significant identification with the Hashemites. On the other hand, the Palestinians were all tied to the Arab lands (as well as to their relatives who lived in Amman and Beirut) by the umbilical cord of the Hashemite Kingdom. Although the Palestinian dream did not fade as time passed, the Palestinians never completely ignored the expediency of a Jordanian solution or of a solution somehow associated with Jordan. A rapprochement between the two opposing poles was most welcome and seemed highly promising. In the early 1980s, therefore, most of the people in the occupied territories looked upon the gradual improvement of relations between Hussein and Arafat with great expectation.

The convening of the 17th PNC in Amman (November 1984) and the embraces of Hussein and Arafat, triggered a wave of optimistic emotions and reactions within the West Bank public: petitions were signed by hundreds of people urging the King and the Chairman to reach an agreement, in many cases omitting any direct reference to an 'independent Palestinian state'. Even a Communist leader like Bashir Barghuti, critical as he was of the timing of the PNC, called for 'national unity'. The agreement finally reached between Hussein and Arafat on 11 February 1985 generated political reactions along these lines. This was not a 'new political party born', as it was erroneously described by the weekly, *al-'Awda* (14 July 1985), but rather a document signed by twenty-eight well-known figures – lawyers, businessmen, journalists, politicians, etc. Their 'Committee for Support of Jordanian–Palestinian Joint Action' clearly stressed their belief in the PLO as 'the sole legitimate representative of the Palestinian people', and they declared themselves 'willing to push forward for the attainment of Palestinian national goals'. These goals were the realization of the 'right of self-determination of the Palestinian people in their homeland within a confederated state with the Hashemite Kingdom of Jordan'. In the outline of their programme, they went a step further toward clarifying their political stand. They openly criticized those who 'spread demagogy and empty slogans' in schools, or those who 'regard themselves as trustees of nationalism and understand patriotism only through rejecting whatever is proposed'. Their opposition to the rejectionist elements within the PLO and among its supporters was one side of the political coin; their support for a more moderate PLO that would act within a Hashemite context was the other. Although relatively small in number, this group projected an overall mood of optimism that with varying nuances was shared by wide circles in the West Bank as a result of the Hussein–Arafat accord.

The rapprochement, however, proved to be short-lived; a year later King Hussein announced his profound disappointment with the PLO and the discontinuation of his attempts to coordinate his moves with theirs. Once again, the Palestinians under Israeli administration were forced to make a difficult choice and to take sides. Once again, the internal splits among the Palestinians reflected the external stresses and strains dividing the entire Arab Muslim world. As a result, there are now three major political groups in the West Bank and Gaza Strip: Islamic, pro-PLO and pro-Hashemite.

CURRENT POLITICAL ALIGNMENTS

Islamic Groups

Palestinian history has known more than one episode in which Islam was deliberately and most successfully used by astute politicians ('Izz al-Din al-Qassam, haj Amin al-Husayni in the 1930s and 1940s) as an expedient focus for identity. In later years, the Muslim Brethren inaugurated active branches in the major urban centres of the West Bank. Subsequently, in the early 1950s, the Islamic Liberation Party of Taqi al-Din al-Nabhani was founded in Jerusalem and became an extremely active rival to the Muslim Brethren. In the overall political picture, however, Islam has had relatively little political importance. This was also true after 1967, when the new circumstances did not bring about a significant upsurge of religious fervour or unusual activity

Eleven years later, there were new developments in this context. In the Gaza Strip, where traditional bonds with Egypt were coupled with social backwardness and lack of political experience, religious consciousness had always been more dominant than in most of the West Bank. *Al-Majma' al-Islami* was registered in 1978 as a welfare organization in Gaza and it became increasingly active following the Iranian revolution. *Al-Majma'* ('the meeting place') is the community mosque where the masses receive social, cultural and other guidance; borrowing this name for the new organization, therefore, had important symbolic value. The activities of this group were not always of a peaceful nature; in 1980, for example, they ransacked, then set fire, to the offices of the left-wing (Islamic) Red Crescent in Gaza. In 1983 one of their leaders, Shaykh Yasin was caught organizing an underground network that was well provided with arms and explosives. Although under Israeli occupation, their aim was to rectify the behaviour of Muslim members of the community who went astray. It is small wonder that PLO supporters accused them of lacking nationalist zeal and being too lenient *vis-à-vis* Israel. The fact that they gave priority to social or religious aims rather than to the Palestinian national cause was regarded by the PLO as a major error on their part, but so far they have withstood all pressure to revise their objectives.

Al-Jihad al-Islami is another political group that for the past few years has been active in the Gaza Strip, and although exclusively Sunnite, they draw inspiration largely from the Iranian revolution (and are therefore occasionally referred to as *al-Khomeiniyya*). They attract the same circles and harp on the same emotions as *al-Majma' al-Islami*, but their main thrust is against Israel. The two groups combined enjoy the support of about 80 per cent of the 5000 students of al-Azhar university in Gaza, thus presenting a major potential threat to the PLO's claim of overall ascendency in the occupied territories. Dr Ismail al-Khatib, head of the Faculty of Islam there, was assassinated by a special death squad sent by Abu Jihad. The message was clearly understood: the PLO would not tolerate any competition among the youth. But this had little effect on fundamentalist feelings and their political expression.

The Islamic groups have managed to increase their political weight in the Gaza Strip by entering trade unions there (e.g., the pharmacists). *Al-Majma'* uses an additional tactic that is helping it to make successful inroads in the general population as well as among the youth: they sponsor the building of new mosques in various neighbourhoods, or replace incumbent preachers with their own people. This phenomenon, although most conspicuously felt in Gaza itself, is widespread throughout the Strip. In Khan Yunis, for example, the manifestation of fundamentalist activity is a group known as *al-Salaflyyun* ('those who follow the example set by the early generations'). These people zealously attempt to implement a strict moral and religious code to the extent of censoring the films shown in local cinema houses, and even forcing recalcitrant establishments to shut down. Throughout the Gaza Strip, these Islamic groups represent a real, grass-roots trend, as is the case in other parts of the Arab world. It should be noted, however, that they are strongly influenced (and substantially supported) by the Egyptian example, by explicit Jordanian policies and by Saudi money.

Although on a smaller scale, the Jordanian and Sa'udi elements are also present in the revival of Islam that is taking place in the West Bank – primarily in the Hebron area. Saudi money as well as Jordanian funds constitute a significant element in financing the outcropping of family mosques there. In Hebron University the Muslim Brethren enjoy the support of about 40 per cent of the entire student population and with only few exceptions (e.g., 1986) its adherents have attained a majority in all the student bodies. Even in the more radically oriented universities of al-Naj'ah in Nablus and of Bir Zeyt near Ramallah, the Muslim Brethren enjoy the support of about 30 per cent of the student population. On the more popular level there have recently been attempts to close down wine-shops in Nablus, while in Dheisha (near Bethlehem) in 1985 an internal struggle pitted the Muslim Brethren against a PLO front: their calls for a revival of pure, true Islam were almost drowned by the din of roofs caving in as they tore down the houses of their political opponents. Recently even inside Israeli prisons there has been noticeably bitter rivalry between pro-Islamic elements and pro-PLO groups. Generally speaking, however, it becomes apparent that whenever possible the fundamentalists try to avoid close contact with Palestinian nationalist groups. The growing importance of the former makes them a coveted target for the mainstream of the PLO – the Fatah, which this past year scored a few successes (in Jerusalem, for example). But the major obstacle so far has been a conceptual one: in mid-1981 a lecturer at al-Naj'ah university stated: 'Territory has no sacred value, nationalism is a beastly, a base instinct, whereas Islam is the loftiest value system that should guide our footsteps'. Although Palestinian by definition, they do not endow the nationalist element with particularly high value. As they see it, the struggle against Israel should be viewed in the context of the ongoing war between Islam and the non-believers. Hence the misguided path followed by the PLO should be replaced by the only true way – that of Islam.

PLO Adherents

PLO supporters represent the largest political camp claiming Palestinian identity as the quintessence of its existence. Like the organization itself, these PLO adherents embrace various political elements and ideological shades. The most important – politically and otherwise – are the Fatah supporters. Attempts to set up a Palestinian National Front in 1973–5 are usually viewed as an unsuccessful episode wherein the relatively small left-wing tail tried to wag the whole dog; since the Rabat conference of 1974, Fatah has borne the main brunt of political activity. Left-wing slogans such as 'reconstruction of a National Palestinian Front' were replaced by total negation of any attempt to establish a central leadership – which might eventually become an 'alternative leadership' (*qiyada badila*), a pejorative term conveying what is still considered a most dangerous concept. Hence Fatah sponsored the creation of as wide and as decentralized an infrastructure of national bodies as possible. Most conspicuous here were the municipal elections of 1976: the PLO, withdrawing its earlier ban on participation, was successful in that many of its supporters were elected as councillors and mayors. Municipalities became political strongholds, and the tens of millions of dollars that were funneled to them after 1978 by the joint Jordanian–Palestinian committee were rightly regarded as Fatah-inspired sums aimed at bolstering the strength of their own people in office. As of 1982, when Israel began to dismiss the pro-Fatah mayors, the relevance of these positions as centres of political gravity substantially diminished.

Institutions of higher education proved to be of more lasting value from the Fatah perspective: there they had to compete with rivals from both left and right, and they did so with impressive results. Al-Naj'ah of Nablus was initially pro-Hashemite; Bethlehem was under radical left influence until 1986; substantial sums of money had to be channeled to Hebron University in 1982–3 in order to gain a foothold on the otherwise predominantly Muslim-influenced campus. At present Fatah supporters are a majority among the students in four out of six major universities: Bir Zeyt, Bethlehem, al-Naj'ah and Abu Dis.

To create and maintain the impression of widespread public support, Fatah paid special attention to the press. Most dailies and weeklies (*al-Fajr, al-Sha'b, al-Quds, al-'Awda, al-Bayadir al Slyasi*, etc.) are pro-Fatah. The 'Institute of Palestinian Studies' and 'Law in the Service of Man' are examples of institutions basically dedicated to the promotion of research into past Palestinian history and the current Palestinian situation, but many staff are Fatah supporters who openly promulgate a pro-PLO line.

The political branch of Fatah has managed quite successfully to take over organized Palestinian activity in most fields although in some areas, such as the trade unions, they had to contend with stubborn rivals. (The twenty-four existing trade unions, pro-Hashemite until 1967, had been captured by the Communist Party or its front organizations.) In the wake of the 1973 war, Fatah persuaded the 12th PNC to adopt a new strategy: although the final goal will always remain an unrelenting struggle for the liberation of all of Palestine, a tactical compromise – an interim solution (*hall marhali*) – may be useful, perhaps mandatory. Through proclaiming a 'strategy of stages' and a 'national authority' in the West Bank and Gaza Strip, the ideal democratic state in historic Palestine may eventually be attained. From a Fatah perspective, the formula for an interim solution may be applicable to the goal as well as to the road leading to it. Unlike its minor, more radical partners (the Popular Front and the Democratic Front for the Liberation of Palestine), mainstream Fatah tended to adopt the political process as a means of achieving its ultimate ends. In the daily realities of the occupied territories this meant not just a passive *sumud* (steadfastness) policy, but an active presence in all walks of organized life. From 1975 on, they would no longer rely on the sympathy of the Communists (even after 1981, when the Palestinian Communist Party was formally declared) but would also attempt to work within the trade unions. After the Camp David Accords and the Egyptian–Israeli peace treaty, it became almost imperative for the PLO to prove that all sectors in the West Bank were united in total negation of Sadat's approach. Attempts were made to convince the Communist Party to enable Fatah supporters to take over the trade unions, but to no avail. Bashir Barghuti's reaction was 'one seat here [in the West Bank] in return for one seat there [in the PLO executive committee]', which was tantamount to a refusal. Fatah decided, therefore, to set up its own 'parallel trade unions' (*niqabat muwazlya*), an example later followed by the Democratic Front. No wonder that on May Day three different 'Workers' Unions' published separate manifestos addressed to the masses!

Pro-Hashemites

In the strictly legal sense of the word, all Palestinians in the West Bank are Jordanians; many of them have vested interests in the Hashemite Kingdom and some – probably many – may have an incentive to support the continued association of the West and East Banks of the Jordan. Very few, however, would dare take a public position in favour of a Jordanian – as distinct from Palestinian – identity. Erosion of loyalty to the Jordanian concept is part of a long process that started before 1967, but it has gathered momentum in the past twenty years. Even avowed pro-Hashemites thought it expedient to dilute their political position with ample portions of Palestinian zeal. This process became more deeply entrenched as a result of King Hussein's 'hands-off' policies after 1974; to outside observers, it seemed as if all the Hashemites could do (if indeed they were still interested, which many doubted) was cut their losses and succumb to the 'tide of history'.

Ever since 1982 there have been increasing indications that the Hashemites have launched a long-range plan directed at a comeback in the West Bank. New members of the Jordanian Parliament were chosen from among younger, but loyal, West Bank Palestinians. Municipal councils are gradually resuming their pro-Jordanian character under more lenient, docile Palestinian mayors. Manipulation of the religious Establishment – which has always been a most powerful tool – has been undertaken; it is being reorganized and brought under stricter control of the Hashemite powers-that-be. Ten thousand teachers appointed by Israel after 1967 in the West Bank and the Gaza Strip were made eligible for a regular monthly Jordanian subvention. In 1982 committees for export of agricultural produce were introduced to all major farming centres in the West Bank, and they have become active in promoting Hashemite interests in a society that is still predominantly rural. Some of these projects combine aspects of image-building with the practical benefits they confer.

Other venues explored and then utilized are in the realm of the mass media. Jordanian television and radio have inaugurated special programmes beamed to the West Bank. A new daily, *al-Nahar*, allegedly the recipient of generous financial support from Amman, has in the course of 1986 increased its scope as well as its unmistakable pro-Hashemite message. On the governmental level a five-year development programme promising substantial annual subsidies to the West Bank was announced in 1986. In fact only a small fraction of these sums reached Palestinian pockets, but they served to buttress Jordanian interests as well as to promote a benevolent image that augurs well for the future.

The present rupture between Jordan and the PLO has enabled the former to impede PLO efforts and to harass any of its supporters who cross the Jordan and can be targeted for direct pressure. Various indirect threats (and promises) are also being made further to impress the Palestinians with the seriousness of Hashemite intentions. None of these have created major changes of mind among the Palestinians, but there are various indications that the traditionally pro-Hashemite forces are gathering strength; for the first time in a decade, some of them dared to come out openly in support of the Jordanian option.

MATURITY AND UNCERTAINTY

When considering the emergence of a Palestinian identity, the importance of the Israeli presence cannot be overestimated. Throughout the period of the Mandate the Jewish performance served as an example for the Arab community in almost every conceivable field, politics included. The very creation of a Jewish state, then the repeated Arab attempts to undo the tenacious, flourishing Israeli national existence, was a further spur for the Palestinian Arabs. Their incorporation into the Hashemite Kingdom involved an attempt to infuse them with a Jordanian national identity. But history informs us that this attempt, although formally successful, did not actually bring an end to their Palestinian memories, consciousness and dreams.[1] The drastic outcome of the 1967 war severed direct links for the Palestinians in the Israeli occupied territories, the Jordanian presence – and in the Gaza Strip, the Egyptian presence – became a distant image rather than a reality. Quite naturally this brought to the fore and reinforced Palestinian feelings and national dreams, making them much more than simply amorphous emotions.

As early as 1959 a small underground Palestinian group had emerged, calling itself Fatah ('the Movement for the Liberation of Palestine'), and in 1964 it became part of a larger body – the PLO, which convened its first National Council in Jerusalem in May of that year. After 1967, it became impossible for the PLO to meet in the occupied ex-Palestinian territories; in 1970 the organization was also forced out of Jordan – from the Palestinians' standpoint, historically a part of Palestine. The PLO emerged, however, as a significant terrorist organization that sometimes cloaked its diabolical nature and enjoyed increasing international recognition as the spokesman for all Palestinians. In the West Bank and the Gaza Strip, the movement thus gained the admiration of the younger generation as well as the respect and heightened identification of a substantial part of the general public.

The Israeli occupation has thus served as a twofold stimulus: it is both an enemy to be hated and a rival to be imitated in that it sets the example of a recently-created national state. The positive aspects of the occupation (such as a significant increase in standard of living, a better understanding of the democratic process, etc.) are not always acknowledged, nor do they attenuate national feelings – just the opoosite is the case.

This background might lead one to expect a noteworthy national movement in the territories, but the past twenty years have thus far provided us with only a sketchy picture. The Israeli 'open-bridges' policies implemented in 1967 contributed to the creation of a relatively peaceful existence. Israeli military might and the security measures taken to counteract destructive elements have played a major role in preserving law and order. But it does not do to ignore the overall situation in the Arab world and its divisive, weakening effect on the Palestinians who are moreover prevented from creating a mature national movement in the occupied territories by internal schisms and controversies. The PLO is forever torn between radical, rejectionist forces and more rational elements. The Palestinian dream constantly collides with the Jordanian reality that refuses to relinquish its very *raison d'être* as a nation and a state. There are also fundamentalist groups that observe the entire scene with different eyes altogether. And there are always – as there have been throughout the modern history of the region – the Arab states that covet their share of the Palestinian cake.

Twenty years after the 1967 war, the Palestinians seem to agree readily about what it is they do not want, but they still find it difficult to agree on a unified programme to achieve what they do want. The philosophical melancholy overriding both public and private commissions is understandable: the human urge to attend to basic needs and daily mundane matters, the awareness that there is no imminent solution and the overriding internal social and political splits – these all converge in a Palestinian society that is definitely more mature and conscious of its particular traits and potential, but is still groping for the right way to a better future.

Notes

1. See A. Cohen, *Political Parties in the West Bank under the Jordanian Regime*, 1949–1967 (Ithaca, 1982).

7 A Palestinian Perspective
Hanna Siniora

Since the beginning of the Arab–Israeli conflict – whether one considers it to be the emergence of the Balfour Declaration in 1917 or the 1948 creation of the State of Israel – the heart of the matter, so to speak, has always been Palestine and the Palestinians, the land and its people. The Palestinians remain the core of the debate which has on five occasions to date thrown the entire region into armed confrontation and which continues to command the attention of nearly every capital between Moscow and Washington. But despite their long history in the disputed territory and their undeniable centrality to the conflict, it was only after the third such confrontation, the June 1967 war, that world public opinion took notice of them. The Palestinians were, after all, more affected by that war and the subsequent military occupation of the West Bank and Gaza Strip than any other people. The changes brought by the 1967 hostilities in Palestinian society, in the Palestinian revolution and in the Arab–Israeli conflict as a whole are indeed profound.

For months after the June war, and in some circles until today, the public continued to ignore the Palestinians, choosing instead to debate such mundane academic questions as who actually began the battle – Israel or Egypt. But such inquiry loses meaning quickly next to the reality of the terrible injustice done not once, but twice to an entire population. Such an injustice, which has yet to be redressed, is the cause of both past and future Arab–Israeli wars. Shortly after the 1967 conflict, the Reverend Henry H. Bucher, Jr, then Field Secretary of the University Christian Movement, wrote in a response to Issues magazine:

Sooner or later . . . given the explosive condition of the area, a further flare-up was bound to occur. And in these circumstances, the question as to who actually fired the first shot is of relatively little importance. What is important is the root-cause of this explosive situation. What is important is first to understand and, from understanding, to try to resolve the issue which lies at the core of the bitter running conflict between the Arabs and Israel of the last 20 years. This issue is quite simply and briefly the issue of Palestine and the Palestinians who, over the last 20 years, have been evicted from their homes and farms in Palestine to make way for the establishment of a Zionist state on land which has been theirs for the past 1300 years, and who have been made to pay with their suffering the debt which Europe owes to persecuted Jewry.[1]

IDENTITY

It was indeed the 'shock' of 1967 which brought about the greatest change in Palestinian society, giving birth essentially to the Palestinian revolution. When the smoke had cleared from around the walls of the Old City of Jerusalem and Palestinians began to realize that there was not one Arab soldier left on Palestinian soil and that they were now completely and totally alone, in the control of the Zionist occupier, the people, as a whole, began to wake up. They now knew that no Arab army could save them, that their destiny was in their hands, that they – the people of Palestine – must fight alone to regain their lost country. In a sense, to use a phrase made popular in the hippie era, they had 'found themselves'. Their identity as Palestinians, both individually and collectively, became of prime importance to their existence and the revolution became the means by which they both preserved and publicized this identity.

Before 1967 this was not the case. The history of the Palestinian people has unfortunately been one largely of service to a foreign occupier – be it the Turks, the British, or the Zionists. This did little to foster a sense of independence, or a belief in one's ability to take control of one's destiny. Therefore following the 1948 loss of Palestine, the Palestinians on the West Bank of the Jordan River and in the Gaza Strip naturally fell back into their pattern of relying on another occupier, this time the Arabs, for deliverance from the Zionists who had taken over their country. The Palestinians, renamed 'Israeli Arabs', within the 78 per cent of the country lost to the new Jewish state were not even allowed the mental balm of reliance on the Arab states as they were cut off completely from the other Arabic-speaking countries. The Palestinians forced out of the country altogether as refugees relied on the Arab host states for more than political promises – they relied on these states for the livelihood that the meagre rations from the United Nations Relief and Works Agency could not provide.

As Abdullah Schleifer points out, the reliance on the Arabs was tragic. Indeed it was 'one of the most tragic symbols of Palestine's past impotence, that almost hysterical necessity for a people without faith in themselves to believe in the greatness of distant leaders who will painlessly deliver them from their oppressors'.[2]

Political events in the Arab world at the time between the 1948 and 1967 wars further facilitated Palestinian belief in distant deliverers. With the rise to power in Egypt of President Gamal Abdul Nasser, the focus shifted from the various nation-states of the Arab world and their diverse interests to an all-encompassing philosophy called Arab nationalism. The goal was for pan-Arab unity and through such unity, the liberation of the Holy Land. There was no real talk of a Palestinian state, a separate Palestinian identity. Palestine was instead a rallying cry for the masses, its people just a sub-group of the greater Arab whole. Leaders like Abdul Nasser and King Hussein of Jordan promised the Palestinians the recapture of the holy sites and surrounding areas, not as a step to national independence, but as a step to incorporation of that piece into the Arab empire.

The Palestinians were, after all, a people just awakened from 500 years of Turkish rule which had created a trend towards backwardness. They were virtually political and historical illiterates capable of believing in an easy deliverance. But with the destruction of the Arab armies in 1967 came the destruction of the Arab nationalist dream in Palestine. Before 1967 expressions of Palestinian nationalism as opposed to Arab nationalism were not tolerated by the host Arab governments. Although before 1948 there had been Palestinian political parties, trade unions, and other professional organizations, after the war Palestinians were not allowed to organize along independent or indigenously Palestinian lines. For Palestinians gathered together on the West Bank this denial of any national expression – either through traditional forms like carrying a flag or writing a textbook on the history of the country, or less traditional forms like the establishment of indigenous Palestinian groups such as the teachers' unions – was particularly severe. After 1948 Jordan clearly attempted to incorporate the West Bank into the Hashemite Beduin Kingdom although it paid lip service, like the other Arab nations, to the return of all of Palestine. After 1967 it was clear to Palestinians that Jordan and the other Arabs had indeed done little more than exercise their vocal cords.

This attempted Jordanization of the West Bank had the effect of leaving Palestinian identity a vague issue. Only the dedicated generation of hardcore nationalists left over from the 1936 general strike were still speaking publicly of a Palestinian state. The rest, particularly those with commercial interests in the Hashemite Kingdom, spoke of Jordan and/or the pan-Arab unity mentioned before. Those in the Diaspora who were financially successful did not risk antagonizing their host states with nationalist 'rabblerousing'. Only those misfortunates in the refugee camps who had little to look forward to anyway clung tenaciously to the idea of return and the re-establishment of their nation on their own native soil.

Hisham Sharabi, editor of the Journal of Palestine Studies, recalls: 'Those of my generation who found themselves, as I did, engaged in professional work had, prior to 1967, long accustomed themselves to repressing their feelings concerning Palestine. We felt that it was futile to speak out – and we stood to suffer professionally. Whether in the Arab countries or abroad, Palestinians lived for that day. But, on the whole, we were successful; personal success seemed somehow to make it easier to endure the national disaster. To be sure, the poor and unsuccessful among us, particularly those living in refugee camps, did not enjoy the same rewards and compensations. Palestine to them was a living daily agony. They thought only of one thing – the return.'

He continues: '1967 made us see ourselves and our situation in a new light. Over half of our people were now living under Israeli rule. The Palestinians had now become the "Jews of the Jews". But unlike the Jews, we did not amount to much. The Jews were in their homeland, a stirring spectacle in the eyes of the world, while our loss of homeland was of little moment. We suddenly saw ourselves for what we were in the eyes of the "civilized" world: another species of Third World sub-humanity, existing outside history – the new Red Indians, the Blacks of Israel'.[3]

This sudden awareness for Palestinians of their position in global society, so to speak, caused both a negative and a positive response. On the one hand, they began to care far less what their Arab brethren or the world community in general thought of them. They had not received much help in the past and now knew not to expect it. On the other hand, they began to see themselves for who they were and who they wanted to be in their own eyes – an independent people with an independent will. Their identity as a Palestinian nation seeking all of its national rights was crystallized in the minds and hearts of each member. They now became virtually obsessed with that one goal – the realization of their national dream.

This entailed a number of new developments, among them a renewed emphasis on cultural roots and national folklore. Palestinians no longer depended solely on Cairo, Beirut or Damascus for a definition of what was Arab and, in particular, what was Palestinian. Instead they rediscovered their own folktales, began writing in earnest their own poetry and short stories, began dancing the national dabkeh and sewing the traditional multi-coloured embroidery. They began to write the history of the nation from their experience, essentially contradicting the Zionist and pro-Zionist versions of events in the Middle East. They opened universities and emphasised higher education like none of the other Arab peoples. Today they have one of the highest rates of higher education degrees *per capita* in the world. In short, in rediscovering their roots they began to reassert themselves as a special nation, a nation with a unique history that would eventually overcome the varied attempts to erase it.

In this period of reflection following the 1967 War, the so-called 'Israeli Arabs' actually rediscovered their families and friends on the West Bank and in Gaza. They were reawakened to their heritage and realized instinctively that the fate of each of the two 'halves' of Palestine was inextricably linked. Today, in fact, much of the cultural revival in Palestine goes on within the 1948 borders of Israel. One of the first cultural centres was set up in Taibeh, a village well inside the 'Green Line' in the Triangle.[4]

In addition to this cultural revival another distinctive factor of the new generation of Palestinians was their attention to politics. A Palestinian youth growing up since 1967 is more politically aware than his foreign counterpart. He or she can explain at a moment's notice the particularities of the Palestinian–Israeli conflict, the position of Palestine in relation to the Arab world, and the status of the Palestine problem on the international agenda. The clear conflict in which they are engaged heightens this political consciousness.

Prior to 1967 those who might have otherwise been involved in nationalist politics, particularly on the West Bank, had their energies instead directed into one of four main channels, as Pamela Ann Smith points out in her text *Palestine and the Palestinians*. The four main channels of action were: (1) the movement to achieve liberal democracy in Jordan; (2) pan-Arabism and Arab nationalism; (3) the Communist Party and other Marxist organizations; and (4) Islamic reformism.[5]

That is not to say, however, that there was not some expression of nationalist tendencies in the post-1948 war period. But these expressions were largely confined to clandestine groupings which were most successful among the Diaspora refugee population. The refugees even opposed the setting up of the United Nations Relief and Works Agency for Palestinian refugees on the grounds that their claim to the homeland would thus be obscured through assimilation into their various host countries. Smith writes: 'Throughout the area the refugees took to the streets to protest against the plan to assimilate them into the neighbouring countries and to demand the right to continue the fight against partition and against the creation of a Zionist state in Palestine. By 1952 several clandestine groups had formed which sought to channel refugee discontent into concrete political and military action aimed at regaining their homeland.'6

In addition to a cultural revival and a heightened political awareness, this newfound sense of identity contributed in a direct way to the Palestinian revolution. A truly indigenous Palestinian revolutionary movement – the Palestine Liberation Organization – emerged and the nation gave it total support, expressing confidence that a movement which drew its ranks from nearly every family of Palestinians would be more effective in liberating the country than the Arab guardians had been. This issue of 'identity' contributed significantly to swelling the ranks of the new guerrilla movement. PLO officials, interviewed about their motives for joining the revolution, also spoke of national identity, of personal dignity.

Ahmad Yamani, of the Popular Front for the Liberation of Palestine faction, said, 'National feeling comes first, then the class motive. I remember I was twelve years old in 1936, when my father, who was a poor peasant, sold the only cow he had to buy a machine gun. The price was thirteen pounds sterling. I also remember another day when British soldiers attacked our village and tortured my father in front of us, then took him to jail. Our story is very simple: we fight for our national cause and dignity.' Shafiq al-Hout of the PLO, answers, 'To me the question is a surprise. To ask me, Why do you fight for your country? is to ask me, Why do you breathe? or Why are your eyes brown? If for no other reason, I have to fight for the identity of my children, who never stop asking me, Who are we, Daddy?'

Zuheir Mohsen, of Salqa, responds, 'National feelings to restore the land and Arab dignity come first. The problem of the Palestinian was that he was unable to answer such questions as: Who am I?

Where do I belong? and Where will I live? When they are after me
in Jordan, I escape to Syria; and then they follow me to Syria. I
escape to Lebanon. What is the solution? My family is in the occupied
territories. The Israelis have one solution for me, to accept my fate
as an exile.'

Perhaps Ali Salameh, of Fatah, who was later killed by the Israeli
Mossad, put it most eloquently when he said:

The Resistance Movement is to me a substitute for the land. The
Palestinian fights to gain respect. As long as I fight, I feel I am
respected. I am not sure when Palestine will be liberated, but still
I fight. The slave does not fight, and I am no more a slave.

Before 1967 a Palestinian was regarded as an unrespected, unpro-
tected, dishonoured fugitive who sold his land. I rejected being
that man.

Thousands of times people pointed at us, whispering: 'That one is
a Palestinian refugee.' Oh, my God, the whispers tortured me!

I can never forget one day when I was a teenager. I had to deny
my identity. I was afraid of saying 'I am a Palestinian' to a group
of vagabonds, so I said that I was a Syrian.

Going back to Haifa is not the problem. The restoration of identity
is the problem. For me, to be proud of my identity and my national
feelings and aspirations is the problem. When I die fighting, I will
know that my death will make my son proud to be the son of a
Palestinian.[7]

In this sense of regaining their identity, Palestinians benefited from
the 1967 conflict. Paradoxically speaking, the war was a blessing in
disguise. Though they lost further land, they regained the right to
hold their destiny in their own hands. Naseer al-Aruri writes,

But while Palestine ceased to exist as a political community, it
continued to exist in the collective consciousness of its own
people. After two decades of futile reliance upon the international
community and the Arab states, Palestinians in the mid-sixties
seized the initiative and took their destiny into their own hands.
With an unwavering commitment to the restoration of their national
rights, they opted for armed struggle, and gained international
recognition of their rights. Their transformation from refugees to
guerrilla fighters was the principal factor that redirected the

character of the Arab–Israeli conflict in the aftermath of 1967 to a struggle between Palestinian Arabs and Israeli Jews.[8]

Thus, with the 1967 conflict, the loss of all of Palestine, came a renewed struggle, a regained identity, a sense of self-reliance. It paved the way for a new leadership. Professor Michael C. Hudson, of Johns Hopkins School of Advanced International Studies, explains it thus:

> If one could chart a relative deprivation curve for the Palestinians. It might well have corresponded to the hypothesis of Tocqueville and his modern interpreters: sufficient well-being, especially in education, among the dispersed Palestinians after their eviction from Palestine in 1948 to inspire a growing awareness of the injustice suffered. The disaster of 1967, suddenly lowering the level of well-being and renewing the injustice, served to precipitate a climate receptive to new leadership.[9]

BREAKAWAY FROM ARAB STATES

Palestinians as a whole began to weigh the benefits of a Palestinian leadership against the continued ineffectiveness and sustained humiliation of their Arab guardians. This climate receptive to new leaders affected all sectors of Palestinian society after 1967, including the refugee population from which the clandestine guerrilla movements had long since been drawing support and from the more financially comfortable sectors who had tended to set dreams of Palestine aside in favour of their professional futures in the Arab world.

For the refugee in the Arab Diaspora, 1967 and its crystallization of Palestinian identity and the birth of the revolution meant not only liberation of the homeland but a long-awaited stab at the Arab governments. Fawaz Turki, who fled Haifa as a child in 1948, wrote:

> As I grew up my bogeyman was not the Jew, nor was he the Zionist, nor was he . . . the imperialist or the Western supporters and protectors of the state of Israel, but he was the Arab. The Arab in the street who asked if you'd heard the one about the Palestinian who . . . The Arab at the Aliens Section who wanted you to wait obsequiously for your work permit, the Arab at the police station who felt he possessed a carte blanche to mistreat you, the Arab who rejected you and, most crucially, took

away from you your sense of hope and sense of direction. He was
the bogeyman you saw every morning and every night and
every new year of every decade tormenting you, reducing you,
dehumanizing you, and confirming your servitude.[10]

Just as the Palestinian refugee internalized this new spirit of nationalism as a means of freedom from the Arab host states, so did an
entirely different sector of Palestinian society turn to the revolution
and the dream of their own state as a means of securing their financial
futures. The Palestinian bourgeoisie, many of whom operated prior
to 1967 in the Arab Diaspora, came to nationalism just before the
June War as the result of a curious incident – the failure of Intra
Bank, the brainchild of Yusef Baldas. This incredibly successful
Palestinian financial institution had taken the Arab world by storm
in the years before the June conflict, and just as suddenly in 1966
failed as the result of a run on the bank by the Kuwaitis. Palestinians
have since felt that the bank was the direct victim of Arab jealousy
of Palestinian success in the Diaspora. Smith points out:

> Whatever the merits or faults of Intra – and the controversy about
> it and bribes still continues – Palestinians of all walks of life draw
> the conclusion that the bank had failed, or been allowed to
> fail, solely because it was Palestinian. Henceforth, they argued,
> Palestinians would either have to share their profits with their Arab
> rivals – and so defuse potential jealousy – or invest their funds in
> an area where Palestinians had a say in the government and in the
> way affairs of the economy were handled. Since no Arab state
> except Jordan gave the Palestinians a right to participate in
> governmental affairs – and there they had little power to decide
> policy – the only answer to many Palestinian businessmen in the
> Diaspora after the collapse of Intra seemed to be the creation of a
> place where economic influence could be secured and maintained
> by political power, namely through the establishment of a state of
> their own.

Less than a year after the collapse of Intra the loss of the entire West
Bank and Gaza to the Israelis during the June War led to even
greater support for Palestinian nationalism among those elements in
Jordan who, unlike their colleagues in the Gulf states, had up to then
eschewed active involvement in Palestinian politics.[11]

The Arab states, particularly Jordan, had discouraged any Palestinian involvement in politics despite their overheated rhetoric about regaining Palestine. Yet after the shocking two to three-day defeat in June 1967, the Palestinians realized the uselessness of the Arab military and determined that both the birthing and nurturing of Palestinian nationalism would have to be done alone.

Despite the military and political posturing by the Arab confrontation states before Israel began the actual hostilities in June 1967, their performance on the field belied the true intentions behind their bravado. They had not prepared adequately for war, and indeed did not really seek it. Their posturing was entirely for the sake of public image. Though Fatah, by then openly operating as a guerrilla force, had wanted war with Israel and had in a sense drawn the enemy out, as Donald Neff, author of *Warriors For Jerusalem*, points out, because they believed that liberation would come through Arab unity and Arab unity only through battle, the Arab states were in reality not seeking conflict, preferring instead merely to vocalize their vow to liberate Palestine in front of their respective news media.[12]

Schleifer quotes Hassanein Heikal, the well-known Egyptian journalist, on this subject of Egyptian posturing:

> Throughout the sixties Egypt had never sought more than an ideological 'open field' or sphere of influence in Jordan, Heykal wrote, for fear that a violent or radical change of regime in Amman would have forced the UAR into an unwelcome military confrontation with Israel over the West Bank. There was a bitter edge for the Palestinian in Heykal's frank admission. Prior to that cruel eye-opener, the June 1967 War, no other people in the Arab East could rival the Palestinians for simple faith in the UAR – in its massive army and revolutionary promise – as the historic agent destined to recover the lost homeland. More than the Syrian or the Iraqi, the Palestinian would have welcomed nothing less than the political union of Jordan with Egypt, as partner in either of the two attempts at a united Arab republic. Yet it was Ben-Gurion who had stayed the deliverer's hand.[13]

It was the hypocrisy of the Arab states which ultimately dealt them out of the game as far as the Palestinians were now concerned. With the Arabs never really seeking open conflict with Israel in the first place for the sake of the liberation of Palestine and certainly not for the sake of the liberation of their own masses, and with their utterly pitiful performances when faced with the enemy, the conflict could no longer rightfully be named an 'Arab–Israeli' conflict. It now changed to a more black and white confrontation, a confrontation between the two parties directly involved, the two peoples sharing and fighting over the same land, in actuality now a Palestinian–Israeli conflict. The Arabs after all were then and now, whether openly or secretly, seeking accommodation with Israel.

The 1967 war, and Israel's astonishing military success, pushed the Palestinians away from their weakened Arab guardians to a stance which would be indigenously Palestinian and increasingly militaristic. Hudson explains it thus:

> A political culture inherently fragmented because of primordial culture divisions, external divisive forces, and uneven modernization, had been subjected to a new Israeli intrusion. The success of Israel's aggressive stance was continually reaffirmed by new victories. To many Arabs non-violent alternatives appeared ever more naive.[14]

What the Palestinians opted for initially was the takeover of an organization which up to this point had been theirs in name only. The Arabs, particularly Nasser, had created the Palestine Liberation Organization in 1964 because they had no plan to solve the conflict and needed to appear to be doing something. But between 1964 and the 1967 war the organization operated as a puppet of Nasser's. Smith chronicles this change:

> While on the surface the formation of the PLO appeared to the outside world and to Israel to herald a new era of militancy and of joint Arab–Palestinian struggle, it in fact represented an attempt by the Arab regimes to prevent the Palestinian movement from taking over action on its own and to use Palestinian militants to defend the interests of the Arab governments against Israel. Under the terms of the Charter the existing state boundaries were formally recognized, including Jordanian sovereignty over the West Bank, Egyptian control in Gaza and the Syrian annexation of the Himmah. Rather than establishing the means whereby the Palestinians would launch an armed movement to regain their land, the establishment of the PLO in 1964 represented a move by the Arab governments to reconcile the points of view of President Nasser, King Hussein and the Ba'athists while preserving unity and the status quo in the face of Israeli threats to divert the waters of the Jordan Valley and to launch hostilities against Jordan, Syria and Egypt. The PLA (Palestine Liberation Army, a military arm of the PLO), which

even after the rise of Fatah continued to oppose the arms and tactics employed by the guerrillas, was totally under the control of its respective Arab government hosts, most of whom had no intention of letting the Commander-in-Chief enjoy real power.

Demands by Palestinians active in the various pan-Arab and leftist movements for participation in the formation of the PLO's constituent bodies were ignored and it became instead a talking shop for the Palestine notables allied to the various Arab governments. The reluctance of some of the Palestinian militants, including George Habash and the other future leaders of the PFLP (Popular Front for the Liberation of Palestine) and the DFLP (Democratic Front for the Liberation of Palestine), to undertake armed struggle independently without the prior commitment of the Arab governments to a war with Israel also split the young generation of Palestinians who had criticised the PLO from its outset and who had been particularly disillusioned at the choice of (Ahmed) Shuqairi and other traditional notables to serve as the representatives of the Palestinian people. Only after the unexpected defeat of the Arab armies in June 1967 and the Israeli occupation of the West Bank and Gaza Strip did all the Palestinian guerrilla movements agree on the necessity of independently launching military action immediately.[15]

Although the 1967 war had not brought about the expected unity of the Arab world through battle, it did cause the even more unexpected unity of the Palestinians under one goal and one tactic – liberation of the homeland through armed struggle. Thus the shock of the war caused by means of a ripple effect, the crystallization of Palestinian identity, led the Palestinians to realize the impotence of the Arab world they had previously relied on, brought about the breaking away of the Palestinians from the Arab states, and gave birth to a unified resistance. The PLO was no longer a tool of the Arab world, but was an independent organization. With the battle of Karameh only months after the June War, when Palestinian fedayeen defeated an advancing Israeli army in Jordanian territory, Palestinians knew their time had come. The PLO began to draw recruits from every sector and every family in Palestinian society. It did not need a public referendum to establish its sole representation because it truly was of and by the people. As it became stronger and the outside forces were weakened, even the Arab states had to recognize that legitimacy at the 1974 Rabat Summit.

The Arab defeat of 1967 had pointed out to the new generation of Palestinians not only the diseased condition of the Arab ruling elites who had previously waged the war of liberation of Palestine but also made it very clear that radical solutions were in store. Sharabi recalls:

The defeat of 1967 also revealed the hollowness of the social and political structure of the Arab status quo. It broke the hold of the old nationalist ideology and forced the emergence of a radical perspective. Palestinians who had belonged to the Ba'ath party, to the Arab Nationalist Movement, to the Syrian Nationalist party, to the Communist party, to the Moslem Brothers, began to see things in a different manner. The old cliches, nourished by the humiliations and ambitions of three generations of petit bourgeois Arab nationalists, began, for the first time perhaps, to lose their meaning. Society at large – its institutions, its political, economic, and social organization – now came under hurried, angry, often incoherent criticism. But this criticism was based on an actual experience of total disaster.

As the rationalizations justifying the collapse fell by the wayside, the proposition that a radical transformation was needed assumed concrete, specific meaning. This perception represented the beginning of the first serious change in this generation's consciousness. But the formation of radical sensibility required going beyond mere generalizations. The new consciousness lacked the theoretical foundations necessary for comprehensive analysis. It also lacked the capacity to produce a political programme and a strategy around which the newly available social forces could organize. The disarray in the social structure now revealed itself in the structure of consciousness itself . . .

To be sure, picking up the gun demonstrated lessons which no theory alone could have taught. The first days of resistance showed not only what human will could generate, but also affirmed revolutionary action as the only way to self-transformation. It became clear that nothing could free society from the shackles that bound it except the force stored in its oppressed and exploited masses. We saw the New Arab Man emerging in the shape of the Palestinian fedayeen. We envisaged the Arab revolution being born out of the Palestinian resistance movement. The immediate aftermath of the 1967 defeat was the heroic period of Palestinian resistance. The courage and determination of the fedayeen injected new life in the Palestinians and all the Arab masses. Never before in their history had the Palestinians felt so strongly bound together. The fedayeen crossed the river and for the first time in twenty years were able to hit back at the enemy.[16]

Schleifer explained the existence of this New Man as the result of a kind of mass catharsis. He writes:

Frantz Fanon saw armed struggle against racist colonialism as a mass catharsis for psychic as well as political-economic liberation in the Third World, and the thesis holds up well in the hills of the occupied territories and the rear bases on the East Bank.

These fedayeen are 'new men', untouched by the Palestine refugee syndrome – the twenty-year emotional burdens of dependency. They are free from waiting on world bodies for charity, free from appealing to the great powers for justice, free from counting only upon great Arab leaders (and their armies) instead of on themselves for liberation.[17]

REJECTION OF THE WEST

Another result of the 1967 war was a turning away by the Palestinians from dependence on foreign governments, particularly those in the West. The Palestinians no longer believed in the efficacy of demanding justice from the so-called 'free world' since the West had proven incapable and even unwilling to pressure Israel into even the slightest concession. Many Palestinians, as a result, began to reject the West and any attempts made by the West to influence them, turning instead for help to the Eastern bloc. Other more radical Palestinians even reckoned that the West would only be made to come around if it was made to feel some of the Palestinians' suffering, thus the advent of so-called 'international terror'.

The history of the United States in the region was never one of neutrality despite a US claim to that effect. It was, after all, President Harry Truman who moved to recognize the new Jewish state immediately, never with so much as a word of sympathy for the suffering the new state had caused the Palestinians. And in 1967, it was the United States which stood ready to assist Israel and which even praised Israel's bravado in bringing about the humiliating defeat and in occupying the rest of Palestine. There is some indication that

US officials may have realized, at least in private, the negative impact the war would have on US–Arab relations and on the Palestinians' feelings toward America in particular. President Lyndon Johnson himself may have realized this. Donald Neff quotes from the National Security Council meeting notes of 7 June 1967: 'The President said that by the time we get through all the festering problems we are going to wish the war had not happened.' Neff continues, 'Those were the wisest words uttered that day, for what was now unfolding in the Middle East would set the region on a course of hatred and war far worse than ever before'.[18]

Some US diplomats in the region also recognized the danger of the US concentrating on Israel's war effort to the detriment of the sentiments of the Palestinian and Arab peoples. Neff quotes Dick Nolte, a US diplomat in Cairo during the war:

> Nolte, looking ahead, presciently warned that the current fighting was doing nothing to redress the major problem between Israel and the Arabs – the Palestinians. 'Necessary to recognize very real passion mobilized in whole area by Nasser on Palestine issue', he wrote. 'Present defeat would only make that "anger of inferiority" all the more ready a few years hence for the next hero. . . . Maybe now, on basis of new security, Israel can be made to see wisdom of settlement along less one-sided lines. Impartial and constructive US role here could go far toward reversing universal loss of respect for and influence of US in whole Arab world.'[19]

The failure of the US government to take Nolte's advice and push Israel into negotiating over the central issue of Palestine right after the war caused an irreconcilable breach in US–Palestinian relations. It did much to push the liberation movement into an armed struggle. Naseer al-Aruri chronicles the move to armed struggle thus:

> Outside Palestine, the struggle against the occupation was also waged along broad nationalist lines. During the two decades that elapsed since the 1947 conflict, the Palestine question had been confined largely to the agendas of charitable international organizations. The dispersed Palestinians retained an unwavering commitment to the restoration of their sovereignty over their homeland. At no point did they acknowledge the legitimacy of the state of Israel. They retained their national identity and resisted all schemes of settlement outside their homeland and all attempts at national subjugation and assimilation. Their struggle, however, remained

passive throughout the twenty-year period while their cause was being advocated, without success, by the Arab states and international organizations. It was the failure of these 'guardians' to obtain redress for the Palestinians that induced them to opt for the armed struggle. Without doubt they were inspired by the process of decolonization and the success of liberation movements in the third world. They began to learn that one does not address moral and legal arguments to his oppressor. They began to view their adversary as a System – a System that assumes their negation. Resistance to that System thus became an act of self-affirmation and a cogent expression of dignity.[20]

This new radicalization of Palestinians caused them even to reflect on the usefulness of the charitable bodies that had given them a hand in the past. These organizations were also seen as ineffectual and basically themselves suffering from a dependence on, and thus submission to, the West. The liberation movement in response worked hard at creating its own aid programme for helping its own orphans, widows and disadvantaged. The PLO succeeded in offering much more to the refugees than UNRWA had ever done. In 1966 the then UNRWA secretary-general expressed sympathy and regret for the meagre assistance the Palestinians were receiving from his organization. He wrote, 'During the long period of their dependence on international charity their life has been one of hardship and privation. The relief accorded by UNRWA, though indispensable, has been no more than a bare minimum . . . The rations are meagre and unvarying and would hardly sustain a person who depended solely on them for any long period.'[21]

In developing their own answer to UNRWA aid, particularly in the camps in Lebanon, the PLO was imitating the more socialist agenda of the other successful anti-colonial and anti-imperial revolutions. Again, they were turning from the West and towards the East. Dr P. Edward Haley, a professor of international relations at Claremont McKenna College in California, recalls a reunion he had with his former teacher, the well-known Palestinian intellectual Fayez Sayegh, shortly after the war in 1968. Haley had at the time taken offence at some of Sayegh's seemingly anti-American remarks. He wrote later:

He [Sayegh] had concluded that the goal of Palestinian self-determination could not be achieved without the support of anti-colonialists everywhere, including the Soviet Union. Slowly, painfully, I began to realize the impact of the 1967 War on developments in the Middle East and on the lives of my Arab friends. I also saw that what I had reacted to was not simply a harsh, anti-American line but a statement of the new international realities as seen by the Palestinians themselves. Eventually I realized that the Palestinians were not so much eager to turn away from America as they were determined not to shrink from their goal of self-determination.[22]

Sayegh was not alone in his reflections. This turning from the West in what the West saw as a radicalization was indeed a by-product both of the 1967 War with the Palestinians' realization that neither Israel nor the West were interested in self-determination for the Palestinians, and of a realization that their own Western-oriented elites had done nothing effectual to achieve their national goals in the past. Thus, it was up to them, the younger generation, to ensure that nothing stood in their way, particularly not old alignments, from governing themselves in a state of their own.

Hudson explains:

> The radicalization of Palestinian ideology, both in its substantive and instrumental aspects, was particularly dramatic within the liberal, American-educated professional elite, previously classifiable as 'moderate' or 'pro-Western'. In searching for an explanation, two factors seem to be important. One, of course, is the trauma of the 1967 War and the intransigence in postwar Israeli behaviour. This behaviour unquestionably forced many Palestinians into advocating radical counter-measures. The other factor was the realization by many young Palestinians that non-radical politics failed to achieve national and social goals. The experience of the Palestinian community during the Mandate was to them sufficient evidence that the traditional elite had lacked vision, was naive in terms of tactics, and thus was inadequate to the challenge of Zionism and British colonial power.[23]

NOW A PALESTINIAN–ISRAELI CONFLICT

As Sharabi pointed out, much of the radicalization in the Palestinian camp and the impasse at which the two adversaries see themselves is the result, from a Palestinian viewpoint, of Israeli intransigence on the issue of the occupied territories after the 1967 war. Despite some hope shortly after the war that Israel would trade the territories for peace, the Jewish state insisted instead that all of Palestine belonged to 'Eretz Israel'. This was not apparently even a position that Israel's ally, the US, favoured. Wally Barbour, the US ambassador in Tel Aviv at the time of the war, wrote that 'despite the heady atmosphere of victory and the temptation this may provide for territorial expansion, the voice of wisdom will prevent them from changing fundamentally the assurances given at the outset that they will remain within their present borders'.[24]

Perhaps Barbour's knowledge of the Israelis and how they would react to such a temptation was not as good as he had imagined. One thing was for sure – at the time of the war and the occupation of the West Bank, including East Jerusalem, and the Gaza Strip, the Palestinians, except for those living inside the 1948 borders of Israel, knew next to nothing about their Israeli adversary. Until then the Palestinians in the occupied territories had had no personal contact with Israelis. There was no television station, no open bridges, only radio broadcasts to give them an idea of the other side. The separation was more total than that between the two Germanys. This isolation helped to create an atmosphere in which the enemy was depersonalized. And by depersonalizing the enemy, the Palestinians could believe in its total annihilation. Turki writes, 'To the Palestinian, the young Palestinian, living and growing up in Arab society, the Israeli was the enemy in the mathematical matrix; we never saw him, lived under his yoke, or, for many of us, remembered him. Living in a refugee camp and growing hungry, we felt that [while] the causes of our problem were abstract, the causes of its perpetuation were real'.[25]

For the most part, as Turki explained, the conflict was broad, between the Arab states and the Jewish state; the Palestinians played a role in the play only as the silent sufferers, the forgotten dispossessed. After the war, however, Palestinians found themselves catapulted onto centre stage. The former leading men, the Arab states, were incapable of carrying on with the production almost as if they had forgotten their lines. And the suffering dispossessed, though still both of those things, were however no longer silent. They were now no longer involved in an abstract, mathematical equation, they were part and parcel of a direct conflict, a direct confrontation with the enemy. With the occupation of the West Bank and Gaza Strip, Israel had brought the 1.5 million Palestinians living there under its yoke and changed the dynamics of the struggle to a

Palestinian–Israeli conflict, relegating the Arab states to a minor part, like mere understudies waiting in the wings.

The first image Palestinians in the occupied territories had of Israelis were not as daring pioneers, as much of the West continues to view them, but as soldiers, as occupiers, as an immediate and very real threat. Every Palestinian family in the West Bank and in Gaza has some horror story to tell about where they were and what they were doing when the soldiers came. Israel was not seen as a liberator, freeing the Palestinians from an oppressive Arab regime, but was and still is seen as an outsider, a usurper, an enemy with imperial designs on the people and the land.

Shortly after the occupation the second view most Palestinians had of Israel was of the settlers, many of whom were Western emigrants, particularly American, with wild-eyed ideas of playing David and Goliath. They positioned themselves on rises overlooking Palestinian villages and fenced themselves in, making the difference between them and the occupying military very small. Neither of these images of Israel has changed much in the 20 years of occupation, and in many instances has become worse. It is still relatively easy for the Palestinian inhabitants of the occupied territories to depersonalize the enemy when speaking of the soldiers and settlers. Both groups have placed themselves in adversarial positions and are universally regarded as outsiders.

However, following the 1967 war, Palestinians began to learn gradually about Israeli society inside the 'Green Line'. Israeli TV was inaugurated with an Arabic language programme, which of course broadcast what the Israeli Government wanted the Palestinians to hear. Nevertheless, this was the beginning of some contact between the two populations. As the contacts increased so did Palestinians' awareness that the Israelis in large measure were here to stay. They began slowly to realize who the Zionists were and what they wanted, and to accept the existence of the Jewish state within its 1948 borders. At least they saw the presence of a large number of Jews in Palestine as a fact.

The war and the subsequent occupation also gave Palestinians their first real look at a democracy in action. Although democratic principles have no bearing on Israel's treatment of the Palestinians under military rule, nevertheless these Palestinians got occasional glimpses of how Israeli society operated within itself and they realized the efficacy of adopting democratic organization in their own groupings such as unions. In a sense, because they were cut off from the Arab world with its more autocratic rule, the Palestinians were forced to use Israeli democracy as a model.

One outcome of their introduction to representative rule was a weakening of tribal control in the villages. It was no longer acceptable for one person to speak for whole communities. Traditionally the *mukhtar*, or village head, had maintained ties to the ruling government and thereby maintained both his legitimacy as a representative of the government and a leader of his village. Under Israeli rule this changed, although, ironically, the Israeli military authorities have sought to maintain this traditional system as a means of having their own agents, or collaborators, in the leadership positions. But by and large, the Palestinian community has rejected the leadership of tribal heads and insisted that the leaders of the PLO, the government in exile, spoke for them.

This change was best illustrated in the spring of 1986 when Jordan's King Hussein announced he was ending coordination for a peace settlement with the PLO. He called on Palestinians in the occupied territories to choose their leadership, broadly hinting that they choose him. There were a few traditional leaders of villages and small towns who journeyed to Amman and presented themselves at the palace as representatives of the population pledging their support for the King. Immediately, demonstrations broke out in some of the towns and inhabitants of the villages, even the families of these leaders, placed advertisements in local newspapers disassociating themselves from these leaders' actions and declaring that these leaders represented no one except themselves. The population once again stood solidly behind the PLO.

For the most part, Palestinians in the occupied territories have very little to do with the Israeli population. Those who can find no work in the captive economy are now day labourers in Israeli factories, but their only contact with Israeli individuals is with their bosses and the soldiers who stop them at checkpoints making sure they get back across the border before dark. For Palestinians, contact with Israel some 20 years after the war is still a humiliation. There is no equality between the two. It is akin to the relationship between the 'haves' and the 'have nots'. As Sharabi poignantly explained:

To the Palestinians, Israel today is nothing more than what it has taken away from them, Israeli happiness is made of Palestinian tears. If today the Israelis are a people with a country, it is because the Palestinians are a people without a country. Israel's victories are the Palestinians' defeats, its pride their humiliation, its might their weakness. As time passes Israel grows and moves forward, a state among states, while the Palestinians slowly disappear as a people, stateless, dominated, and in exile. In the full sense of the word, Israel's being is the Palestinians' non-being.[26]

Palestinians are aware that this image of Israel – the builder of a nation on top of the blood and bones of another – is not the image the Western world has had of the Jewish state. It is certainly not the image Israel has of itself. And after 20 years of occupation and nearly 40 years of the existence of the state these images have not in large measure changed. Despite contact with Israel after 1967, the Palestinians feel they are no better off and may be no closer to a solution. The hope through such contact is that Israel will come to see itself for the imperialist nation it has become. Sharabi maintains that only after the Palestinians went public with their suffering through the armed struggle did a few Israelis and world Jewish leaders start to notice the contradictions between Israeli propaganda as a pioneering miracle and the truth of its existence by virtue of Palestinian non-existence.

He continues:

When the Palestinians picked up the gun in 1967 and organized for armed struggle, the beginnings of self-doubt for the first time set in some Israeli minds: the Jewish state looked less utopian and more colonial. Many Jews inside and outside Israel – Zionist settlers, Jewish *pieds noirs*, Zionist and non-Zionist supporters of Israel – felt somewhat ill at ease; they had either consciously to ignore the facts or to suppress their moral instincts or to rationalize the new knowledge away. Self-doubt, suppressing moral feelings, rationalizing the sense of guilt, are among the first signs of ripening internal contradictions.[27]

IS PEACE MORE OR LESS POSSIBLE?

With the June war and the subsequent military occupation of the West Bank and Gaza Strip Palestinians were subject to a new form of atrocity they had previously not known. In addition to the torment of refugee status for many, the entire population of the occupied territories faced expropriation of their land, a change in their means of livelihood often with no viable alternative, deportation, arbitrary imprisonment, lack of political or civil rights, and other forms of harassment. The atrocities had a dual effect: on one hand, they radicalized the population and on the other hand, they caused many to wonder what caused Israel to behave as it had done. If the shoe were on the other foot would the Palestinians have done the same thing? Palestinians realized as a result of this reflection that a solution must be found that would be acceptable to both peoples living on the one plot of ground. Realizing that living together in a democratic state was both undesirable in some ways and impossible in others, they turned more and more towards the partitioning of the country into two states. By suggesting that a Palestinian state be formed on the West Bank and the Gaza Strip they were even willing to take the smaller fraction.

Yet the victory of 1967 went to Israel's head. Israel decided to keep the occupied land, a decision that made peace less and less possible. While there was a change in Arab and Palestinian public opinion towards negotiation and partition, there was a new arrogance in Israel which now relied solely on military might and gave only lip-service to negotiations while maintaining a policy of creeping annexation. This made a two-state solution nearly impossible.

Peace was thus made more difficult by the June war largely because of Israel's postwar attitude. Israel now refused to talk peace on equal terms. Palestinians, who now saw a monstrous Israel riding high on its horse believing it could keep pushing for more and more, felt they had conceded enough. They were not the obstacles to peace, the Israelis were.

Immediately after the war there was a chance for peace. There was even a plan. In his book *My Friend, The Enemy*, Israeli journalist Uri Avnery details a peace plan he sent to the then Prime Minister Levi Eshkol immediately after the June cease-fire. He writes:

In the midst of the whirl of events, fatigued as we were, it was quite clear to us what had to be done. A moment of historical importance had arrived. A dramatic opportunity was staring us in the face. The historical homeland of the Palestinian people was in our hands. All barriers between us and the Palestinians had come down. We could address them directly, talk to them face to face, offer them the thing most precious to every people on earth: a national state of their own . . . After congratulating the prime minister on the victory, I wrote: 'Now, Mr Prime Minister, all our thoughts must be devoted to the achievement of a permanent peace, which will safeguard for generations the independence, security, and development of the State of Israel. The wisdom of the politicians must reap the harvest sown by the blood of the soldiers . . . I take the liberty of submitting to you, for your consideration, the following plan for the establishment of peace: (1) Within three months the inhabitants of the Gaza Strip and the West Bank will be invited to take part in a plebiscite. In this referendum they will be called upon to determine their future in a democratic way. (2) The voters will be asked to vote yes or no on the principle of the establishment of a free and independent Palestinian state, which will include the West Bank and Gaza.'

The sections of the plan that followed dealt with federative arrangements between the Palestinian state and Israel, the status of Jerusalem, UN supervision of the referendum, the return of the refugees, the links between the Palestinian state and the Arab world (parallel to the links between Israel and the Jewish world), and the attainment of peace treaties between Israel and the Arab states.

I suggested that Eshkol make a dramatic gesture at this very moment of turmoil and disorientation, when all established ideas had come crashing down, when mental patterns were disintegrating and there was a chance for the creation of totally new ones.[28]

But, of course, Avnery never received a reply from Eshkol, and now 20 years later, many people can see that was a mistake. Strangely enough, history in our particular conflict with respect to the chances of peace has come full circle. For the first 20 years, from 1947 to 1967, Israel often spoke about negotiations and the Palestinians, the leaderless people, did not. But from 1967 until now, the Palestinian leadership has sought every avenue to negotiations and Israel has stubbornly refused to talk without setting up a variety of preconditions that one suspects are merely designed to insure there will be no negotiations and thus no threat to the status quo.

Instead of a fair and just peace, Israel has opted for the very last phrase of Avnery's plan – 'the attainment of peace treaties between Israel and the Arab states' – and ignored the entire process preceding that. Thus, in the view of the Palestinian people and much of the Arab world, the Israelis have chosen to place the horse before the cart, so to speak. This actually decreases the chances of peace rather than increasing them. Palestinians, almost to a man, woman and child, are willing now more than ever to accept some kind of lasting and just peace with Israel, but they are less likely to accept the continuation of the completely unacceptable status quo. And Palestinians will use any means available to them to win their liberation.

Within the Palestinian camp there is a great desire for territorial compromise if that is the only way currently to resolve the conflict. The two-state solution, with a Palestinian state on the West Bank, including East Jerusalem and the Gaza Strip, is more popular now than ever before. However, if there is no movement towards this end in the near future there is also more likelihood for war than in previous years. There is also within Israel an ever increasing movement of radical rightists who advocate the outright expulsion of the Palestinian people *en masse* from their homeland, and to Palestinians who have witnessed two massive tides of refugees this possibility does not seem so remote. Depression is setting in as we watch Israel annexing more and more land, deporting our leaders and committed nationalists, imposing unrealistically heavy taxes, creating more and more settlements, depriving our economy of any form of independent base.

All of this means that though Palestinians are willing to negotiate a just peace, they are on the other hand being increasingly radicalized as they see the seemingly unending horror of Israeli military occupation. In the 20 years since the war they have seen that 'might is right', and that power rules the day. A generation of young Palestinians is more willing to use violence to reach a solution.

The two-state solution has indeed been part of the political spectrum for some time now. The leaders of al-Fatah, the largest PLO faction, began calling for a mini-state in the West Bank and Gaza after 1973. Yet, since 1973 Chairman Yasser Arafat has had little to show for his peaceful efforts. Even the young within his own organization are now advocating a renewed emphasis on armed struggle as a result of Israel's refusal to take heed. Smith writes about the conflict within Fatah:

The ideology of armed struggle was once again in the forefront. Stripped of his olive branch by US and Israeli intransigence and plagued with internal strife, Arafat was left with the gun. His unwillingness to use that option against Israel after years of diplomacy threatened to undermine his future and that of the unified PLO which he headed. Once again the resistance movement was torn between those, like the Mufti in the 1930s, and the pro-Abdullah faction in the 1950s, who advocated negotiation and a peaceful settlement, and those, like the rebels of Galilee and the hill country, and the demonstrators in Jordan, who were ready to use arms to repel the invader.[29]

After 1967 the Palestinians made their political goals clear, sometimes through military means and sometimes through diplomacy. What is left now is for these goals to be realized, or for the conflict to rage on. Michael Hudson writes:

> After the 1967 War the Palestinians were able to fashion a new political identity and re-activate their just claims to self-determination in Palestine. Whether or not, their goal of a secular, democratic, unitary state of Palestine was achievable, their emergence made it likely that Palestinian political claims in some form would be part of any future settlement. In the absence of a settlement, the likelihood of continued turmoil remained strong, with the possibilities of new suffering and peril for Israel, frustration and economic regression for the Arabs, further decimation of the Palestinian people, destruction of American interests, and continued risk of the superpower confrontation.[30]

In the absence of a settlement over the last 20 years, everything that Hudson predicted has come true. And still despite efforts to ignore it, the root cause of the Arab–Israeli, Palestinian–Israeli conflict remains – the dispossessed, stateless Palestinian people. Yet victory is theirs in one area – they have made known to the world their just claims and it is not likely that they will be forgotten. Smith writes following the 1982 Lebanon war:

> What was easily forgotten amidst the frightening scenes of death and destruction which filled the world's television screens and newspapers during 1982 and 1983 was that the long years of exile and struggle had also produced an impressive victory on the international front. 'Palestine' and 'the Palestinians' had become household words once again and whatever the fate of the various solutions proposed by the US, the Soviet Union, Israel and the Arab states, it was clear that the PLO's basic demand for an independent state was supported by world public opinion and by almost all of the world's governments. Only the US and Israel still seemed determined to prevent the Palestinians from fulfilling their dream.[31]

As America's Martin Luther King, Jr, said, 'I Have A Dream', and we are not about to relinquish it. It is a dream of the future, not a monument to the past. As my friend, Uri Avnery, often says to Palestinians with whom he engages in dialogue, 'We cannot agree on anything that belongs to the past, so let's concentrate on the future and agree to disagree about what happened'. Indeed, what has happened is emblazoned on Palestinian hearts as it is on Israeli hearts, and, albeit to a different degree, they share a past of pain. What we are saying now is let us not repeat that painful past, but work towards a happy future where two peoples can share in their own states this blessed and holy land. Our hope is that in 20 years we will be publishing another volume celebrating a 20-year-old peace rather than decrying a 60-year-old conflict.

Notes

1. Henry H. Bucher, 'A Symposium: The Significance of the June, 1967 Israeli–Arab War', *Issues*, 21(2) 1967(16).
2. Abdullah Schleifer, 'Al-Fatah Speaks: A Conversation With "Abu Amar"', *Evergreen Review* (July 1986) 45.
3. Hisham Sharabi, 'Liberation or Settlement: The Dialectics of Palestinian Struggle', *Journal of Palestine Studies*, 2(2) (1973) 33–4.
4. Cluster of Arab villages in the Galilee, so-called because of their formation on the map.
5. Pamela Ann Smith, *Palestine and the Palestinians 1876–1983* (New York, 1984) 177–8.
6. Smith, *Palestine*, 148.
7. These statements were part of individual interviews with 22 Palestinian leaders conducted by Bayan Nuwaihed Al-Hout and reported in a chapter by Al-Hout, 'The Nature of the Palestine Liberation Organization', in *Palestine Rights: Affirmation and Denial*, Ibrahim Abu-Lughod (ed.) (Wilmette, Ill., 1982) 18–19.
8. Nasser al-Aruri, 'Dialectics of Dispossession', in *Occupation: Israel Over Palestine*', AAUG monograph 18, Nasser al-Aruri (ed.) (Balmont, Mass., 1983) 5.
9. Michael C. Hudson, 'The Palestinian Resistance: Developments and Setbacks', *Journal of Palestine Studies*, 1(3) (1972) 66.
10. Smith, *Palestine*, 150, cites Fawaz Turki, *The Disinherited: Journal of a Palestinian Exile* (New York, 1972).
11. Smith, *Palestine*, 141–2.
12. Donald Neff, *Warriors for Jerusalem: The Six Days That Changed the Middle East* (New York, 1984).

13. Abdullah Schleifer, *The Fall of Jerusalem* (New York, 1972) 54–5.
14. Hudson, 'The Palestinian Resistance', 67.
15. Smith, *Palestine*, 191–2.
16. Sharabi, 'Liberation or Settlement', 34–5.
17. Schleifer, 'Al-Fatah Speaks', 83.
18. Neff, *Warriors*, 244.
19. Neff, *Warriors*, 240.
20. Aruri, 'Dialectics', 9–10.
21. Neff, *Warriors*, 149, cites UN document A/5812,5.
22. Aruri, 'Dialectics', viii.
23. Hudson, 'The Palestinian Resistance', 79.
24. Neff, *Warriors*, 244.
25. Smith, *Palestine*, 151, cites Turki, *The Disinherited*, 53.
26. Sharabi, 'Liberation or Settlement', 43.
27. Sharabi, 'Liberation or Settlement', 45.
28. Uri Avnery, *My Friend, The Enemy* (London, 1986) 32–3.
29. Smith, *Palestine*, 177.
30. Hudson, 'The Palestinian Resistance', 84.
31. Smith, *Palestine*, 176.

Part II

International Dimensions

8 American Middle East Policy

Steven L. Spiegel

As late as November 1966, President Lyndon Johnson told a news conference: 'We are increasingly interested in the African continent and the Middle East. Our reports give us a reason to believe that things are going as well as could be expected'. By contrast, in a commencement address in May 1968, his earlier complacency had vanished: 'Today in two areas of danger and conflict – the Middle East and Vietnam – events drive home the difficulty of making peace'.

As these contrasting comments shortly before and after the Six-Day War suggest, the dramatic events of May and June 1967 had an immediate impact on American thinking about the Middle East. Beforehand, it was an area of minor concern, a backwater region considered a top priority only during the first years of the Eisenhower administration. Afterwards, the problems of the area were rarely unattended from the halls of Congress to the Oval Office to the press and media. In the perspective of forty years, the Six-Day War stands as the seminal event which led American policy makers to reassess the importance of the Middle East – and, perhaps more important, the perils its instability holds for American interests, including the threat to oil supplies, the possibility of Soviet expansion, and the dangers of confrontation with the Soviet Union. On a wider dimension of American concerns, the Six-Day War can be seen to have led to prime changes in the US approach to the area.

THE IMPACT OF THE SIX-DAY WAR ON SOVIET– AMERICAN COMPETITION

In order to understand the critical importance of the Six-Day War to the competition between the United States and the Soviet Union, it is useful to consider briefly the prior history of the superpower confrontation in the area. The Truman Doctrine, the basic American declaration of the cold war in 1947, was oriented to two nearby countries, Greece and Turkey. Yet, except for discussion of a Middle

East Defense Organization in 1952, US engagement in the region prior to 1953 had largely been economic – the product of American companies seeking expanded involvement, often at the expense of European competitors.

Eisenhower and Dulles entered office committed to a more active American policy in order to address the threat of expanded Soviet involvement and influence in the region. In order to block Moscow, they devised a multifaceted strategy: (1) the British could no longer be trusted to protect American interests in the area, so America would take over; (2) the United States would try to encourage a group of states in the area to organize a 'mini-NATO' to thwart potential Russian influence (later the Baghdad Pact); (3) arms sales would be stepped up to the Arabs (especially Iraq, hopefully Egypt); (4) the United States would keep its distance from Israel and would try to settle the Arab–Israeli dispute.

Eisenhower and Dulles had correctly identified the threat of Soviet involvement and they had developed a sophisticated strategy, but it did not work. Khrushchev, anxious to develop a strategy for challenging the West in the Third World, simply 'jumped over' the Maginot Line Eisenhower and Dulles had created in the form of the Baghdad Pact when he began selling arms to Nasser's Egypt and to Syria in 1955. During the Suez crisis the following year, the Russian leader was able to pose as the protector of the Arabs while threatening to punish the British, French, and Israelis. The United States pressured all three to cease their activity and eventually to withdraw; the Russians got the credit. By tying his fate to the nationalist Arab movement led by Nasser, Khrushchev had catapulted the Soviet Union into a central role in the area. When a radical coup overthrew the pro-western government in Iraq in July 1958, the Russian role appeared to constitute an even wider menace. In response, Eisenhower intervened in Lebanon.

By the end of the 1950s, the Russians were pursuing large programmes of arms transfers to Egypt, Iraq, and Syria; they were engaged in demonstrative aid projects like the Aswan Dam; larger numbers of Arab students were travelling to Moscow. The United States, though heavily involved in the region, had no effective means of countering Russian inroads and was attempting to bolster regimes still ready to align with the West.

In the 1960s, the Kennedy administration attempted to improve relations with Nasser, but was thwarted by the Yemen War which seemed to hold the prospect of Russian influence and Egyptian troops at the border of oil-rich Saudi Arabia. The Johnson administration, trying to develop a new programme for containing Soviet expansion, began to expand arms sales to several conservative Arab states and Israel. During this period, the Russians had gradually been increasing their involvement in the region, especially through continuing military aid. Yet they too were hindered by quarrelling Arab clients. Particularly after 1966, a new radical Syrian government began calling for a 'national liberation campaign' against Israel and complained that Nasser's involvement in the holy campaign was marginal. In order to resolve these divisions, the Russians began warning Nasser of imminent Israeli plans to attack Syria. This action was consistent with the Russian pattern of stirring up local conflict in the hope of furthering their own political gains. All parties knew this accusation was false, and Nasser at first ignored it. By May 1967, however, with his army bogged down in Yemen and his economy deteriorating, Nasser flirted with the tides of history by ordering a partial withdrawal of the United Nations Emergency Force which had been stationed in the Sinai since 1957. He thus set in place the events which led to the Six-Day War three weeks later.

From Moscow's perspective, the consequences of the war were horrifying, and indeed it has never fully recovered its former position in the region. The two Arab states most closely associated with the Soviet Union, Egypt and Syria, were roundly defeated. Both lost significant pieces of territory; their armies were decimated. As these defeats occurred, the Russians could do little but fulminate in support of their Arab clients at the United Nations and increase their presence in the Mediterranean. Even their confrontation with the United States in protection of Syria during the last hours of the war appeared to be little more than posturing.

Yet in the immediate aftermath of the war, the balance did not appear totally negative from the Kremlin's perspective. Although the Israelis won their victory largely with French rather than American weapons, the United States was blamed. As a consequence, several Arab states broke off diplomatic relations with Washington and de Gaulle's abrupt snub of Israel forced America for the first time into the position of protector of Jerusalem. Moscow's enormous resupply of weaponry to the Arabs partially compensated for the dismal showing of the USSR and its arms during the war. It forced the United States to step up its arms transfers to Israel in order to maintain the regional balance of power. By 1969, when Nasser started his War of Attrition along the Suez Canal, the Soviets could justifiably argue that the return of Arab power had begun under their sponsorship. They were also heavily engaged in training and support for the Palestine Liberation Organization, which intensified its terrorist attacks against Israel after 1967.

The Six-Day War certainly increased the immediate dependence of key Arab states on Moscow and of Israel on the United States. In more subtle terms, however, the nature of the Soviet–American competition was altered. For the first time, the means of Russian involvement in the region had contracted and America's options had expanded. In frustration at the successful Israeli attack and its inability to reverse the outcome of the war, Moscow broke diplomatic relations with Israel. It was to prove a terrible blunder. Henceforth, the United States was the only superpower in close touch with both sides. Since the results of the war necessitated diplomatic discussions on conditions under which Israel might return the territories, a negotiating process of some kind was inevitable. The Soviets, always fearful of losing their Arab support purchased largely with arms transfers, continued to align with the radical ideologues. They thereby proved themselves irrelevant for serious negotiations.

The changed atmosphere could be seen immediately after the war. It was the United States which took the lead in trying to reach some kind of *modus vivendi*, a process that led to UN Security Council Resolution 242 in which an agenda for discussions was set. In 1969 it was the United States which promulgated the first major post-1967 peace plan for the area, the Rogers Plan, and the United States which arranged the ceasefire which ended the War of Attrition in August 1970. When Syrian tanks invaded Jordan the following month, the United States and Israel demonstrably manoeuvred to strengthen King Hussein. The Syrians and their Palestinian allies were defeated.

Nasser's successor, Anwar Sadat, was progressively frustrated in his attempts to regain the Sinai through reliance on Moscow. Indeed, in 1972 he expelled the large contingent of Russian advisors who had entered Egypt during the War of Attrition. The country applauded. After the Yom Kippur War, the Kissinger shuttle, Carter's diplomacy and the Reagan plan all epitomized the supremacy of American diplomacy.

The initial outcome of the Six-Day War was confusing: America's client had won, but Washington's relations with the Arab world suffered severe setbacks to the advantage of the USSR. Viewed in perspective, however, it was the Six-Day War which was the turning point: a consistent tide of frustration for Washington was transformed into a period when opportunities emerged. By contrast, Moscow's fortunes began to decline. While these developments were certainly not inevitable, Russian errors and clever American initiatives concretized advantages that the 1967 War had made possible.

THE AMERICAN POLICY RESPONSE TO THE SIX-DAY WAR

The opportunities created by the Six-Day War, and their effect in particular on Soviet–American competition, can be seen only in retrospect. At the time, Americans greeted the war with a combination of exhilaration, relief, and fear.

There had been earlier Arab–Israeli wars in 1948 and 1956, and even the American intervention in Lebanon. There had been previous attempts at peace efforts and at blocking the Soviet Union. But the national response to the Six-Day War was unusual in its emotion and as an event which seemed to necessitate new policies and attention.

The sudden onset of the crisis made it all the more compelling by comparison with other Mid-East crises. The 1948 war had been evolving for years; the Suez Crisis was the culmination of a period of regional tension which began with the Soviet–Czech arms deal in September 1955. Despite its surprise beginning, the Yom Kippur War occurred in a period when the Middle East was a point of attention in the United States. For Americans, easily jolted by shifting tides of mood and fad, the Six-Day War was a bolt as if from nowhere.

The shock was intensified by America's preoccupation with Vietnam in 1967. By this time, the dissension and self-doubt were emerging from their incubation period into a state of full-scale convulsion. The outbreak of hostilities in the Middle East challenged the administration's concentration on Southeast Asia. The Vietnam War had been sold to Americans by the Johnson administration as crucial to defining America's global role and the future of the conflict with international communism. Yet the events in the Middle East reminded Americans that there was more to the world than Saigon. As several senatorial critics pointed out, on various scales of determining the national interest the Middle East appeared more significant than Indochina because of its crucial location astride three continents, the direct threat of Russian expansion, oil, the threat to a democracy (Israel), and the impact on the Suez Canal. By challenging the contemporary dominant world view, the Six-Day War contributed to the disintegration of the Vietnam-centred complex the Johnson administration had propounded.

Americans crave moral clarity in world affairs: good v. evil; democratic v. totalitarian; no greys. By 1967, the distinction between the communist oppressor and the democratic defender was blurring in Vietnam. At a critical moment, the Middle East conflict appeared, and seemed to offer the contrast between hero and villain that Americans were losing in Southeast Asia. In the conventional perspective, the Israelis were 'minding their own business' when Nasser created a crisis, the Arab states encircled the Jewish state, and then threatened to destroy it. The public's impression was that Israel's survival was at stake. Suddenly, the Israelis attacked, and vanquished all of their would-be conquerors in six short days.

These events seemed to imitate a Hollywood script, and they were accompanied by an emotional concentration heightened by the impact of television. Except for Vietnam itself and the Cuban missile crisis, the Six-Day War was one of the earliest international crises when television operated as a factor in the political equation. It was an equation which aided the Israelis at the Arab's expense, as suggested by the sudden rise of Israel's popularity in the American public opinion polls

Mixed with the public exhilaration were other sentiments, especially within the Johnson administration. First, there was widespread relief that Israel had successfully acted on its own, avoiding the need for American rescue. Second, there was concern at the sudden deterioration of US relations with a large segment of the Arab world. Third, there was fear that the Arab–Israeli dispute could lead to a future Soviet–American confrontation, which made the Middle East even more dangerous than Southeast Asia.

The new-found responsibility for Israel, the search for ways to mend relations with the Arab world, and the danger of Soviet–American confrontation created contradictory requirements for American policy. This is illustrated by the approach to arms sales. Before 1967, the United States still maintained flexibility because Paris was Israel's main supplier. After the Six-Day War, de Gaulle terminated France's special relationship with Jerusalem and the United States was confronted with Russian resupply of the Arab belligerents. Since the United States wished to compete by rearming pro-American Arab regimes, especially Jordan, it was forced to assume major responsibility for maintaining the regional arms balance in Israel's favour. In subsequent years administrations attempted to protect the balance of power by selling Israel sufficient weapons to counter British, French, Russian and American arms sold to the Arabs. This policy has been controversial at home and often based on conflicting and inaccurate calculations. The frequent regional wars attest to the difficulty of managing an arms race in which the US is only one of several suppliers and of preventing conflict by arming the participants on both sides to the hilt.

The Six-Day War itself was a prominent example of this frustrating task. Although the Johnson administration, like all involved parties, was caught off guard and unprepared, it did work to prevent war. For the first time in a crisis the US and Israel both tried to gain the other's confidence, but their immediate objectives were running at cross-purposes. Israel – mobilized and progressively encircled – wanted quick action. The Johnson administration – overcommitted and uncertain – stalled. The result was a war which could have been averted only by an early major US initiative, at least the contemplated multilateral fleet and perhaps an American or multination expeditionary force sent to the Sinai as a replacement for the recently deposed United Nations Emergency Force. In the light of Vietnam, these steps were unthinkable. Even had the US not been at war, it is unlikely that the Johnson administration would have been prepared to act quickly and effectively.

The events of the war reinforced the need to do something about the Arab–Israeli dispute lest it result in another similar crisis. By comparison with arms sales and crisis diplomacy, there were few contradictions and many potential benefits in attempting to ameliorate the Arab–Israeli dispute. Israel's security would be enhanced, the Arabs could be coaxed into improved relations with Washington, the dangers of Soviet–American confrontation would be reduced.

In their approach to peacemaking, many American leaders, especially Lyndon Johnson, were influenced by the experience of 1957 when Israel had been forced to withdraw from the Sinai and the Gaza Strip on the promise of future Egyptian concessions which were not fulfilled. When Nasser unilaterally evicted the United Nations Emergency Force from the Sinai, he destroyed the last vestige of the 1957 agreements. Whatever Arab–Israeli compromise individual American officials might advocate after 1967, no principal figures urged unilateral withdrawals by Israel without an Arab commitment to some type of peaceful arrangement. Before the Carter administration, however American officials might disagree with

Israel's demands for complete normalization of relations with Arab states in return for withdrawals, they were also not prepared to entertain withdrawals prior to a form of Arab recognition of Israel and commitment to non-aggression.

American officials differed markedly from Israel in their belief that in return for Arab commitments to peace the Jerusalem government should ultimately withdraw totally from the occupied territories with the possible exception of the most minor of adjustments. Within weeks of the Six-Day War, they were appalled at Israel's efforts to assume complete control of Jerusalem. They believed that Israel was making unrealistic demands for direct negotiations with Arab representatives and for ultimate normalization of relations as the price of withdrawal. The occupied territories should therefore have been the source of deep division between Jerusalem and Washington. There were certainly frequent tensions between the two governments over the issue, but ironically the occupied territories became a source of agreement as well. The Arab states refused to accept publicly the argument that the Six-Day War had altered irretrievably the Mid-East balance of political forces. At Khartoum in August 1967 they had declared defiantly that there would be no negotiations, no recognition, and no peace with Israel. They were thereby standing firmly in favour of the 1957 formula of unilateral Israeli withdrawals, which the United States would not support. Except for Sadat's diplomacy, this stance assured a minimal common Israeli–American perspective toward the peace process.

Vietnam was sufficiently all-consuming that Ambassador Arthur Goldberg at the UN was left to conduct American diplomacy. The result was UN Security Council Resolution 242, which called both for Israeli withdrawals 'from territories occupied in the recent conflict' and for every state in the area to be acknowledged as sovereign and 'to live in peace within secure and recognized boundaries'. Yet Johnson was content to entrust peacekeeping to UN mediator Gunnar Jarring, whose efforts did not result in major breakthroughs. This passive *modus operandi* was broken only by a fleeting approach to Egypt by Secretary of State Rusk in the fall of 1968 concerning possible discussions about a new peace process. In retrospect, the 1967 crisis occurred too late in the term for a major initiative. This administration's method for dealing with Mid-East conflict resolution was too passive, its diplomatic skills too limited, its engagement in Vietnam too overpowering for it to sponsor negotiations.

In American politics, each new administration attempts to set out in new directions, especially in reaction to previous crises. Richard Nixon thus came to power determined to address the problems for the United States created by the Six-Day War. He therefore sought to re-establish America's shattered image in the Arab world and to resurrect relations broken in 1967; to reduce the Russian role in the area; to promote America's position by facilitating an Arab–Israeli settlement. He was less certain regarding how he might achieve these goals.

During the first term, when the Middle East took a back seat to Vietnam, China, SALT, and détente, Nixon was confronted by two competing strategies represented by his two warring national security aides, Henry Kissinger and William Rogers. The Secretary of State, who was at first given the prime responsibility for Mid-East policy, favoured a region-oriented approach popular at the State Department. The outcome of this strategy was the Rogers Plan of December 1969 which laid out a programme by which Israel would withdraw from all but insubstantial territories captured in 1967 in return for the Arabs registering their 'binding and specific commitment' to non-belligerency. Kissinger argued that the United States could not press for negotiations until the key Arab parties, particularly Egypt, first made a move toward the United States, lest the Soviets receive the credit for any breakthrough which might occur. His arguments were strengthened by the poor reception of the Rogers Plan by both the Arabs and Israelis.

Rogers successfully achieved an end to the 1969–70 War of Attrition along the Suez Canal, but this ceasefire was controversial because of Egyptian violations. He was subsequently unable to arrange even a limited agreement between Egypt and Israel, but his efforts demonstrated that after the Six-Day War the United States would no longer withdraw from peace efforts in the area, even if the President was primarily involved in other regions.

After the Yom Kippur War, the incentive to support conflict resolution was even greater. Kissinger's shuttle diplomacy followed by Carter's flirtation with a Geneva conference and then the Camp David Accords and the Egyptian–Israeli peace treaty demonstrated that American engagement in the Arab–Israeli peace process had become a consistent pattern of Washington's policy toward the area. This pattern only reinforced the lesson decision-makers believed they had learned in 1967 – that it was the Arab–Israeli issue which was the perennial source of instability in the region. Zbigniew Brzezinski even suggested at one point that the energy crisis of the 1970s could be solved by a settlement of the Arab–Israeli conflict.

This concentration on Arab–Israeli issues which was focused by the Six-Day War and then concretized by the Yom Kippur War made it more difficult for policy makers to adjust to the changed circumstances raised by the fall of the Shah, the Iranian hostage crisis, the Iran–Iraq war, and the Soviet invasion of Afghanistan. If the Middle East is defined by the Arab–Israeli dispute and the Palestinian question in particular, then other issues are peripheral events, a part of another drama. Ironically, the Carter administration dreaded a second energy crisis, but anticipated that it would be caused by a new Arab–Israeli conflict. Instead, the 1979 crisis was precipitated by the fall of the Shah.

Thus, while in the public arena there was drama, emotion and excitement, the Six-Day War intensified security concerns for decision makers *vis à vis* relations with the Arab world, the protection of Israel, and both the dangers of confronting the Soviet Union and the necessity to block Soviet expansion. When combined with later events, these lessons were sufficiently powerful that policy makers had difficulty adjusting when the Arab–Israeli dispute became less central to ongoing Mid-East developments.

CHANGES IN THE AMERICAN DOMESTIC ARENA PRECIPITATED BY THE SIX-DAY WAR

The domestic American reaction to the Six-Day War was much deeper than temporary exhilaration. The press and media expanded their coverage of the area – establishing bureaux and stationing correspondents in places where they had not previously been located on a permanent basis. Until 1967, Israel had been pictured in America largely in mythical terms – as suggested by the novel and movie *Exodus* and the oft-repeated description that the Israeli pioneers had turned swamps into orchards. Progressively, with the news media exercising a microscopic examination of the Jewish state, a different picture emerged of a country like any other suffering internal tensions, contradictions, even corruption. The harsh realism conveyed by the intensified news coverage was to have a corrosive impact on Israel's image in America, especially during the 1970s.

Coterminous with a more balanced view of Israel, the Six-Day

War unleashed the Palestinian question on the American scene. Despite a series of airline hijackings and terrorist incidents in the years following 1967, the Palestinian cause, the Palestine Liberation Organization and its leader, Yasser Arafat, gained a degree of respectability, especially in liberal intellectual circles. The discovery of the Palestinians was closely tied to Vietnam. A segment of the war's critics argued that Israel, by relying on the military instrument, was demonstrating its identification with American imperialism. The Palestinians, according to this position, were victims suffering oppression analogous to the harm being inflicted on the Vietnamese people by the United States.

Regardless of the accuracy of these attitudes, they had a powerful impact on one segment of American intellectual and political thought. The Palestinian refugees had been a problem for Israel and her supporters since the 1948 war. Now, however, a vibrant moral argument developed to counter the moral claims of Israel respresented by the Holocaust and the Jewish state's democratic tradition. It was an argument which would come closest to official policy at the outset of the Carter era, by which time the Palestinians had come to symbolize for many American liberals identification with Third World aspirations and concerns.

Support for the Palestinian cause as a moral issue required ignoring or explaining away the PLO's resort to terrorism. This was accomplished by arguing that Israeli actions were either worse, or had driven the Palestinians to desperation, or that the Palestinians were comparable to revolutionaries the world over. It was also achieved by the argument that Israel had been transformed from a David to a Goliath, using military means to subjugate the Palestinians.

The Palestinian cause never gained a following in America comparable to that in Europe. Yet the Middle East question was important in weakening the left because it split opponents of the war between backers of Israel and sympathizers with the PLO. Until 1967, Israel had been a unifying issue of the labour–liberal coalition which had been dominant in American politics since 1932. This coalition was itself disintegrating, divided between supporters and opponents of the Vietnam War. The process begun by the seminal events of 1967 meant that opponents of the war were themselves also divided over Israel, a factor which has quietly contributed to the weakness of the left in American politics ever since.

The crisis preceding the Six-Day War conveyed in the most dramatic and emotional of terms to American supporters of Israel that the survival of the Jewish state could be threatened militarily. As liberals gained a reputation for reluctance to use the military option, the argument developed that no liberal administration could be relied upon to protect Israel in a crisis like the Six-Day War in which Israel might not be so successful. The surprising support for Richard Nixon over George McGovern in some sections of the Jewish community in the 1972 presidential campaign was directly related to this fear. The faith of Nixon supporters was reinforced by the huge airlift of military supplies to Israel worth $2.2 billion during the Yom Kippur War. Although counter-arguments could be made, the Carter administration's diplomatic pressure on Israeli leaders also seemed to confirm a suspicion of liberals which had first emerged after the 1967 war.

It is thus not surprising that several dominant members of the neo-conservative movement in America are Jewish. Before 1967, Israel received major conservative support, but it was the liberals who took the lead on behalf of Jerusalem. Afterward, liberals, especially in Congress, maintained their backing, but it often appeared that Israel's most intense supporters were on the right – militant anti-communists epitomized by Ronald Reagan as well as religious fundamentalists. If some liberals were disillusioned by what they regarded as Israel's over-reliance on the military for its survival, many conservatives admired Israel's 'moxie' (as Richard Nixon liked to put it), opposition to the Soviet Union, and loyalty to America's anti-communist crusade. Once the Israelis became dependent on American weaponry after 1967, they also acquired the ability to assist the Pentagon and American corporations with the refinement of US equipment. Their reliability and consistency eventually became much admired in Washington. The origins of a new view of Israel's importance can be seen after the Six-Day War when the Israelis provided intelligence on Russian equipment being used against them, equipment which was also employed by the North Vietnamese against the United States.

The events of 1967 also had a dramatic impact on the way that many conservative Christians interpreted contemporary Middle East history. Many conservatives, especially evangelicals, began to view the continued existence of Israel as a necessary precondition for the Second Coming of Jesus Christ. Since 1967, the American evangelical movement has become a powerful force in support of Israel. From the Reverend Billy Graham's friendship with Richard Nixon to Jerry Falwell's significant role in the Reagan coalition, the evangelists have become a prime element in the pro-Israeli coalition. In such media as television's electronic church, the link between support for a theological millenial prophecy based on specific interpretations of the Bible and the support for Israeli policies of the moment is drawn.

One publication which had a particularly strong impact in mobilizing religious conservatives in America toward a favourable perspective toward Israel was a book by Hal Lindsey. In *The Late Great Planet Earth*, originally published shortly after the war of 1967, he used biblical passages to substantiate his claims that the Bible predicts such factors in current international affairs as the Russian and Arab (and even Black African) threats to Israel which will 'lead to the last and greatest war of all time', resulting in the Second Coming of Jesus.

An argument for support of Israel, which envisioned the ultimate destruction of Israel, thus paradoxically became a major factor after 1967 in popular lore about the Middle East. It is perhaps not surprising that an event such as the Six-Day War so filled with trauma and emotion should acquire theological interpretations, especially since Israel conquered East Jerusalem with its holy shrines.

Both before and after the Six-Day War, the Arabs and Israelis have been effective in gaining the support of conservatives as well as liberals. The impact of the war, however, was to alter the balance even as it increased popular and official attention. With respect to two very different groups – the international oil companies and the American Jewish community – the war had the effect of reinforcing old patterns. From the perspective of the international oil companies, the events of mid-1967 were not good news. Nasser had falsely accused the United States and Britain of colluding with Israel in its pre-emptive attack against Egypt. These accusations led several radical Arab states to break off diplomatic relations with the United States. That could have meant attacks against petroleum installations in the area. As a consequence, the companies stepped up their efforts to gain a more 'balanced' American policy toward the Middle East. A Senate committee later uncovered briefing papers used by ARAMCO officials in the late 1960s to greet such dignitaries as visiting businessmen, Congressmen, educators. The papers instructed their readers to call for a more even-handed policy by the United States, one less disposed toward Israel and more sympathetic to the Arab states.

The increased insecurity of the oil companies after the Six-Day War intensified their vulnerability to Arab pressure. This growing leverage led Saudi Arabia to encourage a campaign by company representatives to warn the Nixon administration that the key Arab oil producers, especially Saudi Arabia, might soon employ the oil weapon for political purposes. During the Yom Kippur War, the ARAMCO chairmen cautioned against sending military supplies to Israel during the war. In 1973, the oilmen performed as they were instructed.

No one, including the Israelis, had to instruct the American Jewish community how to operate in the wake of the Six-Day War. No American group was as deeply affected by the events of 1967. Of all major Jewish communities, the Americans were the last to embrace the Zionist objective. Only the death of 6 million European Jews placed American Jewry at the forefront of the international effort outside Palestine to create a Jewish state in at least part of the British mandate. From 1945 to 1949, in rallies, speeches, articles, and efforts to influence the American government, US Jews became progressively more active in the Zionist enterprise. Following Israel's war of independence, however, the effort became more quiescent, as many Jews turned to charitable contributions and social service organizations as means of expressing their support for Israel. Even the 1956 Suez War failed to change this pattern, because the survival of Israel was not at stake in that war and even many Jewish supporters of Israel had doubts about the wisdom of the Israeli–British–French campaign. Moreover, the 1950s was a period of emerging Jewish suburban life and rising socioeconomic status, encouraging a more reserved expression of political action.

The events of May 1967, however, served to re-awaken American Jewry's interest. Israel's apparent vulnerability and the unwillingness of friendly countries such as France and even the United States to come to her aid left an indelible mark. Afterwards, American Jewish life would never be the same. Travel to Israel increased dramatically, as did the Israel-orientation of Jewish religious, cultural, communal, and political activity. This focus was sharpened as a result of increased attention to Israel in the American mass media and the succession of crises that occurred in the Middle East after 1967. These developments created ample opportunities for individuals and organizations to become engaged in political efforts on behalf of Israel. The war thus initiated an era in which much of Jewish life in America was defined by problems confronting the Jewish State. This preoccupation with Israel emerged as an important factor in American politics and a powerful constraint to be confronted by any President who sought to deal directly with the Arab–Israeli dispute.

THE UNITED STATES AND THE SIX-DAY WAR IN PERSPECTIVE

With the hindsight of twenty years, then, the Six-Day War can be seen to have had these five effects on the United States and American policy in the Middle East.

1. It created an opportunity for the United States to reverse the adverse direction of its competition with the Soviet Union in the region. Until 1967, the Russians had been on the advance. Although it was not clear at the time, the Six-Day War created the conditions which led to the emergence of the United States as the pre-eminent superpower in the area.
2. American policy makers' concerns about the implications of the Six-Day War for the competition with the Soviet Union, relations with the Arabs, and the security of Israel led to accelerated American involvement in efforts to resolve the Arab–Israeli conflict. Though the Johnson administration increased America's involvement only gradually, the Nixon administration followed with a more active response to the events of 1967. In turn, the involvement in conflict resolution thrust the United States into the central position in Mid-East politics.
3. In relations with Israel, the Six-Day War created a new and symbiotic relationship. For the first time, Washington became primarily and directly responsible for Israel's security, leading eventually to the Jewish state's dependence on the United States for both economic and military assistance. The Six-Day War also precipitated a cultural interdependence that was subsequently to have a far-reaching impact on Israeli politics and society, as the Americanization of Israel began. The United States, as the powerful partner, could have used Israel's new need for support as leverage to press for diplomatic concessions. At times after 1967, American leaders were tempted to exert pressure and even to consider imposing the conditions of peace. Yet they invariably retreated because of the difficulties of forcing Israel to undertake policies it rejected, the constraints imposed by domestic favour-

itism toward Israel, the rejection by the Arabs of most American initiatives and the belief shared with Jerusalem that territory should be traded only for some form of peace.

4. The territories also created an Arab attraction to the United States. However many arms the Russians might ship to their Arab clients, only diplomacy seemed capable of dislodging Israel from the territories. The Arabs were largely unsuccessful in their military campaigns, but almost always unprepared to deal directly with Israel. This peculiar combination of requirements brought several key Arab states to rely on Washington, since Moscow had no influence in Jerusalem. Despite America's sponsorship of the Arabs' chief adversary, an enemy which occupied territory they viewed as their own, several Arab states were gradually brought to increased dependence on Washington as the only available avenue for influence on Israel. The results of the Six-Day War thus brought the Arabs – like their Israeli adversaries – to regard the United States with greater respect and awe.

5. Not only the American role in the Middle East, but domestic attitudes toward the Arab–Israeli dispute were eventually altered by the Six-Day War. For America's liberals, the Israeli victory exacerbated divisions between supporters and opponents of the Vietnam War, and even among opponents of American intervention in Southeast Asia. Henceforth, Israeli policy in the occupied territories and Palestinian claims for independent statehood (non-existent when the Jordanians controlled the West Bank and the Egyptians ruled the Gaza Strip before 1967) became a source of concern and controversy on the left of the American political spectrum. Israeli dependence on military instruments and apparent Palestinian deprivation became powerful forces for sympathy with the new Mid-East underdog, which Israel's liberal supporters were constantly forced to confront. On the other hand, both political and religious conservatives were fascinated with the determination of history in favour of the Israelis. As a beacon of eschatalogical hope or a strategic asset to America's security concerns, the Six-Day War began a conservative flirtation with Israel. Meanwhile, oil companies active in the area revived efforts to gain a more even-handed American policy in the wake of Washington's increased identification with the Jerusalem government, while the American Jewish community emerged from the crisis committed more than ever to engagement with Israel.

Any analysis concentrating on the impact of a particular event necessarily risks over-emphasizing the importance of that development. In retrospect, patterns of history emerge. Yet the lessons and decisions we have discussed here were not inevitable. The Six-Day War was a significant event which led to changes in American policy and a greater involvement by Washington in the area. As always, these policies were conceived and implemented by individuals at the pinnacle of power. If different Presidents had been elected, or if they had chosen different advisors, the policies the United States pursued might well have diverged dramatically. In this respect, the Johnson and Nixon administrations were particularly important in determining the lessons which would be drawn from the Six-Day War. While strongly backing Israel's right to Arab concessions, their decisions to pursue the peace process provided a foundation on which subsequent administrations would build in the wake of later crises and challenges.

The peculiarity of the Six-Day War was its sudden arrival, swiftly altering maps, assumptions, and the destiny of an entire region. The shock, emotion, and impact still linger, even after twenty years. Washington is still adjusting to the consequences of the events set in motion by three short weeks in 1967.

9 Soviet Policy and the Six-Day War
Alvin Z. Rubinstein

The Six-Day War was a watershed for the Soviet Union. It set in motion currents in Soviet policy that have continued to be strong and deep, down to the present day: the increased commitment of Soviet military aid on behalf of prime Arab clients; the fostering and exploitation of regional antagonisms in order to advance Soviet aims; the funnelling of massive quantities of advanced weaponry to the protagonists of the Arab–Israeli conflict in order to sustain regional polarization; the blatant use of anti-Israeli and anti-Zionist propaganda to undermine US influence in the area through a linking of Israeli 'aggression' to US 'imperialism'; a readiness to jeopardize improved relations with the United States in order to entrench forward positions in the Middle East; and a willingness to pay the price of stoking conflict and forestalling reconciliation. What was tentative, episodic and cautious in Khrushchev's policy in the Arab world became, after June 1967, forceful, continuous and characterized by a higher level of risk-taking.

THE CONTEMPLATED AND THE CONTINGENT IN 1967

That this all came to pass should not be taken as evidence of the Kremlin's cunning and foresight in 1967, though the temptation to do so is strong and has indeed been argued by some scholars. More sophisticated assessments, however, show the possible connections between the contemplated and the contingent.[1]

That Moscow bears major responsibility for precipitating the crisis of 1967 is generally accepted as a given in analyses of the factors that led to war. Moscow fed Nasser falsified information that was acted upon in unanticipated fashion. Granted that Moscow wanted Nasser to take some action that would ensure Syria's security and discourage Israel from following up its successful air skirmish with Syria on 7 April with a bolder strike, still it is difficult to ascribe an *a priori* Soviet design to the sequence of events that happened once Egypt moved into the Sinai. From mid-May on, there were too many possible choices open to Nasser, to the UN and to Israel; and there were too few opportunities for Moscow to control the actions of the key protagonists. For example, Moscow may or may not have known that Nasser would request UN Secretary General U Thant to remove UNEF from the Sinai, but it could not have known that U Thant would acquiesce immediately, without in any way trying to dissuade Nasser or mobilize support in the UN Security Council for a partial retention or a phased withdrawal. Moscow began to lose most of whatever control it once had over events from 23 May after Egyptian forces had reclaimed control of Sharm el-Sheikh from UNEF forces and Nasser announced the closure of the Gulf of Aqaba to Israeli shipping, a move that his confidant, the editor of *al-Ahram*, Mohamed Hasanein Heikal said, on 26 May, meant war.

Did Moscow fear war and counsel caution? We do not know. There is no Soviet account of Soviet decision-making and behaviour during the four to six weeks that preceded the June War[2]. But the Soviet government could not have anticipated that the Egyptian leadership would mis-deploy its forces in the Sinai so egregiously or be so negligent in protecting its air force as to provide the Israelis with the opportunity to achieve their stunning victory.

Moscow also had another reason, too seldom factored into evaluations of its manipulation of Nasser, for assuming that Egypt would avoid provoking an Israeli riposte: namely the maintenance in Yemen of approximately 100 000 Egyptian troops. In underwriting Nasser in the Yemen, the Kremlin sought to advance several objectives, among which the most important were to deepen Nasser's dependency in order to obtain naval facilities which the Soviet Mediterranean Fleet needed to enhance its ASW (anti-submarine warfare) capability against US Polaris submarines and offset the loss of naval facilities in Albania in 1961; to intensify pressure on the British in Aden, and to a certain extent on Saudi Arabia as well; and to establish close ties with a new 'progressive' force and prevent its being overthrown by 'reactionary' Western-supported leaders. Throughout, Moscow played up the threat from 'imperialism' and fostered Nasser's overseas venture, which was to become Egypt's Vietnam.

Soviet policy was thus determined by strategic and military considerations. While aid to Egypt did not bring the Soviet Union the coveted naval privileges until after the June War, it did induce Nasser to persist in a policy that narrowed his options and heightened his dependence on the USSR – and just possibly made him overconfident

and cocksure, convinced that Moscow would back him no matter
what happened. Herein lay the Kremlin's miscalculation for, after
the middle of May, the pace and character of developments were
shaped primarily by Egypt and Israel. Most likely, a surprised Moscow
found it needed to react to fast-moving events over which it had little
if any control.

THE AFTERMATH: THE BREAK WITH ISRAEL AND
NEW COMMITMENTS TO EGYPT AND SYRIA

The war came – and ended – with the suddenness of a summer storm.
The Soviet media's coverage of events in the days preceding the
outbreak of open hostilities reflected official unease over the deepening crisis, but matters had already passed the point of no return.
Shortly after the outbreak of fighting in the early hours of 5 June,
the Kremlin activated the 'hot line' to Washington for the first time.
It called on the United States to force Israel to stop its attack on
Egypt, Syria and Jordan. Later in the day, in an official statement,
Moscow denounced Israeli 'aggression', which it alleged was encouraged by the 'covert and overt actions of certain imperialist circles'. It
affirmed the 'resolute support' of the USSR for Arab governments
and peoples, demanded that Israel 'stop immediately and uncondition-
ally its military actions . . . and pull back its troops beyond the truce
line', and concluded on an ominous note: 'The Soviet Government
reserves the right to take all steps that may be necessitated by the
situation'.[3] By 7 June the magnitude of the Arab defeat was clear.
There was nothing the Soviet Union could do through diplomacy in
the United Nations or militarily on the battlefield to prevent a
catastrophic defeat.

On 10 June Moscow made the first of its two fateful decisions
which were profoundly to affect the future of the Arab–Israeli
conflict, Soviet–American relations, and Soviet–Israeli relations. At
a meeting of representatives of East European states which had
opened in Moscow the previous day to condemn Israel, and which
pledged to 'do everything necessary' to help the Arab countries, the
Soviet Government announced that it was breaking diplomatic
relations with Israel. The USSR's second critical decision was to
rearm and protect Egypt and Syria from further attack. Both moves
had the immediate effect of stiffening Arab resolve not to settle with
Israel and had profound long-term consequences.

If Moscow had not broken off diplomatic relations with Israel but had contented itself with rearming the Arabs, championing their cause and extracting its political and military advantages, the conflict might have taken a different, less destructive, turn. In addition, had Moscow not (unexpectedly) emerged in the summer of 1967 as an uncritical, generous patron-protector of the Arab States, seemingly willing to back their intransigent position against dealing with Israel, the Arab leaders might conceivably have been more receptive to a formula for returning territory in exchange for recognition. With Soviet support, the Arab heads of state were free to adopt their policy of 'no recognition, no negotiation, no peace' towards Israel at Khartoum at the end of August 1967. Furthermore, without the Soviet blank cheque, the War of Attrition and the October War might never have been fought or have been thought necessary in order to set in motion a peace process which led eventually to a partial settlement. And in the absence of these wars the incipient US–Soviet detente of the 1970s might not have been scuttled, nor the entrenched Soviet position in Egypt been terminated.

The reasons for these two Soviet decisions must remain a matter of speculation. However, it may be useful to consider a cluster of plausible explanations, both for the light they may shed on Soviet policy after the Six-Day War and for an appreciation of the continuing constraints that may affect Soviet policy towards its prime Arab clients and towards Israel in the future.

Moscow was apparently aiming:

1. to offset its sense of impotence and the widespread anti-Soviet sentiment that surfaced briefly in the Arab world in the wake of the June War;
2. to demonstrate solidarity with the Arab cause as forcefully as circumstances permitted;
3. to harden Arab resolve not to make concessions that would thereby put Israel (and the United States) in a better position than before the war;
4. to acquire bargaining chips and a role in the negotiations that would inevitably follow.
5. to manifest the USSR's open alignment with the Arabs in contrast with the USA's upholding of Israel's insistence on direct negotiations with the Arab governments and a formal end to hostilities; and
6. to exploit the wave of anti-Americanism that expressed itself

diplomatically in the severing by most Arab states of relations with the United States.

Soviet Premier Aleksei Kosygin's address to the fifth emergency special session of the UN General Assembly on 19 June 1967 did not specifically explain why Moscow had broken off relations with Israel but it did set forth a position that lends credence to the significance of the considerations noted above.[4] Kosygin attempted to do three things: fix the blame on Israel, vindicate Soviet behaviour and align the USSR with the Arab position. First, he accused Israel of unleashing the 'aggression', demanded its withdrawal from all occupied territory and insisted on restitution for the damage inflicted on the Arab countries. In his condemnation, Kosygin likened Israel's actions to those of the *Gauleiters* of Hitler's Germany, a characterization which initiated a virulent, blatantly anti-Semitic propaganda campaign reminiscent of the latter years of the Stalin era.

Second, to dispel the shadow from Soviet policy and ingratiate Moscow with key Arab leaders, Kosygin implicitly apportioned some of the blame for what had happened to the Egyptian government, suggesting that it was not only the Soviet government but others too, who 'began receiving information to the effect that the Israeli government had chosen the end of May for a swift strike at Syria in order to crush it and then carry the fighting over into the territory of the United Arab Republic'. Finally, Kosygin maintained that the diplomatic support of the Soviet Union and other anti-imperialist forces in the world had kept Israel from toppling the progressive regimes in Syria and Egypt, and that the USSR would now do everything in its power 'to achieve the elimination of aggression, and promote the establishment of a lasting peace in the region'.

Moscow's break with Israel was an act of political animosity unprecedented in Soviet diplomacy. The Soviet Union's vital interests were not involved, no Soviet personnel or property were affected, no challenge to Soviet prestige or status was at issue. Never before had the Soviet government broken off diplomatic relations with a government over an issue in which no Soviet interests were directly threatened. For an adequate explanation, one must look beyond political, military, economic or ideological interests and consider the possibility of what Joseph Govrin called 'the antisemitic sediment deposited by history, which certainly became weightier with Israel's victory in the campaign against Egypt and Syria'.[5]

The second key Soviet decision, to rearm Egypt and Syria, was even more momentous in its eventual consequences. This came as a surprise to decision-making circles in Washington which, initially elated by the blow to Soviet prestige, had jumped to the conclusion that the USSR's position in the Arab world had been completely undermined and that Moscow would not be able to recover from the humiliation it had helped bring upon the Arabs. This elation was short-lived, as the Soviet re-supply effort began almost immediately after the fighting stopped. By the end of June, Moscow had replaced 200 MiG-19s, 50 to 150 Sukhoi-7s and 20 Ilyushin-28s. By late autumn, 80 per cent of the aircraft, tanks and artillery that Egypt had lost in June were replaced.[6] On 23 July 1968, Nasser acknowledged Egypt's political debt to the USSR: 'Had it not been for the Soviet Union and its agreement to supply us with arms, we should now be in a position similar to our position a year ago. We should have no weapons and should be compelled to accept Israel's conditions under its threat.[7]

The military relationship between the Soviet Union and the two main Arab confrontation states – Egypt and Syria – intensified dramatically after the June War. Egypt was the prime beneficiary because of the threat of Israeli forces along the Suez Canal within striking distance of Cairo, Nasser's central political role in the Arab world and the significant naval and air reconnaissance privileges which Nasser provided the Soviet military. From approximately 500 Soviet military advisers before the war, the number leapt to several thousand; from a purely advisory role relating primarily to the technical operation of weapons, Soviet advisers moved into all phases of training, planning and air defence; and from advising mostly at the divisional level, Soviet personnel were assigned to all levels of the Egyptian armed forces. The magnitude of the USSR's military commitment surpassed in both quantity and quality the aid provided North Vietnam or any other Third World country up to that time. The military aid programmes demonstrated Moscow's determination to strengthen the regime in Cairo (a comparable effort went into the strengthening of Damascus) and to forge close political links.

THE USSR AND THE SEARCH FOR A PEACE SETTLEMENT

Having opted for a policy that led it on to a new path in the Arab world, the Soviet leadership did nothing to facilitate any breakthrough towards an overall settlement. In the summer of 1967, Soviet and American diplomats at the United Nations failed to agree on a formula that would be acceptable to the Arab states and Israel. The crux of the problem was to link an Israeli withdrawal from all occupied territories with immediate Arab recognition of Israel's right to exist and to live in peace in the region. The talks conducted by Soviet Ambassador Anatoly Dobrynin and US Ambassador Arthur Goldberg were low-level negotiations unlikely to commit either the USSR or the United States to what might have been accepted by the Middle East actors. The Soviet emphasis, in line with Nasser's preference, was on political struggle. Subsequent Soviet affirmations of its support for a political settlement offered nothing new to help break the deadlock.

The periodic reports that Moscow was urging the Egyptians and Syrians to reach a settlement at the time lack substance or credibility. Certainly nothing ever appeared in Soviet speeches or commentaries intimating that the stalemate stemmed from the Arabs' refusal to accept the existence of the State of Israel. Nor did they ever discuss the Dobrynin–Goldberg talks. In private, Moscow continued to exchange views with Washington, despite continual sniping from the Arab sidelines. On occasion, however, worried about its image in the Arab world and sensitive to Chinese charges of pusillanimity, Moscow had to deny publicly rumours of an impending Soviet–American deal and denounce allusions to 'some kind of mythical "coincidence of interests" between the Soviet Union and the United States' in the Arab world.[8] It is true that the Soviets upheld Israel's right to exist and encouraged Egypt (Syria remained adamantly opposed to any kind of diplomatic bargaining) to agree to the carefully-drafted provisions of UN Security Council Resolution 242 as the basis for a settlement. However, once the resolution had been adopted, they quickly acceded to Egypt's insistence that the provision affirming that the establishment of a just and lasting peace in the Middle East include 'withdrawal of Israeli armed forces from territories occupied in the recent conflict', and should be interpreted to mean a full Israeli withdrawal from *all* territories occupied in June 1967. Subsequent Soviet proposals for a Middle East settlement invariably reflected the Arab interpretation of the UN resolution. (Since Egypt and Israel signed the Camp David Accords in September 1978 and the Peace Treaty on 26 March 1979, the Soviet Union's position on a Middle East settlement has followed the conditions of the Arab confrontation states, specifically as set down in the 'Arab consensus position' in the Fez Plan of September 1982, and as proposed in the UN General Assembly in the period after the 1973 October War. The main difference, of course, between these proposals and UN Security Council Resolution 242 is the absence in the latter of any specific reference to the Palestinians or to the right of the Palestinian people to self-determination and statehood.)

SOVIET ANTI-ZIONISM AND ANTI-SEMITISM

In the two decades since the June War, the Soviet government has carried on against Israel a propaganda campaign unparalleled in its viciousness since the end of the Second World War. The level and nature of the abuse are such that they cannot be passed over without comment. The calumnies of Israel are staples of the Soviet media. Though the Kremlin's political–military aims in the Arab world help account for many of the attacks on Israel and Zionism, there is also an internal dimension that is important to the Soviet leadership.

When the Six-Day War began, the Soviet government immediately put the blame for its outbreak on Israel, but in relatively temperate language an official statement issued on 6 June condemned Israel's 'adventurism' and 'aggression against the neighbouring Arab states' and its violation of the UN Charter and fundamental norms of international law.[9] A few days later, *Pravda* added a new theme to Soviet criticisms: that Israel's attack had been premeditated and in preparation for a long time at the instigation of 'imperialist circles' – that is, the United States, Britain and West Germany. On 13 June, V Petrov, a pseudonym for a high-ranking official, wrote in *Izvestiia*:

> Israel's aggression was not simply Tel-Aviv's aggression. It was the result of criminal collusion between the imperialists of the USA and Britain on the one hand and Israel on the other. The aggression was prepared, planned and calculated overseas long in advance by those who nurtured, armed and reared all these Moshe Dayans and their troops. Israel is only the point of the spear imperialism hurled into the heart of the liberated Arab world.[10]

Furthermore, by portraying 'militant Zionism' as a tool of 'imperialism' (the United States), Moscow hopes to broaden the base of its anti-imperialist line in the Middle East in particular and the Third World in general.

Recourse to anti-Semitism was not long in coming. Smearing Israel and Zionism with the taint of Hitlerite and Nazi-type behaviour was calculated to be particularly offensive. Moscow knew this would prove to be immediately useful in establishing Soviet *bona fides* with Arab radicals and extremists and in fostering Israel's international isolation. A lengthy article in *Izvestiia* on 2 July, entitled 'The Real Face of Israel's Ruling Clique', openly linked Israel and Zionism to Nazism and Hitler's Germany. A little more than a year later Yuri Ivanov, a propagandist with the CPSU's Central Committee, wrote 'Caution: Zionism!' (Moscow, 1970), a virulently anti-Israel, anti-Zionist and anti-Semitic tract which was published by Moscow in a dozen languages.

It remained only for General Secretary Leonid I. Brezhnev to provide the party's official sanction for the propagation of the view of Israel as a state of the Nazi type. This he did in a major speech at a Kremlin reception for graduates of the military academies on 6 July 1967, saying that 'in their atrocities upon the peaceful Arab population they [the Israelis] apparently are trying to copy the crimes of the Hitlerite aggressors'.[11] Henceforth, especially in the regional press and in newspapers intended for wide audiences, articles appeared regularly which stressed Zionism's reactionary character, chauvinism and anti-Communist essence. On 4 October, *Komsomolskaya pravda* wrote:

> The practical application of Zionism to the affairs of the Near East involves genocide, racism, treachery, aggression and annexation – all the characteristic attributes of fascism.[12]

The Soviets deny that their anti-Zionism is also anti-Semitism and insist that though they may suppress the Zionist movement they have also outlawed and fought against anti-Semitism; however, in recent years condemnations of anti-Semitism have almost invariably been combined with condemnations of Zionism, and though legally speaking it is true that anti-Semitism is forbidden, their propaganda – what is written and broadcast in the USSR on Israel and Zionism – tells a very different story.[13] The cartoons appearing in Soviet newspapers do not differentiate between Zionists, Israelis and Jews, and some would have done Hitler proud.[14]

The years following the Six-Day War witnessed an intensification of Soviet attacks on Israel, Zionism and Judaism. Much of this was targeted at audiences abroad in order to demonstrate Moscow's zeal and credentials in opposing Israel's aggression and occupation of Arab lands. Partly, however, this campaign was directed also at

Soviet Jewry. The Soviet leadership was disturbed by the surge of pro-Israel sentiment that swept this community, the readiness of many to emigrate and the open challenge to authority shown by those who were refused permission to do so. Discomfited by the unfavourable foreign publicity of the special circumstances under which Soviet Jews lived, Moscow reacted defensively, sometimes harshly, to the manifestations of Jewishness and support for Israel.[15] The campaigns fluctuated in intensity and virulence, but not until the advent of the Gorbachev period was there a significant diminution in the volume of anti-Zionist and anti-Semitic propaganda, possibly a part of Gorbachev's campaign to improve the Soviet Union's image in the West. Gorbachev's interest in improved relations with Israel (and the West) is also evident in the increase in Jewish emigration: thus, whereas in 1986 only 914 Soviet Jews were permitted to emigrate, in the first six months of 1987, on average, about 700 a month have left.

SOVIET MIDDLE EAST POLICY SINCE 1967: CONSISTENCY AND DISAPPOINTMENTS

Once the basic decisions that transformed the character of its involvement on behalf of Egypt and Syria were taken, Moscow became a partisan advocate-protector of the Arab side in the Arab–Israeli conflict. In the two decades since the Six-Day War, it has not deviated from this line. That there were disappointments was not the result of any inconsistency on its part. Before assessing the long-term effects of the war on the USSR's policy and position in the Arab world, some brief remarks are in order concerning Soviet achievements and setbacks, and the key developments of Soviet policy during the post-1967 period.

Moscow's pay-off for engaging itself intimately and extensively in the re-equipping, training and overall protection of Egypt and Syria was quick in coming. Egypt's defeat, in particular, paved the way for a massive Soviet military presence and brought the Soviet military the privileges it had sought since 1961 – naval facilities at Alexandria and Sollum and airfields for the use of Soviet aircraft, which could carry out ASW operations and reconnoitre the movements of the US Sixth Fleet. But, as has been aptly said, in the Middle East nothing fails like success.

After unstintingly committing themselves to Nasser's defence in

1970, when his War of Attrition against Israel along the Suez Canal backfired, and sharply raising their ante to the extent of deploying 20 000 combat troops to man missile sites and the air defence of Egypt's heartland, Soviet leaders found their position unexpectedly vulnerable after he died on 28 September 1970. A power struggle that consolidated Anwar Sadat's position and resulted in the virtual elimination of Nasser's entire entourage prompted them to formalize the Soviet–Egyptian relationship. The resulting Treaty of Friendship and Co-operation, signed on 27 May 1971, explicitly committed the Soviet Union to the defence of Egypt (something it had hitherto not done for any non-Communist Third World country), suggesting that Moscow believed it would thereby obtain an important return in influence over Egyptian policy. But Sadat had his own priorities. In July 1972, he terminated the mission of Soviet military personnel and sharply curtailed the once extensive Soviet presence. Only the naval privileges were allowed to remain more or less as before.

A limited reconciliation preserved the Soviet–Egyptian relationship intact until the October War. Again, as in 1970, Moscow very much played the role of the generous and protective patron, shielding Egypt and Syria from defeat and enabling both countries to emerge from the war with significant political gains. It stymied US attempts to arrange for ceasefire resolutions at the United Nations until the tide turned against the Arabs militarily; used the Soviet navy provocatively for the first time in a Middle East crisis; and signalled a readiness, if need be, to risk confrontation with the United States in order to keep Israeli forces from destroying the Egyptian Third Army on the eastern side of the Suez Canal and from advancing on Cairo.

However, hardly had the ceasefire taken hold than Sadat proceeded to reverse Egypt's policy and alignment. He courted Washington and alienated Moscow, notwithstanding Egypt's complete dependence on Soviet arms and reliance on Soviet economic assistance. In March 1976 he abruptly abrogated the 1971 treaty and cancelled Soviet naval privileges. In less than five years the formerly impressive Soviet military position in Egypt had turned to sand. Sadat's historic visit to Jerusalem on 19 November 1977 led to the Camp David Accords and culminated in the Egyptian–Israeli Peace Treaty of 26 March 1979.

In the years ahead, Moscow is unlikely to re-establish a major presence in Egypt, or regain the military privileges that it had between 1967 and 1976. This assessment assumes that Egyptian President

Husni Mubarak will concentrate on the institutionalization of his power and on Egypt's serious internal problems and eschew the temptation to become a dominant force in the Arab world; that, having regained all its territory from Israel (the Taba issue remains a minor irritant), Egypt will not resort to war to advance Palestinian claims or its own ambitions in the Arab world; that the United States is prepared to shoulder a hefty part of Egypt's and Israel's military and economic burden for the foreseeable future; and that, as long as US–Egyptian relations are good, the Soviet–Egyptian relationship will be a limited one.

Unlike Nasser (and Sadat from 1970 to 1973), Mubarak has no real need for Soviet military assistance and political guarantees. He seeks basically to preserve, not overturn, the territorial and political status quo in the region (excepting perhaps for the knotty, vexing Palestinian question) and views the Soviet Union warily. But wariness does not preclude normalization. Since September 1984, when Egypt normalized diplomatic relations with the Soviet Union, economic ties have modestly expanded. This demonstration of Mubarak's independence from the United States helps mollify some of his leading critics and strengthen his situation internally. It may even give him additional leverage in bargaining with Washington over aid packages. But improved Soviet–Egyptian relations do not threaten the evolving US–Egyptian (or Egyptian–Israeli) relationship, if only because the Soviet Union would be hard pressed to provide the billion dollars a year in economic assistance which has come from the United States since 1975, and which is likely to continue.

Mubarak's opposition to Soviet policy in the Middle East and Africa is as strong as Sadat's, and stems from a perception of Moscow's aims as inherently antithetical to Egypt's security.

PRINCIPLES OF SOVIET MIDDLE EAST POLICY

Moscow was undoubtedly disappointed by its inability to retain a firm Egyptian connection, but in the course of the twenty years since the Six-Day War it has fashioned a policy that is credible, far-ranging and strategically coherent, has enjoyed solid support among the key oligarchs in the party, military and government, and which is an extension of Khrushchev's 'forward policy' in the Third World, embarked upon in the mid-1950s. A number of generalizations can be made about the effect of the Six-Day War on this policy.

New Projection of Soviet Military Power

First, the Soviet Union took the giant leap from involvement to intervention. Having succeeded in establishing political and economic relations with key Middle Eastern (and other Third World) countries, it exploited the vulnerability of prime targets to acquire military advantages and a strong foothold in strategically important areas. Whereas Khrushchev had used economic as well as military assistance in his courtship of countries such as India, Afghanistan, Egypt, Ghana and Indonesia, Brezhnev and his successors relied primarily on the latter. It was what the clients wanted and needed and, by 1967, Moscow was able to provide both arms and protection from defeat at the hands of a Western-orientated or pro-US regional actor.

The USSR's ability to project its power came of age in the years after the Six-Day War. In the period immediately after June 1967, this was limited to passive defence (such as the ships anchored in Port Said and Alexandria to forestall Israeli bombardment or air raids, and the training of Egyptian air defence crews), but later on, during the period in which Nasser's army was being reconstituted, it served as an active deterrent. During the worst days of the War of Attrition (January–July 1970), Soviet pilots and air defence crews assumed responsibility for protecting Egypt's heartland from Israeli air power, and Nasser from another defeat. In the October War, Soviet power manoeuvred protectively to ensure against an Israeli victory and to check US moves on behalf of Israel. More recently, in Lebanon, in the period of Syrian vulnerability after the Israeli invasion of June 1982, Soviet power was deployed openly as a warning to Israel and a signal to the United States, and protectively to safeguard the Asad regime.

Having made its initial appearance as a new facet of Soviet foreign policy in the Arab–Israeli conflict, this readiness to intervene forcefully on behalf of beleaguered clients was manifested again in the 1970s in Angola, Ethiopia and Afghanistan. It stems from an impressive and continually-expanding conventional capability, and it reflects a determination to play a major role in every region of the Third World.

New Level of Risk-taking

Second, the Six-Day War and the central Soviet role in the escalating events that led to its outbreak demonstrated the lengths to which

Moscow would go in inciting a client, in the hope of being able to exploit regional rivalries and exacerbate regional tensions. In goading Egypt into taking action on behalf of Syria, matters possibly went further than it had calculated: Moscow may not have wanted war, but it assuredly did not seek peace or amelioration of tensions. It intrigued in a volatile environment for some unspecified morsel of advantage, for reasons that had nothing to do with its clients – Syria's – security, in the process discovering the limits of its ability to control those it was seeking to influence.

The circumstances of May–June 1967 were unusual, but even previously Moscow had relied for its gains in the Middle East (and the Third World in general) on its ability to exploit regional tensions. Trotsky's unsuccessful formula for coping with the German advance on Petrograd in 1918 – no war, no peace – typifies Soviet behaviour in the Third World since the mid-1950s. Khrushchev found that the existing disputes in the Middle East (Egyptian–British, Egyptian–Iraqi, Egyptian–Israeli, Syrian–Israeli, Syrian–Iraqi, and so on) and in South Asia (Afghanistani–Pakistani, Pakistani–Indian) provided the opportunity to establish close relationships with those actors which were at odds with their Western-backed rivals. Brezhnev, guided by the same principle, went further. He demonstrated Moscow's fealty as a patron prepared to intervene to prevent defeat at the hands of a US-backed regional rival. It is this restless probing for advantage in high-tension environments, rather than an underlying political or ideological affinity or shared sentiment, which best explains Soviet policy in the Arab world and on the Arab–Israeli conflict.

Primacy of the Perceived American Threat

Third, the opportunism that guided the Soviet approach to the Arab–Israeli dispute was impelled by a desire to undermine US power and prestige. In the twenty years since the June War, Soviet policy has continued to work not merely for strategic denial but strategic debasement: the erosion of US positions regionally and globally, and the dissipation of its resources in areas of marginal utility to the Soviet Union. Indeed, except with regard to Turkey, Iran and Afghanistan – cases which bring into focus traditional anxiety about the security of Russian frontiers – the USSR's policy in the Third World can be seen as heavily, if not primarily, a function of the ongoing rivalry with the United States.

Time and again in situations of promise or peril, when a fundamental choice has been required, Moscow has opted for commitment to a regional client rather than co-operation with the United States. The effect of its policy has been to stoke regional tensions and aggravate relations with the United States. What is so striking about this approach, apart from the consistency with which it has been followed, is Moscow's readiness to jeopardize prospects for obtaining much-needed Western technology, credits and trade that would undoubtedly flow from lessened US–Soviet tensions in the Third World; also remarkable is the seeming disparity between what the Soviet Union obtains from the Arab world and what it stands to gain from improved ties with the United States. The fact is that the USSR has no economic stakes in the Arab world that are essential for Soviet economic development or security; it has no ethnic, religious, cultural or political ties with any nation-state or key group in the Arab world (most Soviet Muslims being of Turkish extraction). The hard currency that the USSR earns from arms sales is more than offset by its stunted trade with the West and added defence costs.

The explanation for this behaviour is to be found in the Kremlin's view of the threat to its domination from the United States. One way of diverting American attention and resources away from Europe and the Far East – the prime theatres of Soviet interest – is through cost-effective probes in the Third World, and perhaps nowhere has the Soviet Union found a regional environment more conducive to this kind of low cost, sub-strategic involvement than in the Arab world.

Entrenching Stalemate

Fourth, since the Six-Day War – during the War of Attrition, the October War and late 1982 when Syria was vulnerable to Israeli air power – Moscow has amply demonstrated that it is capable of preventing the defeat of an Arab client in a regional conflict. It proved an effective patron-protector, fully supportive of prime clients against external attack, internal opposition and pressure from an American-supported regional rival. In the process, Moscow has earned a reputation for reliability. Once involved, it has stayed the course, irrespective of the military, economic and diplomatic costs or the adverse effects on relations with the United States. Soviet credibility came of age, comparing favourably with US behaviour in the area.

Successful in preventing defeat and enabling ambitious, anti-American Arab leaderships to maintain a military option against Israel, Moscow was nonetheless unable to deliver clear political triumphs for its clients. Sadat's reconciliation with Israel came as a shock, which helps explain Moscow's extravagant support for Syria and its nervousness at any hint of change in the position of Hafez al-Asad or Yasser Arafat that might again make the United States the hub of all diplomatic activity in the Middle East peace process and relegate the Soviet Union to the sidelines.

Moscow benefits from a condition of stalemate. The essence of its policy in the Middle East is predicated on the assumptions that conflict is endemic, that irreconcilability can be sedulously encouraged by providing one side or the other with sufficient weaponry to make a military option seem feasible, and that the USSR's interests are served by such polarization and militarization of regional politics, whereas those of the United States are not. From its experience over the past two decades, Moscow has learned to limit its expectations and settle for success in sustaining whichever rivalries it can.

Learning the Limitations of Influence

Fifth, relations between a patron and a client have turned out to be far more complex and unpredictable than Moscow had originally assumed. Of particular importance in defining the contours of such a relationship is the pattern of preferences and initiatives undertaken by the regional actor, often against the wishes of the superpower benefactor. The Soviet–Egyptian experience is illustrative. From the very beginning, the key to the relationship was the recognition by both parties of its asymmetrical character, both as to aims and advantages: what mattered most to Moscow was of little importance to Cairo, and vice-versa. Stripped of illusions and devoid of trust, the Soviet–Egyptian relationship fed on tactical necessities. Moscow's leverage on issues of importance to Egyptian leaders was at best marginal once Cairo resolved upon a course of action. Gratitude for Soviet support did not carry with it any willingness to tolerate Soviet interference in Egyptian decision-making on key issues.

For example, there is no evidence that the large quantity and high quality of its aid to Egypt enabled Moscow to mobilize or strengthen the position of those Egyptian officials or bureaucratic elites that may have been disposed to be guided by Soviet wishes. The situation of Egyptian Communists did not improve much and Moscow did little on their behalf after it had obtained extensive military privileges. Nor were the Egyptian military or political elites ever reconstituted to the degree that Moscow had recommended shortly after the June War. Soviet propaganda and cultural activities operated under very close scrutiny, and it would seem from every indication that they had no impact on Egyptian life or the political attitudes of the elite. Indeed, even in the heyday of the Soviet presence, anti-Soviet currents prevailed throughout the leadership. Despite much fanfare in the press, neither Nasser nor Sadat really altered the composition of their ministries, or their practices and priorities, in line with Soviet suggestions.

Over the years, Cairo (and the same holds true for Damascus) sought from Moscow the military, economic and diplomatic support which would enable it to pursue its ambitions in the Arab world and provide it with leverage in the context of the Arab–Israeli conflict. For its part, Moscow sought to establish a major presence in Egypt, not principally with the expectation of placing it upon a 'socialist' or incipiently communist path, but in order to acquire strategic advantages of importance to its geopolitical rivalry with the United States. Thus, it was willing to accelerate the Middle East arms race and raise the level of tension, albeit within bounds that it hoped to be able to control. The deterioration in the Soviet–Egyptian relationship resulted from a change in Sadat's policy aims and not as a consequence of any wavering in the USSR's commitments or credibility. In the absence of direct Soviet military domination of a client, as in the case of Afghanistan, it is the regional client that sets the tone and limits of what the USSR can hope to achieve in direct benefits from the courtship. In relations between a superpower and a Third World government, direct influence of a superpower is, as a result of the constraints of today's international system, usually contingent, issue-specific, variable, not amenable to institutionalization and temporary.

Difficulty of Repairing Ties with Israel

Sixth, Moscow's breaking off of relations with Israel did not bring the anticipated reward of a central role in Arab affairs. It neither polarized the Arab world permanently against Israel and the United States nor provided the Soviet Union with tangible benefits beyond those that would undoubtedly have been forthcoming as a consequence of its support for the Arabs. In addition, the break with Israel decreased Moscow's ability to influence Israeli policy, worsened relations with the United States and eventually highlighted the limits of Soviet influence in the Middle East. It appears to have been a political blunder for which the Soviets continue to pay a stiff price.

With each passing year, restoration of Soviet diplomatic relations with Israel becomes more necessary for Moscow and more difficult to accomplish psychologically. Contrary to Soviet expectations, Israel is not prepared to pay a high price for a restoration of ties. Domestic opinion in Israel has become more anti-Soviet. The reasons are several: disillusionment among the generally dovish elements; insistence by those who have emigrated from the Soviet Union since the early 1970s (among whom Natan Sharansky is a powerful voice) that a precondition for renewing relations must be improved treatment for Soviet Jews and permission to emigrate for those who so desire; and the absence of a dominant political party, which means that both Labour and the Likud are wary of uncritically and too hastily embracing Gorbachev's on-again off-again courtship.

Moscow has made conciliatory gestures, but has so far shied away from the big step. In August 1986, Israeli and Soviet diplomats met in Helsinki for official talks for the first time since 9 June 1967; at the UN General Assembly in late September 1986, Soviet Foreign Minister Eduard Shevardnadze discussed normalization of relations with (then) Israeli Prime Minister Shimon Peres; and Shevardnadze's major speech at the UN did not condemn Israel, as has been the Soviet practice at such gatherings. Also, over the past few years, Soviet officials have met with such Jewish leaders and public figures as Edgar Bronfman and Elie Wiesel. As yet, none of these exchanges has succeeded in persuading the Soviet leadership to rectify its misjudgement made in the aftermath of the Six-Day War. Still, the increase in official contacts between Soviet and Israeli officials at the UN and elsewhere, and the arrival in July 1987 of a Soviet consular delegation in Tel-Aviv, attest to the steady drift towards diplomatic normalization.

A Limited Role

Finally, twenty years after the war, Soviet proposals for a comprehensive Middle East settlement encounter a mixture of disdain and lack of interest, the feeling being one of seeing old wine in old bottles, perhaps newly washed at the most. So far, there has been nothing new in Soviet proposals. Nor is there any evidence to warrant the recurrent proposition that 'Without Soviet assent, there is little likelihood that any Arabs will be able or willing to negotiate directly with Israel in the foreseeable future',[16] given what we know of how Egypt came to sign a peace treaty with Israel.

So long as Moscow refuses to normalize diplomatic relations with Israel, what it has to say about a comprehensive settlement is of little importance. Its principal aims are to find a way around the diplomatic puddle it created and to demonstrate to friendly Arab regimes the role that it can play in bringing about a political settlement on terms they would like. It lacks credibility as a diplomatic broker and resents the widespread belief that the United States could, if it wished, duplicate the Camp David episode in advancing a settlement of the Palestinian issue. At some time in the future, Moscow may tire of its role and image in the Arab world of being a bearer of arms and a defender of beleaguered clients. For the moment, however, the strategic benefits in terms of its rivalry with the United States seem sufficient to sustain it along the general lines that have been so clear since the Six-Day War.

Notes

1. For a thoughtful account, see Joseph Govrin, 'The Six Day War in the Mirror of Soviet–Israeli Relations: April–June 1967' (Jerusalem: Hebrew University, Soviet and East European Research Centre) research paper 61 (December 1985).
2. No Soviet scholar has written a detailed account of the Six-Day War. For the most part, Soviet scholars treat the issue briefly, in the broader context of Middle East and Arab–Israeli relations. One of the better Soviet studies devotes only six pages to the June War and focuses on Washington's alleged culpability, with little attention to Cairo's behaviour, much less that of the Soviet government. See E. M. Primakov, *Anatomiya Blizhnevostochnogo konflikta* (Moscow, 1978) 250–6.
3. BBC Summary of World Broadcasts (hereafter SWB) SU/2484/A4/1, 7 June 1967.
4. The following is drawn from Alvin Z. Rubinstein, *Red Star on the Nile: The Soviet–Egyptian Influence Relationship Since the June War* (Princeton, N.J., 1977) 15–16.
5. Govrin, 'Six Day War' 27.
6. International Institute of Strategic Studies, *Strategic Survey 1967* (London, 1968) 37.
7. SWB ME/2830/A/9, 25 July 1968.
8. Gennady Vasilyev in *Pravda*, 8 September 1967.
9. *Pravda*, 6 June 1967.

10. Translated in *Current Digest of the Soviet Press* (hereafter CDSP) 19 (24) (5 July 1967) 7.
11. CDSP, 19 (27) (26 July 1967) 4.
12. CDSP, 19 (39) (18 October 1967) 14.
13. Lukasz Hirszowicz, 'Soviet Perceptions of Zionism', *Soviet Jewish Affairs*, 9 (1) (1979) 53–4.
14. Judith Vogt, 'Old images in Soviet anti-Zionist cartoons', *Soviet Jewish Affairs*, 5 (1) (1975) 20–38.
15. See Jonathan Frankel, 'The anti-Zionist press campaigns in the USSR 1969–1971: An internal dialogue?' *Soviet Jewish Affairs*, 2 (1) (1972) 10.
16. Rita E. Hauser in the *New York Times*, 9 September 1986.

10 Israel in the International Arena
Harold M. Waller

There can be little dispute that the Six-Day War was a watershed in the history of Israel. Its significance is apparent even from our present twenty-year vantage point. One can never be sure how history will ultimately judge an event, but it is likely that when the histories of our time are written definitively, the Six-Day War will be seen as a decisive turning point in Israel's development. During the forty years of statehood to date, there have been several key events, especially during the last twenty years – the Yom Kippur War, the 1977 election, President Sadat's visit to Jerusalem, and the Israeli–Egyptian peace treaty. Yet none of these other events had quite the same impact as the 1967 war.

The uniqueness of the Six-Day War in the history of Israel is found in two key aspects: the overpowering, courageous, and brilliant military victory, and the fact that after the war Israel was in control of a considerable amount of land that had been under Arab control prior to 5 June. Admittedly, the victories in 1948–9 also resulted in Israel assuming control over territories that some people regarded as properly Arab. But at that time the belief that statehood for the Jews was a necessary, if not a moral, requirement, meant that sympathy for the Jews and their struggle outweighed whatever sympathy might have existed for the Arab inhabitants of Mandatory Palestine. It should be noted parenthetically that those whose opinion counted during the early years of statehood were largely found in Western nations and certainly not in the Third World, a situation that was to change dramatically by 1967. In any event, the territory acquired by Israel in 1967 had a different status than the territory brought under Israeli control in 1948–9, both in the eyes of Israel and in the eyes of the rest of the world. After all, it was Israel that identified the West Bank and Gaza as 'occupied', with the government of the day being disposed to trade them for peace, if only the much-awaited telephone call had come.

Despite examples from our own times when territory acquired by force has been retained by the victor, international norms now are such that retention is not a readily available option, certainly not to a small country like Israel. Thus Israel was transformed overnight into a nation that was occupying territory that was not recognized by others as rightfully belonging to it. Israel assumed the risk of being perceived as part of the framework of colonialism, however unjustified the label. The point here is that the outcome of the war created circumstances that later evolved in ways that would not have been possible had the war not occurred. As a consequence, the disposition of the territories – especially the West Bank – and the treatment of the inhabitants became issues of central concern for Israel, which found itself in a position that was fundamentally different from that which had existed prior to 1967.

Until 1967, Israel's concern, in addition to maintaining its security in the face of the constant Arab threat, were matters such as immigration, the absorption of the immigrants, economic development, nation-building, and creating a just society. For the most part – with the noticeable exception of the immigration issues – these were matters that concerned most of the emerging nations of that era. There is no suggestion here that the problems of international relations were insignificant for Israel at the time, only that they were qualitatively of a lower order than the post-1967 problems.

After the Six-Day War, problems of international relations were elevated to a very high priority for the Israeli government. The issue of the control of the territories that Israel brought under its jurisdiction in 1967 became a central subject of international concern, partly because of its intrinsic importance and partly because the Arabs forced it to a paramount place in world consciousness. Israel was thrust to the centre of the United Nations agenda and to the top of the international media's priority list. Foreign offices were continually required to formulate policies regarding Israel and the territories. As a result, Israel even became a domestic issue in some countries. The effect of all this was to place Israel in a defensive position politically, and to force it to try to compensate with military power for its political weakness. The fact that Arab oil power reached its peak a few years after 1967 undoubtedly contributed to Israel's political weakness, but it only acted as an exacerbating factor in an already difficult situation.

In the aftermath of the Six-Day War, Israel was transformed from what appeared to be a frail and threatened new state into an established regional power that was accused of threatening its neighbours. Brilliant diplomatic manoeuvres and public relations

154 *Israel in the International Arena*

offensives by the Arabs and their friends helped to convert Israel from hero to pariah within a few short years, simultaneously bringing the Palestinian problem to the attention of the world in a manner that transferred the sympathy that had been Israel's over to the Palestinian Arab people and the Palestine Liberation Organization (PLO) in particular.[1]

TWENTY DIFFICULT YEARS

The past twenty years have been an unpleasant and difficult period for Israelis and friends of Israel abroad. Setbacks in the UN and its agencies have been a cause of great consternation and even anguish. Media coverage has often been frustrating. Yet one must ask whether it has all really mattered very much. There are two answers that might be suggested, depending on the level of analysis. At one level, it can be pointed out that during the past twenty years the crucial variables for Israel have been military strength and the association with the United States. The capacity of the Israel Defence Force (IDF) to deter possible attacks, repel attackers who do initiate battle and to reach out to retaliate against the perpetrators of terrorist attacks is well known, and has been vital to Israel's continued security. At the same time, the support of the United States in the international political arena has been essential in preventing total erosion of Israel's position. So at the level of the military–security situation, Israel has survived two dangerous decades bruised but basically intact.

Another way to look at the question of whether political setbacks have mattered is to raise the question of the long term, for which Israel's objective is to achieve normalization of its position in the Middle East. The achievement of that goal requires more than the security afforded by the IDF and the cooperation and support of the United States. It requires that Israel find its security not only in armed force, but also in peaceful cooperation with most (if not all) of the states of the world. For the kind of state that Israel wants to be, pariah status is not an acceptable solution. Of course, the question of Israel's ability to divest itself of pariah status is not entirely in Israel's hands. There are no actions that one can contemplate that would guarantee that Israel could achieve its cherished goals of normalization of relationships by acting unilaterally. But even allowing for that point, the role of international outcast – or, at the least, problem case – creates a heavy burden for Israel to carry, one which at some point could have adverse political and military consequences. In a sense, this summarizes the dilemma that the decline in international standing has created for Israel.

The balance of this chapter will be devoted to an examination of several indicators of the decline of Israel's international standing, an analysis of factors contributing to the decline, a comparison of Israel's position in 1967 and 1987, and an assessment of the significance of the changes. Finally, an attempt will be made to suggest what course Israel's standing among the nations will follow in the years to come.

DIPLOMATIC RELATIONS

In a situation such as Israel finds itself, where the state's legitimacy has been questioned from the beginning, the establishment and maintenance of diplomatic relations with various other states constitutes an important measure of international standing. The importance attached to the according of recognition by the United States and the Soviet Union in 1948 is indicative of this thinking. Admittedly Israel's independence – and thus its existence as a sovereign state – was achieved on the battlefields in 1948–9. But that existence and sovereignty were given operational meaning in the context of the international system by the recognition granted by a number of nation states. The United Nations Partition Resolution of 1947, of course, did legitimize the effort of the *yishuv* to declare independence, but it remained for the combination of military victories and diplomatic recognition to realize the promise held out by that Resolution.

In the years following 1948, a major objective of Israeli foreign policy was to expand the list of countries with which Israel had diplomatic relations in order to counter the effect of Arab challenges to the legitimacy of Israel's existence. Those efforts were largely successful, as Israel was able to establish diplomatic relations with most of the countries that mattered, including even some Muslim countries such as Iran and (at a lower level) Turkey. Israel had formal relations with the nations of Western Europe, the Soviet Bloc, and Latin America, as well as with the English-speaking countries of North America and Oceania. Moreover, during the period of decolonization, Israel was successful in establishing contacts with the newly-emerging states of Africa. Thus by 1967, Israel had diplomatic relations with most of the UN member states (with notable exceptions such as the Arab League and mainland China).[2] This situation was important for the morale of a beleaguered nation, but had political implications, too. Opponents of Israel were on weak ground when they challenged the *bona fides* of a UN member that was recognized by most other UN members. Furthermore, Israel could reasonably expect political support from the countries with which it had relations. Diplomatic relations surely do not suggest a blank cheque politically; but on the kinds of issues that Israel faced in the pre-1967 period, the existence of diplomatic relations provided a sort of cushion against political attacks. There was no assurance that friendly countries would come through when the chips were down; in fact, Israel had a major confrontation with the United States after the Suez War of 1956. More importantly, during the crisis period of May 1967, Israelis had the perception that they stood alone against the massed Arab armies. Admittedly the response of the international community to the closing of the Straits of Tiran and the threat of aggression by Egypt and Syria was not very impressive. But in the wake of Israel's sweeping victory there was substantial support for Israel's position in certain quarters, even as many Third World and Soviet Bloc countries were breaking diplomatic relations. The content of UN Security Council Resolution 242, adopted in the autumn of 1967, reflects the view among key UN members that the occupied territories were not the only important issue, that the question of Israel's legitimacy and right to exist in peace behind recognized and secure borders was equally important. In the context of that period Resolution 242 can be seen as a strong endorsement of Israel's position, despite the ambiguous phrase on withdrawal 'from occupied territories'.

The breaking of diplomatic relations by the Soviet Bloc countries (except Romania) and nearly all of the black African states in 1967 and 1973 represented a serious blow to Israeli foreign policy and international legitimacy. Despite all of Israel's development assistance to the African countries over the years, formal relations were negated in a flash, in response to strong Arab pressures and perceptions of Israeli expansionism at the expense of other so-called non-aligned countries.[3] The message of this action was loud and clear: in the eyes of these states Israel's legitimacy could no longer be assumed. Even though the breaks in relations constituted a response to the nature of Israel's victories in the 1967 and 1973 wars, it proved useful for the Arabs to interpret them as undermining Israel's legitimacy *per se*. The infamous 1976 UN resolution on Zionism as Racism furthered that objective, for if a country's central ideology were found to be racist, could that nation reasonably expect to be accepted among the community of nations in the future? And if such a nation were to be eliminated and replaced by a non-racist regime, would not that be an acceptable solution to the problem? In retrospect, the dissolution of diplomatic relations by so many states made the political offensive that much easier because those who had broken diplomatic relations were well disposed to follow through on the implications of their move.

The breaking of diplomatic relations (or the refusal to establish them) is not a very common course of action in today's world. When the United States withheld recognition from the Soviet Union after the 1917 revolution and from Communist China after the 1949 revolution, it was sending the strong message that it did not accept the legitimacy of those regimes. There have been other examples of using breaks in diplomatic relations to signify displeasure with particular actions of a nation state, but there has been nothing in the diplomatic history of the world since 1945 comparable in scope to the massive break of relations with Israel in 1967 and 1973, when several African states that had held out after 1967 joined the diplomatic boycott while Israel was holding Egyptian territory west of Suez – i.e., African territory.

Israel was thus singled out for unique treatment, especially by the Third World. The only comparable case might be South Africa, which is also the object of condemnation. The resulting isolation complicated the conduct of foreign policy by Israel, but not beyond manageable limits. The saving feature of the situation was Israel's ability to maintain other forms of relationships with many countries aside from formal diplomatic ones. In particular, Israel continued to trade with numerous countries that had cut off relations. But in addition ways were found to have political contacts with such countries, as well as with countries that had never had diplomatic relations with Israel. In many cases such contacts had to be carried out in clandestine fashion; for example, it is widely known that Israel has maintained a continuing relationship with at least two Arab countries, Jordan and Morocco. Direct talks between the monarchs of those countries and representatives of the government of Israel are widely believed to have taken place. Moreover, in recent years there have been well-publicized meetings between the Israeli and Soviet Foreign Ministers. Given that such activities are well known, it does not require much imagination to conclude that Israel is probably maintaining more discreet political contacts with other

countries with whom it does not have formal diplomatic ties. Therefore the absence of diplomatic relations has had a symbolic effect
above all else. One cannot dismiss the symbolic effect as irrelevant,
however; symbols are important in politics. Given that the major
arena for Arab struggle against Israel since the 1967 war has been
the political and not the military, any symbol of the delegitimation
of Israel can have adverse consequences. In summary, Israel's
international standing has undoubtedly declined, as indicated by the
reduction in the number of countries with whom Israel has diplomatic
relations, but the problem is less severe than it appears to be on the
surface because of the presumably wide network of official contacts
outside of the usual diplomatic networks.

ISRAEL IN INTERNATIONAL ORGANIZATIONS

The period since 1967 has been an exceptionally difficult one for
Israel in international organizations, where it has been constantly
subjected to abuse, vilification, and condemnation. The task of
representing Israel in such organizations is a daunting and frustrating
one. The victories, such as they are, primarily involve thwarting
attempts to pass anti-Israel resolutions, to expel Israel from the
organization, or to deprive it of various rights or privileges. Of course
the struggle within these bodies is part and parcel of the general
political struggle by Israel to maintain its international position and
legitimacy. Many of the specific issues are thus of little consequence.
But the totality of the issues, the pattern that is set, contributes to
Israel's overall standing on the world scene.

The most serious dilemmas have arisen in the UN itself, where the
campaign against Israel has become an annual autumn rite when the
General Assembly meets. The low point from Israel's perspective
was probably the passage of the Zionism is Racism resolution in
1976. In addition, there are the annual General Assembly resolutions
on a variety of topics, usually concerning the occupied territories,
the rights of the Palestinian people, etc. There are also resolutions
in response to specific Israeli actions. Each year Israel's credentials
in the Assembly are challenged. And there are predictable efforts to
allege a close connection between apartheid and Zionism, between
the racism inherent in South Africa's treatment of its black majority
and Israel's treatment of the Arabs under its control in the occupied
territories, between the Israeli government and the South African

government. The votes become the official position of the Assembly and can be utilized for propaganda and political purposes in a variety of forums. The Security Council is less prone to such posturing. Despite numerous decisions that may not have pleased the Israeli Government, most concern specific Israeli actions. General attempts to delegitimize Israel would meet a likely United States' veto. Still, the United States has felt constrained on occasion to go along with the passage of resolutions opposed by Israel, resolutions which can be used internationally against Israel's interest – for example, when the Security Council passes a resolution calling upon Israel to cease creating settlements in the occupied territories.

Other international organizations, generally UN organs, have tended to resemble the General Assembly because their procedures do not include a great power veto. Israel has thus encountered difficulties in bodies such as UNESCO, WHO, the ILO, and the Human Rights Commission. In most cases, the accusations brought against Israel relate to conditions in the occupied territories, such as assertions that Israel is providing inadequate educational facilties, allowing health conditions to deteriorate, denying rights to workers, or depriving individuals of human rights. Such accusations are also made about Israel proper, but they are more effective when made in reference to the territories, where they cannot be considered an internal matter. Moreover, the very nature of a military occupation leads to events which are ideal targets for those trying to embarrass Israel in front of the world community. One example should suffice: it is unreasonable to expect that conditions under a military regime can afford the degree of protection of human rights as might be found under a civilian regime ruling its own country. The fact that Israeli military rule over the territories pending a peace settlement is implicity acceptable under Resolution 242 is a point which is overlooked when these various resolutions are debated.

Perhaps the remarkable aspect of Israel's twenty years of opprobrium in international organizations has been that Israel has withstood the verbal onslaught and that the situation has begun to improve. Israel's demonstration at Camp David that it would trade territory for peace under the appropriate circumstances certainly contributed to a relaxation of the hostility toward Israel, especially in certain African states. Divisions in the Arab world and the decline in the oil price also helped. Consequently in recent years Israel's position has improved. The antagonistic majorities are still there, but they are not as large. The more outrageous schemes, such as expelling Israel from the UN, are not very threatening. And much of the attack on Israel has been reduced to a ritual that is often performed without conviction. For the longer run, Israel has to assume that the tide will turn eventually; but until this happens, the record can be used as a powerful indictment of Israel as a nation that regularly departs from international forms of behaviour.

LINKAGE TO SOUTH AFRICA

There is little doubt that opponents of Israel have had some success in linking it to South Africa. In each case, it is argued, a light-skinned people exercises dominion over a dark-skinned people, depriving the darker group of its fundamental right to self-determination. This is a powerful argument in an environment where opposition to racism unites diverse peoples and countries. Obviously the nuances of the Arab–Israeli conflict are overlooked amidst the simplistic talk of a Tel Aviv–Pretoria axis. But it has proved to be an effective angle, especially in Africa, where the South African question is probably the leading international issue. The problem is compounded by the existence of some superficial similarities. For example, the white South Africans are the descendants of Europeans who colonized and settled the region some time ago, but are of much more recent vintage than the blacks, while the Jews are descended from European settlers who came to Palestine during the last century. Never mind that the Jews trace their connection to the land back to the Biblical patriarchs or that over half the Jews in Israel are non-European in origin. Also, Israel is establishing settlements in the territories, suggesting that it is inserting people into areas where they are not indigenous. And the residents of the territories are not permitted to exercise full political rights, a situation which is seen as parallel to that which exists in South Africa. Furthermore both the Jews and the Afrikaners see themselves as isolated and set upon and try to protect themselves by rigorous security measures against largely internal enemies. The list of comparisons can be as extensive as it is misleading. Israel has been hurt by this accusation of similarities and also by its links to South Africa, even though a number of major Western nations have far greater and more significant trade and political links to South Africa than does Israel. However, the attempt to show that military, political, and trade links between the two countries follow necessarily from the similarities between the two societies is difficult to counter because of the complexity of the effort required.

Israel is no more racist than any other nation-state that exists to fulfil the aspirations of a particular people. However, the occupation since 1967 has left it vulnerable to accusations that it treats the inhabitants of the territories in a racist manner. Israel's policies in the territories can be defended, even as the debate about those policies continues within Israel. But the debate within Israel is based on the premise that control over the territories was a necessary consequence of a war of self-defence and that retaining control over the territories until the successful conclusion of a peace agreement is therefore justified. If outsiders do not share that premise, then the assessment of Israel's policies will differ. It creates situations which can be exploited by those whose objective is to pin the racist label on Israel. Hence the utility and the potency of South Africa-based accusations against Israel has been greater than they would have been had the Six-Day War not occurred.

PUBLIC OPINION

There are two levels of public opinion that ought to be considered: the level of the mass public and the level of opinion leaders and influentials. The second would appear to be more important, even in those countries where public opinion often has an impact on public policy. Generally the formation of foreign policy is less likely to be influenced by mass public opinion than is the formation of domestic policy. The expression of opinion on foreign policy is often the preserve of opinion leaders, people who speak and write for public consumption, who may influence the direction of mass opinion, and who often will have the ear of those who are responsible for decisions. On matters of foreign policy they can play the vital role of articulating the context in which policy should be formed.

It is within this sector of society that a serious erosion of Israel's position has taken place. It is certainly not true that all elite opinion in all countries has turned against Israel since 1967. But even if we confine ourselves to Western countries where these processes are more highly developed the change in outlook has been dramatic. Whereas prior to 1967 Israel generally enjoyed strong support in the media and in intellectual circles, since that time it has become both fashionable and acceptable to take a sharply critical stance toward

Israel and its policies. The hostile position has not become universal; far from it. But in a situation where questions of majority and minority positions may not be terribly consequential, the presence of a significant body of opinion that opposes Israel's position makes it easier for governments to adopt stands that are contrary to what Israel perceives as its interests. Over a period of time, the presentation of opinions and information unfavourable to Israel in the news, in newspaper columns, in books and magazines, on radio and television can also make public opinion in general more tolerant of policies that conflict with Israel's.

The events of 1967 created a situation where opinion leaders would find more reason to express unfavourable sentiments and opinions about Israel than had been the case in earlier years. Again, the occupation provided considerable material for many opinion leaders, especially as the time period appeared to become open-ended and as the government of Israel began to consider long-term retention of the Golan Heights, Judea and Samaria and Gaza. Moreover, we live in an era where it is fashionable to sympathize with an underdog. After 1967, Israel was no longer an underdog and the Palestinian Arabs established a claim on the world's sympathy. Israeli hubris in the years between the Six-Day War and the Yom Kippur War did not help the effort to retain the support of opinion leaders. The danger of these developments is that continued exposure to criticisms of Israel makes people less likely to jump to Israel's defence in a time of crisis. Thus the deterioration of elite opinion since 1967 is not only an indicator of a weakened political position, but also a warning sign of possible difficulty in the future.

There is some indication that, at least in the United States, the problem may not be as great as some may have feared. In a recent study, Eytan Gilboa has demonstrated that American mass opinion has remained quite strongly in Israel's camp, despite short-term perturbations caused by actions such as the Lebanon War.[4] Gilboa, who concentrated on national sample survey data, did not deal with the problem of elite opinion in particular, and one cannot therefore infer from this data exactly what the state of elite opinion is or has been, nor what the influence of opinion leaders on policy-makers with regard to the Middle East conflict has been. What opinion leaders have accomplished is to make Israel an easier target of criticism than it had been in the past.

WHY ISRAEL'S STANDING DECLINED

It is clear that in international affairs Israel is subject to a different kind of treatment than virtually any other state. The fact that Israel is singled out for such special handling in itself constitutes convincing evidence of Israel's deteriorated position. In searching for an explanation for this development, it would be easy to conclude that there is an inherent bias against Israel that eventually became an operative factor. Was there simply latent anti-Semitism lurking in the background, attitudes that were dormant from the end of the Second World War until 1967 but which surfaced when the Jews shed their cloak of powerlessness? Surely that may be part of the explanation, but it is far from the whole story. There are a number of objective factors that have influenced attitudes toward Israel and its policies.

Israel has suffered politically because of a number of developments, most of which have nothing to do with Israel at all, but which affected the international environment within which Israel operated. One of the most important of these is the emergence of the Third World as a major player in international politics. Israel's statehood coincided with the beginning of the era of decolonization, a process that occurred quite rapidly during the two decades after 1945. By 1967 the Third World was a force to be reckoned with on the world scene – not in the conventional sense of the great powers, but rather as increasingly adept players in the diplomatic arena, particularly in international bodies that operated on the principle of one state, one vote. Israel, despite a reasonable claim to be on the right side of the decolonization process itself, had the misfortune to become identified with the twin bogies of imperialism and colonialism. There were a number of reasons for this. The first was Israel's European face, a prominent feature for many years despite the growing presence of Jews with Asian and African roots. To the sophisticated observer, there was a vast gulf between the children of downtrodden Eastern European Jewish communities and the Western European powers that had constructed colonial empires in the Third World. But to others, Israel was simply another case of European interlopers maintaining an enclave in Asia. The identification with imperialism resulted in part from the joint venture with Britain and France (the classic imperial powers) in 1956, and in part from the reliance on the Western nations for political and material support. Whether deserved or not, the Soviet Union had appropriated the mantle of anti-imperialism and anti-colonialism, so that in the eyes of the Third World a country, especially one located in Asia, that concentrated its ties in the First World, was hopelessly entangled with the imperialists. This was the case despite Israel's notable involvement in the development of numerous Third World countries. Finally, the events of 1967, which brought substantial numbers of Arabs and new territories under Israeli control, fit into the model that much of the Third World used to analyze politics: a European nation ruling over non-European people in part of Asia. Thus it was inevitable that disaffection between the Third World and Israel would result. Furthermore, while it was difficult for the Third World to do much that would harm the interests of the major pillars of imperialism and colonialism, Israel was small, relatively weak, and vulnerable. Thus Israel simply suffered from a major shift in the political constellation.

A related factor is that of ideology. Despite Israel's long-term involvement with socialist ideology, whatever revolutionary ardour that might have existed had by 1967 worn off. This is not an unusual phenomenon; even that most revolutionary of societies, the Soviet Union, has not been immune. But at the same time as Israel was tempering the imperatives of socialist ideology in the face of the reality of running a state that faced complex challenges, the Third World, along with many of its enthusiastic advocates in more affluent areas, were being carried away by the certainties of a rather unsophisticated Marxism. It was comfortable for them, politically and ideologically, to be anti-Israel, and there were few costs involved. So Israel provided a painless way for socialist and developing nations to remain true to their ideological principles. This was true for the Soviet Bloc countries as well as the Third World. By cutting ties with Israel, denouncing it in political forums, and providing aid and comfort to its enemies, the communist countries made significant political gains and earned considerable support, not only in the Arab world – where the Soviets had to overcome a significant Islamic bias – but in Third World countries that had no particular axe to grind with Israel.

In 1967 Israel came to symbolize the success of power. This was a value that was questioned by many and beyond the reach of others. Israel's success with power thus prompted feelings of both envy and resentment, both of which could contribute to a somewhat hostile disposition to Israel politically. Unfortunately Israel's success was often accompanied by over-confidence and braggadocio, so that the country became an inviting target to those who wanted to see it cut down to size. International organizations frequently provided a forum where Israel's battlefield prowess was neutralized and its opponents could score victories that would provide psychological satisfaction. As a result it seemed that winning at the expense of Israel had become a form of international sport, a game that could be played by almost any state with very little cost to the players (aside from Israel).

What part did anti-Semitism play in these developments? Undoubtedly there were people in the Christian and Muslim worlds who could not abide a strong Israel because they could not come to terms theologically with the end of Jewish powerlessness.[5] Simply by being victorious in 1967, Israel acted as a provocation to such people. The continuing rule over the territories symbolized Jewish power and constituted defiance of the proper order of things. Other forms of anti-Semitism were exploited by the Soviet Union as a means of drumming up support against Israel. Yet despite the kinds of pronouncements emanating from the Soviets and from certain Arab countries, in which vile anti-Semitic canards were used with impunity, anti-Semitism never became the primary motivating factor in the anti-Israel crusade that reached its peak during the 1970s. It may have been a factor with certain individuals, some of whom played key roles in shaping the foreign policy of their nations, and there were indeed gauche outbursts from time to time. But the tendency simply to equate anti-Israel stances and policies with anti-Semitism would appear to be misguided. The causes are much more complicated. Even the anti-Zionism campaign cannot be explained merely as anti-Semitism with a different name, though the question of why one particular people's national ideology should be singled out for international denunciation has not been answered satisfactorily.

The sharp and sudden increase in oil prices in 1973, with the concomitant transfer of wealth and power to the Arab oil-producing states, is another factor that contributed to the decline in Israel's international standing. Overnight the Arabs were elevated to become major actors in international politics. Given their already established position as part of the Third World bloc of countries, they were well situated to capitalize on the opportunity to further their political objectives, which mainly involved Israel. In effect, they were able to buy political support for their cause to the detriment of Israel's interests. The power of oil blended with considerations of pragmatic politics to aid the Arab cause. Despite the lofty pretensions, the UN and other international bodies often operate in accordance with practices that would make the most seasoned and cynical party machine boss blush; the practice of horsetrading is at least as well developed in the General Assembly as in the United States Congress. In a period when the oil states were riding high, they had a great deal to offer many of the small countries that make up such a large portion of the UN membership, while Israel had very little to offer. The consequences were entirely predictable. The relevance of this analysis is enhanced by an examination of the last six or seven years, during which the price of oil has declined. The effectiveness of the oil states in international organizations has declined in step with the oil price, thereby reducing the threat to Israel.

Finally, opponents of Israel – and especially proponents of the cause of the Palestinian Arabs – have mounted and executed very effective propaganda and public relations campaigns for many years. In the midst of defeat in Beirut in 1982, Yasser Arafat was masterfully using the media to further his longer-range objectives. Israel, which had held innumerable debates over the relative ineffectiveness of its own information activities, has been very much aware of the success of efforts by and for the Palestinians. Despite a number of attempts to rectify the situation, Israel has not been very successful in getting its message across. Meanwhile the plight of the Palestinians – both the refugees and those living under occupation – has been seared into the consciousness of thinking people all over the world, largely in the context of people suffering because of Israel.

If one is to compare Israel's political position today to the situation that obtained twenty years ago – realizing that the balance in strategic terms may be different – the inescapable conclusion is that Israel finds itself in a less favourable position now, but that the situation is improving. Israel has been on the defensive in the international arena since the early 1970s. Although the intensity and virulence of the opposition to Israel may have moderated somewhat in recent years, Israel continues to be the object of regular attacks in international forums and ongoing attempts to undermine its legitimacy.

Ironically, the acquisition of the territories west of the Jordan River, which have provided Israel with a greater measure of military security than had previously been the case, has created a conundrum for policy-makers and the public alike. Israel has not been able to find a route to a peaceful resolution of the linked issues of the territories and peace with Arab countries in addition to Egypt. Without the resolution of both problems, there are inherent limits on the extent to which Israel's international position can improve.

Therefore Israel will probably have to be content with marginal improvements which, though not insignificant, cannot be expected to lead to the removal of the genuine sense of grievance that Israel is entitled to hold in light of the history of the last twenty years.

As has been argued above, the problem of the decline in Israel's international standing is a by-product of the military success of 1967.[6] It is pointless to speculate on what Israel's international position would have been had the war not occurred. Surely there was a political price to be paid for the military and strategic success of 1967, but it was probably a necessary price. The relevant question is whether Israel's policies since 1967 have been optimal and whether different policies would have lessened the decline in the nation's international standing. With the benefit of hindsight, and without going into detail, a case could be made for alternative policies.[7] Nevertheless the fundamental reality of the occupation had a more significant impact on Israel's international standing than Israel's own policies.

There are two specifically troubling aspects of international reaction that deserve attention. First of all, there is an essential unfairness in the way Israel has been treated. States with unclean hands have been in the vanguard of those denouncing Israel and advocating the imposition of disabilities on it. Moreover, there is a selectivity at work here in the way that Israel has been singled out for more elaborate and more careful scrutiny than is applied to other states and is brought to task for actions that go unnoticed when carried out by other states. Despite all of the explanations for the treatment of Israel, which do make sense, there remains a residual variation that cannot really be explained. Have Israel's actions differed so much in kind from those of all other states in the world as to warrant the extent of international attention that is focused on them? Israel has become an obsession of international organizations and the world media. Anti-Semitism is too simplistic an explanation. But what then is the answer? Is it simply a coincidence of history?

The second troubling aspect was the unpredictable and unreliable support of the Western democratic nations. They clearly lacked the will for a political fight, partly because of ambivalence about Israel's actions, partly because of a desire to be conciliatory toward the Third World, partly because of anxiety about oil supplies, and partly perhaps because of a lack of confidence about their own positions. Whatever the reasons, Israel was let down in the UN, in the European Economic Community, in various international bodies and even in the Socialist International that the Israeli Labour Party had worked so closely with over the years. In a sense Israel had to exercise leadership to demonstrate that the forces of history were not necessarily heading in one direction only, and that democratic countries need not cower before authoritarian regimes and worse. By withstanding the political onslaughts of the past twenty years, Israel has performed a distinct service to the small community of democratic nations.

It is unlikely that Israel can hope to regain the standing that it held prior to 1967 within the next few years. Yet there are unmistakeable signs that the situation is improving. Diplomatic relations are being reestablished, anti-Israel majorities in international bodies are declining, language is becoming more temperate, and a strong base of support for Israel remains in a number of countries. Some of these changes can be attributed to modifications of the external environment, while others are the result of shifts in Israeli policies themselves. The progress of the past few years suggests that additional improvements reasonably can be foreseen during the coming years.

Notes

1. Irving Louis Horowitz, 'From Pariah People to Pariah Nation: Jews, Israelis and the Third World', in Michael Curtis and Susan Aurelia Gitelson (eds), *Israel in the Third World* (New Brunswick, N.J., 1976) 361–91.
2. A discussion of the early attempts to establish a relationship with China is found in Michael Brecher, 'Israel and China: A Historic "Missed Opportunity"', in Curtis and Gitelson (eds), *Israel in the Third World*, 218–33.
3. Susan Aurelia Gitelson, 'Israel's African Setback in Perspective', in Curtis and Gitelson, (eds), *Israel in the Third World*, 182–99.
4. Eytan Gilboa, *American Public Opinion Toward Israel and the Arab–Israeli Conflict* (Lexington, Mass., 1987).
5. The anti-Semitic aspects of Islam are the subject of Bernard Lewis, *Semites and Anti-Semites* (New York, 1986).
6. The opposite result occurred in the wake of the 1956 Suez War. See Nadav Safran, *Israel: The Embattled Ally* (Cambridge, Mass., 1981) 368–80.
7. A useful analysis of some policy options can be found in Daniel J. Elazar, *Israel: Building a New Society* (Bloomington, 1986) ch. 9.

Part III

Inside Israel

11 Israeli Society and Politics

Itzhak Galnoor

Has Israel undergone a transformation in the last twenty years? The main question addressed in this chapter is: 'What type of discontinuities can be attributed to the 1967 war?' Sudden human changes should always be suspected for their ephemeral nature; and transformations – that is, a complete break of continuity in the system's main features – are rare indeed. Nevertheless, we know that Israel has changed dramatically in this period.

Moreover, how many of these changes can be directly attributed to a single event – a war, in this case? Here, the answer is less ambiguous. War is an upheaval in the life of every society, it also subjects the political system to the supreme test of proving its ability to guarantee the collectivity's most decisive interests. A democratic political system – particularly when it fails this test – tends to forfeit its power of survival and must change or disappear. This is particularly so in Israel, because – irrespective of whether the assessment is objective or subjective – the 'government' is judged according to its ability to cope with security (i.e., national survival). For Israelis the milestones in their collective chronology (especially since 1948) are the country's frequent wars and occasional military operations.[1] This popular approach to Israel's history could be justified if we remember that wars change not only the country's international position or its territories, but also the size of the population, economic markets, military budgets, and also less tangible things – national expectations, sense of identity and self-confidence.

In order to answer the question : 'Has Israel changed?' we need to compare the state of Israeli society and politics in the mid-1960s and the mid-1980s. We shall also examine several features of discontinuity related to the 1967 and 1973 wars and their aftermaths. Of course, one can only speculate about how certain transformations may or may not have taken place without these wars, but one can examine those changes in direction which have taken place since 1967, and how the 1973 war served as a catalyst for those transformations.

ISRAEL IN THE MID-1960s

The second decade of Israel's independence did not bring peace and tranquility. The period following the withdrawal from the Sinai in 1957 was relatively quiet, but towards the completion of the National Water Carrier in 1965 the region began to ferment again. In this section we focus on internal developments only.

Society

In terms of socioeconomic development Israel in the mid-1960s was still a 'developing' or 'industrializing' country. Not only was Israel's level of economic development below that of Western democracies, but – more important – the process of nation-building (or rebuilding) had just begun. The small tribal-like community of about half a million Jews in 1948 more than tripled in the 1950s. It was a society of first-generation immigrants, just beginning the long and agonizing process of profound transformation; in 1965 about 60 per cent of all Israeli Jews, and almost the entire adult population, had been born outside the country.

However, by any set of indicators, Israel's development in the first two decades of statehood was rapid. Table 11.1 presents some aggregate economic and social indicators and compares the first eighteen (1950–68) with the next eighteen years (1968–85).

From Tables 11.1 and 11.2 we can see that within a relatively very short period Israel transformed from a relatively underdeveloped to a modern, urban society. This is exemplified by the fact that within less than four decades the percentage of the civilian labour force engaged in agriculture dropped from 18 to 6 per cent, while employment in the service sector increased from 49 to 65 per cent.

The second conclusion one can draw from Tables 11.1 and 11.2 is that the greatest period of change was during the first eighteen years of independence – for example, in population increase, economic growth, reduction in the balance of payments gap, industrial and agricultural productivity and living standards' rise. This may seem surprising, since this early period included the severe economic recession of 1966–7 while the second included the fastest five years of development in Israeli history (1968–72).

In the mid-1960s there were three main social divisions in Israel, the ethnic, the religious and the national.

Table 11.1 Selected indicators of socioeconomic development

| | 1950 | 1968 | 1985 | Change factor | |
				1950–68	1968–85
Population (10³)	1370	2841	4266	2.1	1.5
GNP *per capita* (index)	100	233	344	2.3	1.5
Gross domestic capital formation (index)	100	253	403	2.5	1.6
Private consumption *per capita* (index)	100	214	326	2.1	1.5
Net imports of goods ($m)	300	1093	8021	3.6	7.3
Net exports of goods ($m)	35	602	6080	17.2	10.1
Cultivated area (dunam 10³)	2480	4132	4370	1.7	1.1
Industrial production (index)	100[a]	306	770	3.1[a]	2.5
Industries engaging 100 + employees	163[a]	332	447	2.0[a]	1.3
Electricity production (10⁶ KWH)	543	5327	15010	9.8	2.8
Vehicles (10³)	10	108	614	10.8	5.7
per 1000 people	7	38	144	5.4	3.8
Telephones (10³)	31	419	1780	13.5	4.2
per 1000 people	23	147	417	6.4	2.8

Source: Central Bureau of Statistics, *Statistical Abstract of Israel*, 20 (1969); 30 (1979); 37 (1986).
Note: [a] Figures are for 1958.

Table 11.2 Distribution of employment in labour force

	1950	1968	1985
Agriculture	18	11	6
Industry	22	24	23
Construction, electricity and water	11	9	6
Public and private services	49	56	65
	100	100	100

Source: CBS, *Statistical Abstract of Israel*, 30 (1979); 37 (1986).

(a) *Ethnic divisions*

In 1967, the division between 'oriental' and 'western' Jews was in its pre-political stage. The ratio between the two groups evened out in the early 1960s, and the oriental community became a majority in 1965. Yet the socioeconomic gap between the two communities remained considerable in terms of income, housing, education and employment. Politically, the 'orientals' were powerless – under-represented in all national institutions and in the country's various elites.

However, in the 1960s a change began to take place. Here and there oriental leaders appeared – in organized groups such as Wadi Salib,[2] in local authorities, in regional branches of workers' committees and in the Histadrut. The 'ethnic problem' was already bubbling in the 1960s. The oriental community began the struggle for the attainment of economic, and eventually, political and social equality. In retrospect the question was: 'What expression would this struggle take?'

(b) *Religious divisions*

Unlike the ethnic divisions which appeared in Israel after 1948, the division between 'religious' and 'secular', observant and non-observant Jews, existed in pre-state period. Under the British Mandate the religious courts were granted jurisdiction in matters of personal status such as marriage, divorce, burial, etc. During the state period, a parallel judicial system of Rabbinical courts was established under the Ministry of Religious Affairs and was given jurisdiction over these matters for the Jewish community. In addition there were also political agreements between the parties which defined the observance of the Sabbath, dietary regulations and the extent of support for religious schools, institutions, etc. This whole package – partly legal and partly not – is known in Israel's political parlance as the 'status quo' agreement.

In the mid-1960s the 'status quo' agreement remained in effect and the religious parties regarded themselves as its guardians, as the old disputes about the role of the state or the observance of the Sabbath, erupted from time to time and caused governmental crises. The National Religious Party (NRP) and Poalei Agudat Israel participated in Ben Gurion's cabinet (1961–3), in Eshkol's cabinets (1963–5) and again after the 1965 elections and in the first National Unity cabinet established on 5 June 1967. It is interesting to note that the religious parties were not deeply involved in the political upheavals of the 1960s. They confined their interests mainly to religious affairs.

In contrast, the Six-Day War transformed the nature and content of the relationship between observant and non-observant Jews;

the religious parties, particularly the NRP, now became a key factor in Israeli politics and in the 1977 change of government. Most observant, non-ultra-orthodox Jews were incorporated into Israeli society and politics and were successfully organized to advance their cause. Nevertheless, the cleavage between the observant and non-observant was maintained and was manifested in separate schools, youth movements, sports clubs, *kibbutzim*, political parties and residential neighbourhoods. The status quo agreement – partly sentimental and partly expedient – meant in effect a series of religious, economic and political concessions made by the non-observant majority. And there was the paradox: despite their incorporation and their successful organizations, many observant Jews, especially the young ones, felt that they had not occupied a leading position in the Zionist revolution and that they were outside the mainstream of Israeli society. This has influenced their attitudes and behaviour in the post-1967 era.

(c) *Israeli Arabs*

The last cleavage to be mentioned here is between Jewish and Arab citizens of the State of Israel. In 1949 about 160 000 Arabs remained within Israel's armistice boundaries – 14 per cent of the total population. In 1967, there were about 350 000 Arabs in Israel (13 per cent of the population). The two communities are divided in terms of nationality, religion, culture, language and residence. The common denominator is the state, and – increasingly – the economic market. The Israeli political system has never sought to integrate the Arabs or subject them to a 'melting pot' policy. Its main concern was to ensure – through military government – their loyalty as citizens and their observance of the law. The Arabs enjoyed formal citizenship rights, religious, cultural and local autonomy, as well as some measures of economic development and welfare. Arab turnout on election day was very high – an average of 87 per cent in the period 1949–65 – but politically they were denied any real power. The majority in those years voted for Mapai and its affiliated Arab parties and about 20 per cent for the Communist party.

In the 1960s many Israeli Arabs became more mobile economically, benefiting from the general rise in the standard of living. They developed a pragmatic approach to furthering their interests which contained an element of recognition of and compliance

with the state and its political system. This trend was enhanced
by the abolition of military government in 1966 and some other
measures of liberalization. For example, in 1960–5 about 40 000
Arabs joined the Histadrut. Yet politically, little changed. To
have permitted Arab independent political organization would
have immediately raised sensitive security issues, as well as
questions about confiscation of land by the state. The result was
that, through a combination of security, bureaucratic and legal
means, no independent Arab party was actually allowed. Instead,
there were regularly seven or eight Arab (including Druse)
members of Knesset, belonging to Jewish parties and their
affiliated lists. The takeover of the territories in 1967 placed this
'internal division' of Israeli society even deeper within the broader
context of the Arab–Israeli conflict.

Politics

The main feature of the Israeli political system from the pre-state
period until the mid-1960s and the source of its strength was the
reliance on the power of organizations and institutions. The political
parties, together with the bureacracy and the mass media were the
main factors that contributed to stability and continuity.[3]

The two main issues to be addressed are whether Israel was
politically developed, and whether it was democratic. The main
features of Israeli politics in the pre-1967 era were as follows:[4]

(a) A considerable degree of consensus concerning the Jewish
state as an instrument for attaining Zionist objectives. On this
fundamental assumption, Israel's political culture was united and
the divisions already described could be bridged. This in turn
contributed to politics through coalitions, compromises and
accommodation.
(b) The pre-state division into three 'political camps' still existed.
The general distribution of votes between the labour camp,
the 'civic' bourgeois camp (General Zionist and Revisionist
Movement) and the religious camp was more or less perpetuated,
with Mapai as the dominating power. Yet these divisions lost their
ideological basis and became mainly political and organizational.
(c) There was a high degree of politicization in Israeli society. The
space between central government and society was densely
occupied by numerous bodies and 'secondary centres'. These

were not independent pressure or voluntary groups and organizations. The most prominent feature of this myriad of bodies was that they were affiliated, in one way or another, with central institutions: the government, the Histadrut, the Jewish Agency and the political parties. In 1965 Israel was still a highly organized society.

(d) It was also still a society of political parties. The main parties acted as clearing houses in the complex and highly divided political system. Accordingly, the 'partisan key' was a series of arrangements between Mapai, the other parties and the affiliated organizations to allocate each a share of the various resources. This central feature of Israeli politics started to change due to the socioeconomic transformation in society.

(e) Israel had a strong executive. It could rely on the party discipline of a parliamentary system, a dominant party, and a loyal centralized public bureaucracy. Toward the mid-1960s there were already shifts in the relative strength of the various governmental bodies in relation to one another. Above all, the power of the executive branch began to weaken.

(f) The judiciary was independent, and enjoyed a high degree of respect. It remained by and large outside party politics. Moreover at that time the judiciary branch deliberately refrained from becoming enmeshed in the political process – hence, for instance, the reluctance to give the Supreme Court the power to pronounce upon the legality of legislation. Israel made a clear distinction between processes requiring political and administrative decisions and those entrusted to the judgement of the courts.

(g) Finally, Israel's political system was a rather closed one with political participation confined to elections or to membership in the parties and the various affiliated organizations. There was relatively little autonomous political activity by individuals or groups, particularly 'non-established' groups such as new immigrants, oriental Jews or Israeli Arabs.

The answer to the first question posed in the beginning of this section, therefore, is that by the mid-1960s, Israel was rather developed politically. There was enough agreement on goals and procedures to enable the system to function; there was only one legitimate political centre, and there were recognized institutions. In short, given the formidable challenges, the political system proved its steering capacity, and the government its ability to cope with threats and to reach binding decisions with little use of coercion. However in the post-Ben-Gurion era, it became more difficult to overcome crisis and potential breakdowns with the old tools of accommodation and compromise.[5]

Was it democratic? In a democracy, citizens have an impact on steering through access to resources and participation. In these very general terms Israel was democratic, and that would have been the prevalent feeling among most Israeli citizens in the mid-1960s. Yet Israel was an 'organized' democracy with access restricted by a powerful network of parties and affiliated bodies. Accordingly, citizens' participation was more of the responsive type – they voted, listened attentively to the news and complained to public officials. But their role as autonomous political factors was rather limited.

TWO INTERVENING PERIODS

The Crisis (1965–7)

These years were characterized by a mood of helplessness and even despair. Jokes could be regarded as an indicator of low efficacy. If so, this was the period in which a small booklet entitled 'All Eshkol Jokes' was very popular reading in Israel. This is the period when the most famous joke circulating in Israel was:

> A sign in Lod Airport: 'last one to leave the country, please turn out the light!'

More concretely, the 1960s brought a number of critical challenges to Israeli society and politics:

(a) The 'Lavon Affair' was a major political crisis which started in 1960 and continued on and off until the 1965 general elections.[6]

(b) Ben-Gurion finally resigned as Prime Minister in 1963; this was followed by a split within Mapai and the establishment of a new party, Rafi, in 1965 headed by Ben-Gurion. To counterbalance this, Mapai formed an Alignment with Achdut HaAvoda and reinforced itself with 'outsiders' such as Alon and Gallili.

(c) The economic recession, 1966–7, was accompanied by a high level of unemployment, particularly of oriental Jews in the development towns. This was a period of unrest with an unprecedent number of strikes.[7] Most of them were directed against the government and the Histadrut.

(d) The 'waiting period' in May–June 1967, between the closure of the straits by Egypt and the war, was collectively traumatic. There was public confusion, lack of confidence in the political leadership and some threats of military insubordination. This forced Eshkol to resign as Defence Minister and bring in Herut, for the first time, as a partner in the unity cabinet.

The 'Lavon Affair' epitomizes the crisis of the political system because it contained almost all possible disruptions. All the major institutions were involved: the Knesset, the judiciary, the Defence Ministry, the Israel Defence Forces, the Histadrut, the press and the other parties. For the first time since Israel's establishment there was a feeling that not only was the political system not functioning but that the country was going nowhere. This subjective feeling of a breakdown was intensified during the economic crisis and developed into a real fear for survival in the period before the 1967 War.

True, the 1965 elections can be regarded as a 'victory of the institutional setting of the existing regime'.[8] The 'labour' camp still had a majority – with the affiliated Arab parties – of 55 per cent of the electorate. But it was deeply divided and Rafi (Ben-Gurion's party) was not invited to join the government coalition. Four years later, in the 1969 elections – despite the fact that *all* the labour parties became part of the new Alignment – it won only 46 per cent of the votes. In 1965, Gahal, a combination of Herut and the Liberal Party and the predecessor of Likud, was formed; in 1967 it joined the cabinet coalition; in 1969 this bloc on the right, headed by Menachem Begin, began its slow ascent to power.

The external situation had been deteriorating since 1965, but the 1967 war caught Israeli society by surprise. Israel entered the Six-Day War politically united and on the seventh day came out divided – a division that has frozen the situation for twenty years, the longest standstill in Zionist history.

The 'Empire' (1967–73)

This cynical title is derived from the fact that in retrospect we know that there was a wide gulf between the deteriorating external situation and the mood within the country. It became immediately clear that the military victory of 1967 would not bring an end to Israel's security

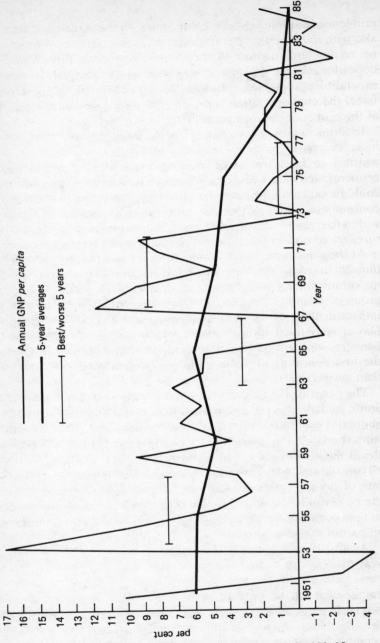

Figure 11.1   Average changes in GNP *per capita* (per cent) 1950–85.
Source: Central Bureau of Statistics, *Statistical Abstract of Israel*, 37 (1986).

problems; hostilities resumed, not only with the Arab countries, but also with the Palestinians. The Arab League's 'three nos' (no peace, no recognition, no negotiation) on 3 November 1967 ended the hopes for a quick diplomatic breakthrough. Consequently, military expenditures remained very high, close to that of 1967.[9] Yet within Israel the euphoria continued right up to the 1973 war. Let us look at the economic developments first.

In terms of GNP *per capita*, the post-1967 five-year period was the most successful in Israel's history. Moreover, it stands in sharp contrast to both the preceding and the following years.[10] Other economic indicators also show a great leap in 1967–73. The same could be said about the standard of living (annual increase in private consumption by 12 per cent); immigration (a quarter of a million within five years); an expansion in welfare services and state expenditures on education, health, housing, community services.

At the same time, many new independent groups began to appear outside the rigid structure of Israeli politics after 1967. The most important among them were the Israeli 'Black Panthers', a vocal group of young orientals which appeared in 1970 and had a strong impact in their demands for equality. Typically, Defence Minister Dayan responded by saying that Israeli society cannot raise 'two banners' – security and welfare – simultaneously. This was one of the first indicators that the Six-Day War produced more questions than answers.

The general climate in the rest of society was one of limitlessness. Some leaders spoke of Israel as a 'military world power', and others about the 'economic Switzerland of the Middle East'. Massive support from the USA, the arrival of Jewish immigrants from the USSR and the availability of cheap Arab labour from the occupied territories – all contributed to an aura of invincibility and visions of the miraculous fate of Israel. The reconstruction of the old political system under the powerful leadership of Golda Meir (since 1969) and the inability to read correctly the meaning of the War of Attrition (1969–70) were all part of the same phenomenon.

Against this background the traumatic effect of the Yom Kippur War of 1973 can be more easily understood. The war shattered the basic faith of most Israelis that their leaders knew what they were doing, even when it came to issues of survival. The immediate result was an unprecedented event in Israeli politics: public pressure caused the resignation of Golda Meir and her cabinet in 1974. There was a genuine desire 'to begin everything anew'. In the long run, the 1973 war changed the unquestioned position of the most important institution in Israel – the defence establishment, which includes not only the IDF and the military industry, but also the secret services, the border police and many affiliated bodies.

The 1967 and 1973 wars – and the five years between – should be regarded as the most critical period in Israel's development since independence. Let us turn now to examine the social and political changes up to 1985 and return to this point at the concluding part of this chapter.

ISRAEL IN THE MID-1980s

Social Changes

Israel in the mid-1980s belongs to the family of modern developed, even post-industrialized, societies. Of course, not everybody in Israel shares this wealth and there are groups that not only did not make it, but became relatively more impoverished. But the overall figures measuring the development of the society as a whole are impressive indeed. First of all, the composition of society has changed. Israel is no longer a society of first-generation immigrants. In 1985, 60 per cent of all Jews, and 94 per cent of those aged 1–19, were born in Israel. Furthermore, changes in the standard of living in the last two decades have been qualitatively different. The same average urban family that we depicted in the 1960s has disappeared completely. In the mid-1980s it resembles the relevant families in other advanced Western countries.

As already shown in Tables 11.1 and 11.2, the society as a whole now demonstrates post-industrial features – for example, in the composition of the labour force, the dominance of services in the economy, the total stock of years of formal education in the country, and in technological progress, including the appearance of a military–industrial complex.[11] We also find an increase in leisure activities and a prominent role played by the electronic mass media, as well as societal stresses that can be associated with rapid socioeconomic changes. To illustrate, a country with 144 private vehicles per 1000 people (i.e., almost 70 per cent of all households own a car), can no longer be defined as 'underdeveloped'. Incidently, 'modernization' is also manifested in the reduction in the *per capita* consumption of calories in the Israeli diet in the last decade.

But in pure terms of economic development, 1973 reversed the trend and it was followed by low (and even negative) rates of growth. Between 1973 and 1985 the average annual change in the GNP *per capita* has been a little above zero. (+ 0.5 per cent). This was a long period of stagnation, coupled with hyper-inflation, social unrest and internal friction. What does it mean in terms of the three social divisions presented in the 1960s?

(a) *The ethnic division*

Very important changes occurred in the role played by the ethnic division in Israeli politics – or, more precisely, by the second and third generations of Jews whose parents had immigrated to Israel from Asian and African countries. In 1965, Jews of oriental extraction accounted for about 47 per cent of the population,[12] compared to 46 per cent of Western extraction. The remaining 7 per cent were Israelis – themselves and their fathers born in Israel. In 1985, the ratio was 43 per cent 'orientals'; 38 per cent 'Westerners' and 19 per cent 'Israelis'. The majority of the 'orientals' in 1985 were born in Israel to an immigrant father. They number close to a million people and their average age is lower than that of the rest of the population. They are the second and third generations of immigrants whose welfare, attitudes and political behaviour determine the present shape of Israeli society. This group is the product of the Israeli educational system, but their average level of schooling is still relatively low.

Table 11.3 Years of schooling: Jews born in Israel aged 14+, by father's place of birth (1985)

	Years of schooling					
	0	1–8	9–12	13–15	16 +	Total
Father born in:						
Israel	0	8	64	18	10	100
Asia–Africa	1	13	72	10	3	100
Europe–America	0	4	50	25	21	100
Total Jewish population	1	9	63	17	10	100

Source: CBS, *Statistical Abstract of Israel* 37 (1986) 567.

Table 11.3 shows, first of all, that compulsory education has granted 1–8 years of schooling for everybody, and secondary education for the great majority. However, the gap is still very disturbing. Only 13 per cent of the 'orientals' attain higher education, compared to 46 per cent of the 'Westerners' and an average of 27 per cent for the total Israeli-born population. Furthermore, if we look at the figures five years earlier, the percentage of 'orientals' to reach the universities was only 10 per cent compared to 40 per cent of the 'Westerners' and an average of 24 per cent for the total population.[13] Accordingly, even though there has been an impressive advance in the 'stock of schooling' among Israeli-born 'orientals', the average gap between them and the 'Westerners' has increased, even in the 1980s.

The same pattern can be discerned when we compare occupation distribution by the father's continent of birth. Israelis whose father was born in Asia–Africa have advanced into professional, administrative, scientific and academic occupations, but their 'westerner' counterparts have done so more rapidly.[14]

What is the meaning of the figures that point to an increasing education and occupational gap? They do not tell the entire story. Well hidden behind the averages are some important changes. First, a small elite of Israeli-born 'orientals' has been 'making it' into Israeli society both in terms of education and occupation. Those figures are difficult to come by, but they are quite apparent in institutions of higher education and workplaces. Second, many of these 'orientals' have joined not only the middle class, but also the relatively wealthy part of it – as construction managers, commercial dealers and shop owners. Again, we do not have the relevant figures on income distribution to substantiate this point. Third, the gap *within* the 'oriental' community has increased significantly and at a higher rate than the gap between Israeli-born orientals and 'Westerners'. In 1985, only 1 per cent of Israeli-born 'orientals' had no years of schooling at all, compared to 18 percent of 'orientals' born in Asia–Africa. This difference is partly responsible for the gap between the income levels of those two groups and in the future it will influence other occupational features.

'Something' has happened within the oriental community in the last twenty years and not only politically. One small part of the 'oriental' community advanced more rapidly than the 'Westerners', another part at the same rate, and a third part (which is much bigger than the first) less rapidly.

Generally speaking, the 'orientals' are now part of modern
Israeli society. Certain groups were left behind and the average
advance has been slowed down because of the relative disadvan-
tage of the non-Israeli-born 'orientals'. The significant fact,
however, is that once the door of social and economic mobility
has been opened to the 'oriental' elite, the chances are that the
next generation will use it even more successfully.

The above conclusion is based predominantly on my estimate
of what would be the consequences for the 'orientals' of their
political revolution that has taken place in the last decade. In
this period the oriental community has gained power, both as
voting citizens and as occupiers of positions in the political and
the economic elites.

The political revolt of many 'oriental' voters brought the Likud
into power in 1977. Note that they voted for an established party,
with an 'Ashkenazi' leader and with a middle-class 'liberal' party
as one of its components. They clearly did not vote for a more
radical, perhaps even alienated, ethnic party such as the 'Black
Panthers'. What the 'oriental' voters were striving for was to
become equal partners in Israeli society. In the 1981 elections,
the ethnic tension became explosive and even though it subsided
later, the tension is still there. 25 097 voters elected Kahane to
the Knesset in 1984, many of them 'orientals' from development
towns[15] – another extreme manifestation of the same phenomenon.

Is this an integration process through which the 'oriental'
community will gain its rightful place in Israeli society? Is this a
power struggle which is bound to produce more friction and
extremism? What is the probability of solving the ethnic problem
in the long run? One can only answer this with a few observa-
tions.[16]

First, the Israeli political system dominated by Mapai and
the Labour movement is responsible for raising the political
consciousness of the new immigrants, particularly those of
'oriental' origin. Within one generation, they and their
children were autonomous enough to decide that they did not
want Labour in government any more, and brought in Likud
instead.

Second, the strengthened Likud is both a result and a cause
of this change. It captured the support of those who felt 'outsiders'
in Israeli society; this contributed a great deal to the sense of

belonging and to the political standing of the 'oriental' community, both subjectively and objectively.

Third, this political 'revolution' is probably the most significant response to the ethnic gap that still exists in most aspects of life in Israel. Once Israelis of 'oriental' origin penetrate the political elite as equals, there is a very good chance that the rest will follow.

Finally, the upward mobility of the 'orientals' is the most important social change in Israel in the last twenty years. However, it coincided with the revival of religious fundamentalism and the appearance of chauvinistic nationalism – led by certain parts of the 'Western' community. A few populist leaders and movements did not hesitate to foment racial tension and under the guise of Jewish religion or nationalism, feelings against Arabs reached an unprecedented level of antagonism.

(b) *Religious divisions*

The three religious parties reached their high point of electoral success in the early 1960s when together they won about 14–15 per cent of the vote. In 1981, together with the new 'Traditional Movement' (Tami) and in 1984, with the addition of the 'Sephardic Torah Guardians' (Shas) they attained only 11–12 per cent. So in those twenty years the religious parties have lost one fifth of their 'net' political power in the Knesset. At the same time, it is commonly believed in Israel that 'religion' was weak in the 1960s and is very strong now, because of the position of the religious parties in the government coalitions. It enables them to ensure the passage of more religious laws, obtain more financial support for religious institutions, and so on. No one has proved, however, that there is also more religious observance. This apparent paradox points out to a profound change that has taken place in the last twenty years in the role of religion in Zionism. It has had two manifestations: the rise of the non-Zionist orthodoxy and the new extremely nationalistic interpretation of the State of Israel by religious Zionists. We shall discuss here the latter development only.

In the early state period, the religious parties, particularly the NRP, sank into the mire of coalition politics as Mapai's constant partners in government. The NRP younger generation became increasingly dissatisfied and blamed the party for the fact that the religious camp had not occupied a leading position in the

Zionist *epos* – in the underground movements, illegal immigration, the War of Independence and statehood. Thus a real opposition of young religious leaders emerged within the religious camp. It might have ended up merely as another group within the faction-ridden NRP had it not been for the Six-Day War, which produced in one stroke a rare combination of historical and mythical elements: a miraculous military victory, holy places, new 'frontiers' and historic lands in *Eretz Israel*. Here, finally, a cure for the malady of the young generation of religious Israelis was found. This change within the religious camp began in 1967, but the Yom Kippur War was even more important. The war that took Israel by surprise was perceived as a heavenly omen, and led to the creation of *Gush Emunim* and the emphasis upon 'redemption Zionism' – i.e., politics wearing the mantle of messianism. As a result, the 'religious camp' as we knew it up to 1967 is no more. 'Religion' has become intricately involved with the future of the state and in this respect some religious groups have become more integrated into Israeli society.

First, the religious parties, particularly the NRP, were the crucial factor that enabled the Likud to form a government in 1977 and to stay in power (or share it) for over a decade.

Second, in the 1980s 'religion' has more direct influence on Israeli society and politics than ever before. The most extreme example is the appearance of an underground religious movement. When some of its members killed innocent Arabs in the name of religious motives, Israel was shaken to its moral and ethical foundations.

Unlike the previous cleavage, this one shows no indication of disappearing even in the long run.

(c) *Israeli Arabs*

The basic problem of the Israeli Arabs – being a minority within a state that strives to be 'Jewish' – has not changed as a result of the 1967 war. Yet the question of the future of the occupied territories involved Israeli Arabs and made them the litmus test of Israeli democracy. Economically, many Israeli Arabs enjoyed the growth of the post-1967 era and suffered from the stagnation and the inflation afterwards. Yet, politically two conflicting phenomena took place.

The first was the emergence of a new generation of Arab

leaders who began to fight for their rights within the rules of the democratic game. They joined existing parties, used their power as local representatives and organized various joint committees to make their political strength felt. The Arab vote in 1981 and 1984 points to internal conflict: more people who abstain and stay out completely; more voters who vote for an Arab–Jewish party (the Progressive List for Peace) or for the Labour Alignment to take advantage of their ability to influence Israeli politics.

Second, within the Jewish community, some extremists advocate the expulsion of Arabs from Israel; while some euphemistically refer to the state as a 'Jewish' or a 'Zionist Democracy'. Such sentiments seem to have influenced the Knesset decision in 1985 to amend the Basic Law: The Knesset to require allegiance from political parties to Israel 'as the State of the Jewish People'. Even though the amendment was introduced to balance another one requiring parties to refrain from 'racism', it shows insensitive usage of the Law for declarative purposes and attests not only to lack of tolerance toward a different minority, but also to a sense of insecurity among some Jews. More concretely, the cabinet majority decision of 17 May 1987 to grant army veterans reductions in university tuition fees (and thereby require Arab students – who do not serve in the Army – to pay higher fees) would have been a step toward making them second-class citizens – and was widely decried as leading to apartheid. The decision was dropped due to public and political opposition, but the damage was done by the encouragement given to extremist positions regarding the Arabs.

Thus, we find two opposing trends, compared to the 1960s. The Jewish community, over-extended by twenty years of occupation and weary of the long conflict with the Arabs, shows signs of withdrawal, insecurity and persecution. The Israeli Arab community, on the other hand, expresses more confidence in Israel's future and in their role as Israeli non-Jewish citizens in it. The most revealing fact in this connection is the existence of a majority among Israeli Arabs, on the one hand, for Israel's withdrawal to the pre-1967 borders and the establishment of a Palestinian state and, on the other, for seeking solutions to their problems within Israel.[17]

The problem of Arabs and Jews in one state cannot be solved in isolation from the regional conflict. But it does serve as a critical test for the Jewish community and for the viability of democratic values in Israel, precisely because the Arabs are different in almost every way.

Changes in the Political System

Was Israel more or less politically developed in the mid-1980s? Let us examine here again the same main features that were presented for the 1960s.

(a) There is less consensus in Israel regarding most issues, and no agreement at all about the future shape of the state. The divisions go beyond party politics or policy options. They reach all the way into the belief systems of individuals and groups in the society. The 1967 war reopened the old questions regarding the purposes of Zionism, the meaning of the state, and the boundaries. Moreover, disagreement 'invaded' the other older divisions in society – ethnic differences and the issue of national integration, the role of religion, the place of Arabs in an Israeli state and also Israel's relationship with the Jewish Diaspora. Once the fundamental consensus on this plane was eroded it also affected the political system and its ability to function through coalitions, compromises and accommodation.

(b) What has remained of the previous 'political camps' is their organizational framework, particularly the Histadrut. In the post-1967 period, the trend toward freeing society from the all-encompassing grip of the pre-state 'camps' has been almost completed. Yet these 'camps' still define the main electoral alternatives for the voters: the Labour Alignment, the conservative Likud and the religious parties. Ideological differences exist in external affairs or in attitudes towards the Arabs, but in internal affairs this trinity does not reflect the real opinions in the society of the 1980s.

(c) Israeli society is still highly politicized, but in the last twenty years one critical change has taken place – namely, in the relationship between government and society and in the power of the 'secondary centres'. These are still relatively strong, yet the network as a whole has lost its centralized character. In the mid-1980s, we find new powerful economic organizations, social groups, voluntary organizations and all kinds of pressure groups. They are not affiliated as before; they represent new interests in their respective fields, and act independently. There are also indicators of corporatism in Israeli society and politics and, to be sure, there are many weak groups which find it extremely difficult to gain a share in public resources. But the system as a whole is less closed, particularly for the Israeli-born generations, and it is in this sense more democratic.

In the two decades since the 1967 war, the role of the parties in Israel has weakened considerably. The dominating Mapai–Alignment was replaced by Herut–Likud in 1977 and 1981, but no party dominates the system any more. The elections put Herut at the head of the coalitions, but the absence of a 'pivot party'[18] proved to be a recipe for instability.[19] For example, for the support of the Camp David Accords and the peace treaty with Egypt votes outside the coalition were needed. The National Unity cabinet, formed by the two major parties in 1984, is a testimony to the breakdown of the old ways of 'doing politics'; it is no more than a temporary, *ad hoc* mechanism.

(d) The Executive, even in the days of Golda Meir's premiership (1969–74) became weak, and more clearly so after the 1973 war. The vacuum created in the centre of the Israeli political system was not filled – as some had feared – by the bureaucracy. Part of the slack was taken up by non-governmental bodies, but the main result has been a considerable weakening of central steering capacity.

(e) The judiciary (and particularly the Supreme Court and the special quasi-judicial Inquiry Commissions) has been required to exercise much closer control over the executive branch. In fact, in many instances the judiciary took over some decision-making functions. It was a decision of the High Court of Justice in 1969 that ensured that TV broadcasting on the Sabbath was permitted; in 1979 that dismantled the Elon Moreh settlement in the occupied territories; and in 1986 that forced the government to institute daylight saving in Israel. The list is long, and if we include the frequent use of Commissions of Inquiry, we must conclude that the judiciary, as a result of the weakening of both the executive and central government, has been called upon to exercise considerable power in Israeli society and politics. We find in the 1980s much more committed participation and voluntary political activity on the part of individual Israeli citizens and groups. The system is more open, politics in general is more fluid and opportunities are more genuine. No change has taken place in the high election turnout or party membership, but we find changes in other aspects of participation, such as direct involvement of citizens in election campaigns; the increased activities of pressure groups and voluntary grass-roots organizations; and the much higher number of political demonstrations.

In short, what we see is a rather confused picture. The change of government in 1977 was an upheaval in Israeli politics. Given that, it is surprising to note, ten years later, how relatively little has actually changed. No real transformation occurred in the way Israel conducts politics. Moreover, the Likud has been trying to do what Mapai used to do in the 1950s and both parties, once they became partners in the 1984 unity government, engaged in unprecedented division of the 'spoils'. No major reform has occurred in the Israeli political system in the last two decades, the only exception being the 1975 law according to which the heads of local authorities are elected directly. It was implemented for the first time in the 1978 local elections and has brought a great number of new faces to Israeli politics and eventually to the Knesset and the cabinet.

Otherwise the political system has not developed much in the last two decades. The change of the ruling party in 1977 – in itself a significant and maturing step – resulted in transient narrow-based cabinets, or temporary solutions such as the National Unity cabinet. Furthermore, the period after 1973 has been characterized by political instability and lack of government steering capacity.

The list of the 'system's' blunders is long and well known: the 1973 war, high-level corruption discovered during Rabin's premiership, illegal activities of the West Bank settlers and the discovery of a Jewish underground, the war in Lebanon, hyper-inflation, corruption in acquisition of land in the West Bank, the conduct of the secret security services and the Pollard affair.

There is also a short list of achievements – the peace with Egypt on top of it, followed by the withdrawal from Lebanon and the curbing of inflation. It is easy, and tempting, to divide the responsibility among parties and leaders, but the cause seems to be more general: Israel has not found a collective answer to the entirely new circumstances created by the 1967 war. The result has been a stalemate and it does not matter whether the 'voting public' or the lack of leadership are responsible for that. The incapacity to make decisions has halted the country in its tracks in both external and internal affairs.

Is there anything wrong with that? Why not regard it as a prolonged state of transition? The problem is that the decisions that must be made now are of the same magnitude as those in 1947–9, which were, then, to accept partition, establish the state, fight the War of Independence and sign the ceasefire agreements. Instead, the political system is practically paralyzed, capable only of making terrible mistakes. Moreover, inertia and indecision have become a threat to Israeli democracy itself.

We noted the important opening up of Israeli society, including increased political mobility, particularly within parts of the 'oriental' community. However, dangers in the development of Israeli democracy have also been exposed during this period. The more formal institutional side of democracy – what could be called the rules of the game – has remained more or less intact. Elections to the Knesset and local authorities have been held regularly; no-one could possibly complain about a lack of parties to choose from; the 1977 transition of power took place smoothly; the press is generally free, and so on. But the other components of democracy – individual and civil rights as a *sine qua non*, civic-mindedness, respect for the law and equality before the law – are still problematic.

One could argue that in light of Israel's external and security problems, it is amazing that even the rules of the democratic game have been observed, but that is cold comfort. As we have pointed out, Israeli society has modernized in many respects and become more 'democratic' in terms of opportunities, access to resources and citizens' participation. Yet the long impasse in the ability of democratic institutions to act decisively, and the recurrence of 'blunders' have taken their toll. Israeli democracy too is hobbling along, and despite the relatively long practice of democracy, democratic values are not sufficiently ingrained in this new society. Even the formal rules and institutions have been occasionally imperilled, as parties, groups and Knesset members have engaged in assaults on the law, while opinion polls reveal a loss of faith in the democratic system, particularly among younger people.[20] For some people in Israel, democracy means *only* certain rules, and they are willing very easily to change these rules to advance their religious, national or any other goal. The potential threat to Israeli democracy stems from a sense of disorientation – a feeling of insecurity that may lead first to frustration and then to xenophobia, racism and all other escapes from demands of rationality.

There are opposite forces at work too and – as noted – in certain respects Israel has become more democratic. Yet some basic attitudes – towards individual and civil rights and equality – leave much to be desired.

THE BROKEN PATH

None of the points discussed in this chapter are 'proof' in themselves that a change has taken place or that it was 'caused' by the 1967 or 1973 wars. The general point here is entirely different: the 1967 war, the occupation and the preoccupation with its aftermath have contributed to a broken path in Israel's social and political development. What would have happened otherwise is not relevant. When we compare the broad features of Israel, twenty years apart, we see a five-year period (1967–73) that wedged itself into the previous flow of development and trends. Historically, one cannot say that it was an intentional intervention, because the Six-Day War was not of Israel's making. Nevertheless, the period after the war signifies a choice. Certain groups regarded the 1967 war as a step on the way to redemption, and the 1973 war as birth pangs of reviving the homeland. Once this viewpoint was not forcefully counterbalanced and became the 'unofficial' official policy, impasse was inevitable. Accordingly, the idea that what had happened in the pre-state formative years of Zionism should be a guide to the present and future is not just an anachronism; it is responsible for the break that occurred in Israel's path of development. The economic, social and political changes presented above illustrate this point very well.

The economy was probably on the verge of take-off in the pre-1967 recession. However, the sharp five-year expansion was probably too strong and rather imbalanced.[21] Israel's economy has experienced a continuous fall since 1973.[22] The two-digit *monthly* inflation that followed can be attributed to government mismanagement of the economy, but the increase in the defence burden and the external debt and the unprecedented dependency on the USA are direct results of the wars.

No one knows what would have happened to the internal divisions in Israeli society under different circumstances. For instance, the demands of 'oriental' Jews for greater equality began before 1967, and would have continued anyhow. Moreover, this process of social change has been accelerated by the post-1967 economic boom, and particularly by the Likud takeover. However, the chauvinistic twist of this process and the association of some 'oriental' Jews with extreme positions are an unfortunate result of the prolonged occupation. It is also the cause of the appearance of a few groups which represent a very dangerous combination: romantic territorialism and religious fanaticism.

What would have happened to the political system? We emphasized its volatile shape in the post-Ben-Gurion era. A slow process of change had begun, with new blocs on the left and on the right and the appearance of the first 'native' Israeli party in the 1965 elections. All of this was stopped and overshadowed by the spectacular military victory and the economic prosperity which followed. It caused a temporary reconstruction of the old political system under the leadership of the Labour elite. It was shaken after 1973, but lingered on until 1977. Again, because of the wars, developments took a different turn, and – given the situation today – probably a wrong turn.

The major decisions of both the Zionist movement and the State of Israel up to 1967 were characterized by the existence of enormous external constraints and the need to find loopholes through which the Zionist dream could be advanced and – later – the state defended. The options – even in the early state period – were very narrow indeed. In 1967 a major change occurred when for the first time Israel was in a position to define the broad options, or at least their range. Moreover, it could for the first time concentrate more on its domestic development: economy, society and politics. Instead, there has been a flight from the need to devote more energies to internal affairs and from taking difficult decisions in these areas. Under the false banner of 'new frontiers' in the occupied territories, twenty years of the potential use of the collective national energy have been wasted.

The ultimate balance of this period in Israel's history is unknown yet. There have been advances in certain areas and potential positive changes in many others. The stalemate and incapacity to take decisions on the most crucial external issue has halted the country in its progress. If a drastic change takes place in the near future with regard to the occupied territories, perhaps those twenty years will be remembered as a tremendous collective learning experience.

Notes

1. 'Wars' usually imply crossing the previous cease-fire lines. Hence most people will speak about the 'five wars' during the state period: (1948–9, 1956, 1967, 1973 and 1982) and occasionally add the 'War of Attrition' (1969–70), and the 'Litani Operation' (1978).
2. The Wadi Salib 'riot' began with a spontaneous demonstration in May 1959 by immigrants from Morocco living in a slum in Haifa. It turned into acts of violence and spread to other North African communities in other cities. The leader was arrested and sentenced to a short prison term. Subsequently a party was formed. It ran in the 1959 Knesset elections and failed to obtain the required 1 per cent minimum.
3. See Itzhak Galnoor, *Steering the Polity: Communication and Politics in Israel* (Santa Monica, 1982) 123–57.
4. See Itzhak Galnoor, 'Transformations in the Israeli Political System since the Yom Kippur War', in A. Arian (ed.), *The Elections in Israel 1977* (Jerusalem, 1980) 119–48.
5. Galnoor, *Steering the Polity*, 295–6.
6. In 1954, while Pinhas Lavon was Minister of Defence, a foiled Israeli intelligence operation ('the mishap') in Egypt resulted in death sentences for two Egyptian Jews and long imprisonment for several others. The question: 'Who gave the order?' – Lavon or a senior intelligence officer – remained unanswered despite numerous hearings and inquiries. In 1960, Lavon demanded that his name be cleared, and the matter quickly deteriorated into a major crisis involving all parts of the political system. The Mapai party removed Lavon as secretary-general of the Histadrut; Ben-Gurion resigned from the cabinet; and the Knesset was dissolved and early elections were held (August 1961). Ben-Gurion's decision to leave his party and form a new one in the 1965 elections are also related to the Lavon affair.
7. In 1965 and 1966 there were close to 300 strikes annually compared to an average of about 100 in the preceding years, Central Bureau of Statistics (CBS), *Statistical Abstract of Israel* 12 (1961) 391 and 31 (1980) 348.
8. S. A. Eisenstadt, *Israeli Society* (London, 1967) 357.
9. E. Berglas, *Defense and the Economy: The Israeli Experience* (Jerusalem: The Maurice Falk Institute for Economic Research in Israel, 1983) 51–3.
10. In 1968–72 the GNP *per capita* grew annually by 8.5 per cent (!) compared with a decline of ((-) 1.4 per cent) in 1967–8 and an increase of only 1 per cent in 1973–4.
11. Alex Mintz, 'The Military–Industrial Complex: American Concept and Israeli Realities', *Journal of Conflict Resolution*, 29 (4) (December 1985) 623–39.
12. 'Extraction' means those born in the Diaspora, or whose father was born there.
13. CBS, *Statistical Abstract of Israel* 31 (1980) 519.
14. CBS, *Statistical Abstract of Israel* 37 (1986) 310–11 and 31 (1980) 328–9.

15. See CBS, *Results of the Election to the 11th Knesset* (Jerusalem, 1985) 30.
16. For a presentation of different approaches among Israeli scholars, see S. Smooha, 'Three Perspectives in the Sociology of Ethnic Relations in Israel', *Megamot*, 18 (2–3) (March, 1984) 195–201. (Hebrew).
17. S. Smooha, *The Orientation and Politicization of the Arab Minority in Israel* (Haifa, 1984) 166.
18. A 'pivot party' is one without which no coalition to its left or to its right can be formed. See I. Galnoor, 'The 1984 Elections in Israel', *Middle East Review*, 18 (Summer, 1986) 54.
19. I. Galnoor and A. Diskin, 'Political Distances and Parliamentary Control: The Knesset Debates on the Peace Agreements with Egypt', *State and Government*, 18 (Autumn, 1982) 5–26 (Hebrew).
20. See 'Opinion poll of young people positions' (Jerusalem: The Van Leer Institute, 1986).
21. For instance in the electronics industry. See M. Sarnat and H. Levi, *The Influence of the Six Day War on the Metal and Electronics Industry in Israel* (Jerusalem, 1973) (Hebrew).
22. Z. Sussman, *Israel's Economy: Performance, Problems and Policies* (London, 1986) 1.

12 Political Ideologies: From Consensus to Confrontation
Shlomo Avineri

Israel is a credal society. It was established as an expression of a political ideology – Zionism – founded on the modern quest for Jewish self-determination in the post-Emancipation era. While Zionism was never a uniform ideology but a set of belief-systems sometimes rather wide apart from each other – from Marxist-revolutionary Zionism to religious Zionism – its core has been the acceptance of the idea that the Jews are a nation and hence entitled to national self-determination and sovereignty in a country of their own.

The dramatic events of the Six-Day War appeared to have vindicated not only the ability of that ideology to maintain itself in the world of power politics but also seemed to have added to its legitimacy. While in the Arab world the defeat of 1967 cast a shadow on the political efficacy of the secular Arab nationalism of the Nasserite type, in Israel profound changes in the national self-understanding of the Israelis took place.

This chapter will try to focus on three changes which have characterized the development of ideology in Israel in the post-1967 period. Two relate to the Jewish population of the country, and the third refers to ideological developments among the Israeli Arab population. The first issue deals with the ideological realignment in Israel, the second with the developments within religious Zionism, which have considerable consequences for the wider political spectrum of Israeli ideology, and the third refers to a restored feeling of Palestinian nationalism among Israeli Arabs. Observers usually focus on developments within the Jewish community in Israel, but developments among Israeli Arabs cannot be divorced from the overall picture.

THE REALIGNMENT OF LEFT AND RIGHT

The first development has to do with a general transformation of the terms of the political debate in Israel, and even with a certain redefinition of the terms 'left' and 'right' within that debate. Between 1948 and 1967, the Israeli political debate revolved around several issues: a 'neutralist' or pro-Western orientation in international affairs; *laissez-faire* v. a mixed economy with social-democratic hegemony; an extreme anti-German attitude, growing out of the impact of the Holocaust, against a willingness to entertain the possibility of forming relations with a 'new' Germany; an activist defence policy, epitomized by David Ben-Gurion, or a more accommodationist policy, formulated by Moshe Sharett; the Lavon Affair, etc. One issue which was central to the political debate within the Jewish *Yishuv* (community) in the late 1930s and the 1940s – the debate about partition – was over. The armistice lines of 1949 were considered by practically all Israelis as the realistic definite borders of Israel. If, prior to 5 June 1967, the Arab countries had been ready to sign a peace agreement with Israel on the basis of the existing frontiers, there would have been an overwhelming Israeli consensus in favour of accepting this, perceiving this Arab readiness as a major concession and a tremendous achievement for Israel. With very few exceptions on the lunatic fringe of Israeli politics, there was no irredentist call in Israel during the period of 1949–67, advocating an Israeli initiative to recapture Judea and Samaria, or even the Old City of Jerusalem.

This post-1948 consensus was visible across the spectrum of Israeli politics. Within the Labour movement, it was seen as the major achievement of the pragmatism of Mapai, which was able to wrest a state for the remnants of the Jewish people out of the debris of the Second World War because it had the wisdom and the practical ability of combining vision with realism. The Herut party was obviously less sanguine about this, but even it relegated its erstwhile irredentist calls for an *Eretz Israel* 'on both banks of the Jordan' to symbolical incantations devoid of practical consequences. When pressed under questioning as to how they could live with a 'truncated' Israel which did not control the Old City of Jerusalem and the 'Triangle' (as Judea and Samaria were then called), Herut leaders would sometimes reply that one should also leave something for the Messiah. The loss of access to the Old City and the Wailing Wall even gave rise to a negative theology: more than one Israeli argued in the 1948–67 period that there might have been some symbolism in the loss of access to the Wailing Wall precisely at the time when Israel regained its independence and sovereignty. So long as the people of Israel were stateless and powerless, the Wailing Wall served as a legitimate focus for their hopes for redemption; once they had regained independence, the symbol of destruction, exile and wailing might not be needed any more. 1967 – which brought with it Israeli control over the West Bank and Gaza, coupled with a universal feeling of redemptive deliverance, associated with Mordechai Gur's (subsequently Chief of Staff of the Israel Defence Forces) historical exclamation 'Har ha-Bayit be-yadeinu' ('The Temple Mount is in our hands') – has subtly but profoundly changed all this. The debate over partition between the Labour and Liberal wings of Zionism on the one hand, and the Revisionists on the other, has been reopened. With one difference: if in the 1930s this was a debate about an ultimate political goal, a desideratum – at a time when Jewish sovereignty did not yet exist and hence did not control even one square inch of *Eretz Israel* – the debate after 1967 was being conducted against the background of Israel's astounding victories, of Arab intransigence and of Palestinian terrorism – and, last but not least, of effective Israeli control over the totality of *Eretz Israel* west of the Jordan river. Possession and the evocation of historical and biblical associations ('We have returned' was a phrase constantly reiterated by such diverse people as Moshe Dayan and Naomi Shemer, a popular songwriter strongly attached to nationalist themes) had a powerful impact on the national mood and the psychological map of the country as it evolved in the political consciousness of the post-1967 days.

What appeared to have been closed in 1948–9 by the dual impact of the acceptance on the part of Israel of the UN partition resolution and the outcome of the War of Independence, became once more an open question. The national consensus that Israel had to be defended, and defended at all cost, from within its 1949 borders, was broken and for the first time since Independence the question of the Israeli boundaries was reopened. While there was virtually no dissenting voice regarding the reunification of Jerusalem, the future disposition of the West Bank and Gaza became the focus for the most acrimonious and divisive debate in Israel since its inception. For the debate is not only about policies, it is about the boundaries of the polity itself. The emergence of new political organizations, from the Movement for Greater Israel and *Gush Emunim* to Peace

Now, revolves around the consequences for the nature of the Israeli commonwealth of a decision on the status of the West Bank and Gaza.

The debate over the future of the West Bank and Gaza has, of course, a number of aspects and the security aspect of that debate is naturally very prominent. Yet security is not the only – or even dominant – issue. Security issues are central to Israeli–Egyptian relations, as they are with regard to Israel's policies along the Lebanese border. Yet they never became the focus of a soul-wrenching debate, as the debate about the West Bank and the Palestinian issue have become. Moreover, it is clear that, by debating whether the area should be called 'Judea and Samaria' or 'West Bank', one is not discussing strategy or security, but an issue of profound ideological significance to Israel's understanding of itself. Similarly, by insisting that Jews have the *right* to settle in Judea and Samaria – not that this is important for strategic and security reasons – one is raising philosophical and ideological issues transcending merely pragmatic security considerations.

TERRITORIAL v. SOCIOLOGICAL SCHOOL

In this ideological debate, the best way to characterize the two approaches – that of the 'hawks' and 'doves' respectively – is to go beyond such simplistic labels. I would suggest labelling one approach (the Likud position) as 'territorial', and the other (the Labour approach) as 'sociological'.

The 'territorial' approach maintains that Israeli control over all areas of *Eretz Israel* is the dominant consideration which should determine Israel's attitude to the question of borders. These areas – Judea, Samaria and Gaza – are an inalienable part of the historical Land of Israel (hence the insistence on calling them by their Hebrew historical names), and should therefore remain an integral part of the Jewish homeland. The Palestinian Arab population should, at best, be granted personal autonomy to run its municipal, educational, religious and cultural institutions, but territorial control should be retained by Israel: the Israeli army and police should remain responsible for external and internal security; public lands should remain under Israeli control (and thus provide a reservoir for Jewish settlements); Israel should retain the right to settle Jews in the areas in question; and it should preserve mineral and water rights in the territories.

The sociological school – the Labour party and its allies – on the other hand, maintains that Israel's national agenda should be determined by considerations of social structure, not territorial control. For the sociological school, the question is not one of historical rights derived from the past but of the future social nature of the Jewish polity. Here the sociological school maintains that a larger Israel, including the West Bank and Gaza, will be a less Jewish and less Zionist state than a smaller Israel more or less within the pre-1967 boundaries (although including East Jerusalem, about which there is no debate). This larger Israel, the sociological school maintains, will include the 1.2 million Palestinian Arabs of the territories which, together with the Arab population of Israel proper, would mean a country with an Arab minority of 40 per cent of the total population. A smaller Israel, on the other hand, which could be brought about were Israel to find partners for a compromise over the West Bank and Gaza, would have an Arab minority of approximately 17 per cent and would thus be more Jewish and more Zionist. The sociological school is aware of the paradox presented by these choices but argues that were Israel to retain control over the West Bank and Gaza, it would either have to extend full civil and political rights to the Palestinian population resident there, or keep it in perpetual non-citizenship status. In the first case, Israel would become a binational state; in the second, a mini-South Africa. neither of these options is what the Zionist dream is about and hence the sociological school looks for partners – Jordan, moderate Palestinians – to work out a compromise under which Israel would be able to guarantee its security interests while getting rid of its control over 1.2 million Palestinians whose very presence under Israeli rule would, according to the sociological school, subvert both the Jewish and the democratic nature of the Israeli body politic.

Moreover, the term 'left-wing' in pre-1967 Israel usually meant that one was pro-Histadrut and a supporter of the welfare state and a mixed economy with a strong public sector; to be 'right-wing' usually meant to be anti-Histadrut, pro-*laissez-faire*, etc. In other words, 'left' and 'right' were usually understood in terms of the socioeconomic debate over domestic policies. Since 1967, being 'left-wing' is understood as being opposed to the annexation of the West Bank and Jewish settlements in these areas, and favouring some sort of territorial accommodation or compromise, either with the

Jordanians or Palestinians; being 'right-wing' is now understood as supporting the retention of the West Bank and Gaza and the policy of creating Jewish settlements in these areas and opposing any compromise with the Palestinians. 'Left' and 'right' have become terms connoting one's stance in the national debate, not the social one.

The changed terms of the political debate also altered the relative relevance of the positions of the 'left' and 'right' for the Israeli electorate. Before 1967, the 'left' and 'right' for the Israeli electorate. Before 1967, the 'left' – i.e. mainly Mapai and later the Labour party - were perceived as addressing the immediate issues of Israeli life: defence, immigration, Ingathering of the Exiles, development of the country and the integration of new immigrants. And though Labour was far from successful in tackling all of these issues adequately at the same time, the national agenda was nonetheless determined by the priorities and ideological matrix articulated by the Labour party and its allies. The right-wing – mainly Herut – appeared as if marching to a different drummer: if it made noises (as it did less and less over the years) about the 'lost territories', such lamentations and exhortations about divine rights to Jericho or Jenin did not help a new immigrant, be he from Rumania or Iraq, who still had difficulties finding his way from Tel Aviv to Haifa.

If Herut branded as shameful Labour's policy of accepting reparations from Germany, this did not really go very far with immigrants who knew that some of their chances of making it in the old-new land depended at least partially on these funds. Moreover, Herut's historiographical exercises about who 'really kicked the British out' appeared as quite esoteric to a population that had other, and no less vital, issues to confront in the here and now, and if the Histadrut's bureaucracy was not always exactly loved by all newcomers (or, for that matter, old-timers) it was still a powerful, omnipresent reality which did, after all, help people find a livelihood and supplied housing and medical services. Herut's anti-Histadrut rhetoric was a poor substitute for that overpowering reality, insensitive as it sometimes appeared to some of the susceptibilities of the newcomers, yet extremely efficient in its catering for immediate problems.

After 1967, and with the relative affluence which was shared by all Israelis – albeit not always equally distributed – the new reality transformed Herut's (the Likud's) rhetoric: Hebron, Bethlehem and Jericho were no longer faraway names, embedded in a mystical past, but real, accessible and hallowed with the glory of recent Israeli victories. By addressing itself to these issues, the Likud was referring to deeply-felt emotions and ideas symbolizing the continuity of Jewish life in the Land of Israel. By embarking on a settlement effort in Judea and Samaria, the Likud (and *Gush Emunim*) were also appropriating for the right the traditional symbols of left-wing Zionism – pioneering *halutziut* and work on the land.

The contrast growth of the Israeli parties of the right after 1967 – and after 1973 – has also changed the Israeli party system from a multi-party system with one hegemonic party (Mapai/Labour) to a virtual two-party system with the small religious parties in the middle, without any one party ever enjoying the preponderance and dominance that Labour traditionally enjoyed in the past. Likud may at the moment be on the decline (the zenith of its power *vis-à-vis* Labour was 1977, and it has since then decreased constantly in electoral appeal), but even if Labour were to win a clear plurality in a forthcoming election it would still be faced with a right-wing party of comparable size such as it never faced prior to 1967. The unquestioned role of a dominant party – which Labour enjoyed prior to 1967 and which guaranteed that it would lead every government coalition, as no alternative coalition was not feasible – is not very likely to return. The rise of the Likud was certainly helped by the protest vote of the immigrants from Middle Eastern countries, but without the message which related to the retention of Judea and Samaria this protest would have amounted to empty rhetoric: for the first time since 1948, 1967 gave the Likud's rhetoric substance and relevance.

CHANGES WITHIN RELIGIOUS ZIONISM

A second, and parallel, development occurred within the religious parties, and mainly within the National Religious Party (NRP). This party, the historical descendant of Mizrahi and Hapoel Hamizrahi, has been since 1948 (and even before) the traditional political ally of Mapai and Labour. This apparently incongruous alliance between Labour Zionists and Religious Zionists gave all Israeli governments between 1948 and 1977 their internal cohesion and political sense: all had at their core the Mapai–NRP alliance, with the occasional addition of some of the other centrist or left-wing parties (General Zionists on the one hand, Mapam on the other). What appeared as incongruous had an inner rationale, deriving from the ambivalence of Religious Jews over Zionism. Religious Zionism, as it emerged in the Mizrahi movement, was a pragmatic compromise between the traditional Jewish orthodox suspicion of what might be classified as false messianism (which is the way Zionism appeared, and still appears, to many orthodox Jews), and a realistic assessment that the rebuilding of the Land of Israel was an effort to which religious Jews could not remain indifferent. This delicate balance, epitomized in Rabbi Abraham Isaac Kook's dialectical understanding of Zionism (even in its socialistic, and sometimes atheistic, formulations), enabled the NRP to become a partner with Labour in a pragmatic effort to secure a haven for the Jews in the here and now, without identifying that political, man-made effort with the coming of the Messiah. Hence the NRP was able to distinguish between its support for a non-militant effort at nation-building, and the messianic hope which remained directed towards an other-worldly total redemption. In short, the State of Israel for the NRP was not yet the messianic redemption, though it could be obliquely referred to as 'the beginning of the growth of our Redemption' ('reshit tzemihat ge'ulatenu'), in the delphic language of the special prayer introduced after 1948 on behalf of the State of Israel.

Politically, this meant that the NRP was on the 'doveish', not the 'hawkish' side of Israeli politics. Throughout the 1950s and early 1960s, the NRP not only followed a line of close co-operation with Labour, but usually sided with the more moderate approach within Labour (as during the Ben-Gurion/Sharett controversy). In the crisis preceding the Six-Day War, the NRP leader, Moshe Haim Shapiro, supported the inclusion of Moshe Dayan in the Cabinet because he saw in his presence the best guarantee that Israel would *not* have to go to war: only a strong Cabinet, not weakened by what appeared as the vacillations of the Eshkol government, could withstand the populist pressure to fight.

The consequences, we know, were different, and 1967 has transformed the NRP from a moderate 'dovish' party to the spearhead of the Israeli settlement efforts in the West Bank. That this development, resulting in the emergence of *Gush Emunim* out of the more militant wing of the NRP, had to do with generational changes within the party itself (the 'Young Turks' of Zebulun Hammer and Yehuda Ben-Meir against the veteran, moderate wing of Moshe Haim Shapiro and later Joseph Burg) forms, of course, part of the background to the story. But, in addition, this younger leadership now had a slogan and a motivating idea which it lacked before 1967 and which was provided by the events of May and June. Neither could one discount the fact that, for religious Jews, what appeared as the wondrous salvation of the Six-Day War could not have occurred without divine intervention in the course of human affairs. The symbolical meaning of the liberation of the Old City, the Temple Mount and the Wailing Wall – events that stirred the heart of every Israeli witnessing them – had for religious people the added significance of a supernatural message, connected with the divine scheme of things. Israel and its military feats for the first time became connected with a theodicy, with the project of a millennial divine redemption: the 'beginning of the growth of our Redemption' turned into the Redemption itself. For the first time since the rise of modern Zionism, religious Zionism found itself on the militant and maximalist side of the Zionist spectrum, freed from its ambivalence over Zionism and its marginal status in its realization. Religious Zionism, for the first time since Herzl, began to set the tone of the national agenda, and not just clamour for more funds for religious schools or interfere with the life of the secular population with restrictive demands concerning the sabbath and dietary laws. As some *Gush Emunim* activists were later to say, it was no longer shameful to be religious within the Zionist camp, it had become a source of pride.

This shift in the political position of the NRP meant that the internal balance which had given Labour a pliant and comfortable ally against onslaughts from the right began to be upset. In the 1967–70 National Unity government (which included Menachem Begin as Minister Without Portfolio), an internal coalition between the NRP, the Likud and Moshe Dayan, created a new political configuration very different from the conventional Israeli political map of 1948–67. The NRP was no longer automatically supporting the more moderate policies of Labour, but became the most outspoken exponent of the views of the Movement for Greater Israel. The weak Labour-led coalition of Yitzhak Rabin, which had the arduous and thankless task of rebuilding Israeli military strength and morale after the Yom Kippur War, found itself, on a number of issues (like the illegal *Gush Emunim* attempt to put up a settlement at Sebastia) at the mercy of a 'hawkish' NRP. Rabin's misguided attempt to oust the NRP from the government and call early elections in the winter of 1976–7 was motivated by the attempt to weaken this pressure from the right. It misfired badly, and the election results of 1977 only consolidated the new Likud–NRP alliance which now became the cornerstone of Menachem Begin's first coalition government. And while today the

NRP is going through a number of complicated processes (prodded, no doubt, by its loss of many of its voters to the Likud because of its rightward swing), it certainly is no longer the moderate party which was once the guarantor of Labour's ability to form centre-left governments. The NRP may again in the future become a partner for a Labour-led coalition, but it will certainly exact a price in terms of a right-wing tilt from such a government with regard to the West Bank. Here, as well as in the general ideological and political map of Israel, 1967 has deeply changed the way in which ideologies have their impact on politics and modes of thinking in the country (and, incidentally, among world Jewry as well).

'PALESTINIANIZATION' OF THE ISRAELI ARABS

The third development relates to a political community which is marginal to the Israeli body politic and whose position within it has always been ambiguous: the community of Israeli Arabs, who make up about 17 per cent of the population of Israel proper (this does not include the Palestinian Arab population on the West Bank and Gaza who do not participate in the Israeli political structure). These Arabs, concentrated mainly in the Galilee and along the old Israeli armistice line with Jordan, are a heterogeneous group: most of them are Muslims, with a minority of Christians and Druze. This is the remnant of the old Palestinian Arab population in these areas, and is made up of those Arabs who did not flee or were not uprooted by the War of Independence of 1948.

It goes without saying that their position is, fundamentally, not an easy one: an Arab minority in a Jewish state constantly threatened by Arab countries and Arab armies has more than adequate reasons to feel ambivalent about its political allegiance and be looked at askance by the Jewish majority. But, despite this, and despite the fact that Israel's Arab citizens do not have to serve in the Israeli army, they are – and consider themselves to be – citizens of Israel. They vote in national and municipal elections, enjoy the benefits of the Israeli welfare system (though they can catalogue a long list of basically justified complaints that the system occasionally does not work in their favour), and have an education system which allows them to educate their children from state funds in Arabic rather than in Hebrew and teach them Arab history and literature. A very sizeable proportion of Israeli Arab citizens have consistently voted over the years for the Israeli Communist party as one way of expressing their protest against the Jewish and Zionist nature of Israel, and the Communist Arab Members of Knesset have always been very prominent and active in utilizing the parliamentary system for the benefit of their constituents. The Communist party also controls many of the Arab municipalities and local councils, the most prominent case being their continuous control of City Hall in Nazareth for many years.

For all of their problems and uneasy situation, prior to 1967 the Israeli Arabs were developing as a breed apart, conscious of their Arabism yet destined to develop in a way different from other Arab communities, including the Palestinian community in the West Bank and the Arab countries. Immediately after 1967, some pious hopes were expressed in the Israeli political establishment that the Israeli Arabs might become a bridge between Israel and the larger Arab community, for here was a community which preserved its Arab culture and identity while living in peace with the Jewish state.

What happened after 1967 was a reverse of these aspirations: rather than having the Israeli Arabs project their relative integration into Israel as a hopeful sign for future co-existence, Israeli Arabs have become 'Palestinianized'. If, before 1967, politically conscious Israeli Arabs were proud to point to their dual identity as both Arabs and Israelis, today a triangular self-image is almost universally accepted among the educated classes of the Arab Israeli community: they are Israelis, Arabs and Palestinians. While before 1967 most political efforts on their part were aimed at securing equal opportunities and better conditions as citizens in Israel, today much of their political activity is aimed at securing political self-determination for the Palestinians in the West Bank and Gaza. Israeli Arabs have been careful – and so has the Israeli Communist party – to distinguish between themselves, as belonging to the Israeli body politic, and the Palestinians on the West Bank and Gaza. But some Israeli Arabs have moved to East Jerusalem so as to live 'in a more Arab environment'; many others serve as teachers in schools, colleges and universities on the West Bank, so that a constant process of osmosis between the two communities, severed in 1948, is taking place. No irredentist ideology has yet developed among Israeli Arabs, and their realism will probably prevent it from developing in the future. But their radicalization and rediscovery of their Palestinian identity is another of the dialectical outcomes of ideological shifts in Israel in the wake of the Six-Day War.

To sum up, 1967 has radicalized and polarized Israeli political ideologies, and the ideological spectrum of Israeli political life has moved from a consensual to a confrontational pattern. No other single event has had comparable impact on the development of political ideologies in Israel since the Six-Day War.

13 Religious Reactions: Testimony and Theology
Michael Rosenak

What is 'a religious reaction' to a startling historical event like the Six-Day War, so heavily laden with relief, gratitude and joy, yet bearing the imprint of perplexity and bereavement? I shall begin by relating four of the many comments and episodes that come to mind, snatches of speech that may suggest parameters for our discussion.

Who in Israel or in the world would have believed *that after a battle of 132 hours* Israel would have in its hands Jerusalem and the place of our sanctuary . . . all of Western Eretz Yisrael . . . all the Sinai Peninsula till the Suez Canal? It is all exactly written in the book of Joshua: 'And no man stood up to them of all their enemies . . . Nothing was lacking of all the good thing which the Lord had spoken . . .'

Master of the Universe: May this be an hour of mercy before You. Lest our spirits become arrogant and we say . . . 'Our strength and the might of our hands have wrought this great deed'. But let us know . . . that we have merited to live in an epoch in which God has returned to His people . . . And our very eyes have seen this.[1]

In the air hung a sense of great and holy hours. When I asked a fellow-soldier, a member of Kibbutz Sha'ar Ha'amakim, at the Rockefeller Museum, before the conquest of the Temple Mount, what have you got to say? He answered me with a verse from the Bible. 'I was glad when they said unto me, let us go to the house of the Lord. Our feet were standing in thy gates Jerusalem, Jerusalem, that is built as a city that is tied together'. The fellow smiled as he cited this verse. Maybe because it isn't fitting for a member of Hashomer Hatzair to speak thus. But I saw his eyes and I knew that that was what he felt.[2]

On [a certain] public occasion, in March 1967, I asked the following question: Would we (like Job) be able to say that the question of Auschwitz will be answered in any sense whatever in case the eclipse of God were ended and He appeared to us? An impossible and intolerable question.

Less than three months later, this purely hypothetical question had become actual, when at Jerusalem the threat of total annihilation gave way to sudden salvation, atheists spoke of miracles and hardboiled Western reporters resorted to Biblical images.

The question *is* impossible and intolerable. Even Job's question is not answered by God's presence, and to him children are restored. The children of Auschwitz will not be restored and the question of Auschwitz will not be answered by a saving divine presence.[3]

Peace in the world will not be built on the foundations of readiness to compromise . . . I maintain that if there will be concessions on Eretz Yisrael, there will also be concessions on peace in the world and the redemption of the world.[4]

Which of these qualify (or qualify more) as religious responses? Is a religious response only (or mainly) one of a religious person, articulating religious perceptions? Is it (also) a 'religiously heavy' statement or outburst, even when made by a 'secularist'? What is the status of a philosophical exploration, made in the wake of an historical happening? And what about an ideological pronouncement about the consequences of an event and its normative significance, made from a religious perspective?

In examining and clarifying these questions, we shall have recourse to two categories of response: *testimony*, spontaneous and unmediated, and *theology* – reflective, sometimes comprehensive, often ideological. The first type of response, that of testimony, takes us back to Independence Day 1967.

FROM INDEPENDENCE DAY TO *SHAVUOT* (PENTECOST) 1967: EXPERIENCE AND TESTIMONY

Each of us Jews knows how thoroughly ordinary he is: yet, taken together, we seem caught up in things great and inexplicable. It is almost as if we were not acting but being acted through . . . The number of Jews in the world is smaller than a small statistical error in the Chinese census. Yet . . . big things seem to happen around us and to us.[5]

In numerous articles, letters and conversations, Israeli and Diaspora Jews testified to acting and 'being acted through' in a drama that placed them, however temporarily, in a dimension of existence they had never known. This drama and dimension had something 'religious' about it, if only because routine secular assumptions appeared suddenly inadequate and trivial, and, for a while at least, religious experiences – even religious people – seemed more serious, as though they knew more about the mysterious Actor and His unfolding plot.

The drama may be said to have begun on Independence Day. It was then, on the evening of 14 May, that the news reached Israel of Egyptian forces on the move into the Sinai. That day, however, despite worry, the country was celebrating. The highlight of the holiday, as usual in those years, was a military parade, held at that year's Independence Day celebrations in Jerusalem. The parade was a small one, conscientiously held to the dimensions of men and equipment required by the demilitarized status of Jerusalem, a city distrustfully shared by Israel and Jordan. Thus the celebration highlighted the pain associated with Jerusalem, divided by a wall and largely inaccessible. On that same evening, at the annual Independence Day Song Festival, Jerusalem was again brought into consciousness, for a young singer, Shuli Natan, performed Naomi Shemer's new song, *Yerushalayim shel Zahav* (Jerusalem of Gold), a sentimental ballad of love and longing about the 'city that dwells abandoned and at whose heart stands a Wall'. None of the listeners suspected that, within a few short weeks, the song would become a kind of anthem, and that a new stanza would be added: 'We have returned . . . the Shofar is sounded on the Temple Mount'.

In retrospect, perhaps the most startling episode of testimony of that day took place in a Jerusalem *yeshiva*[6] *Mercaz Harav Kook*, established by the first Chief Rabbi of modern *Eretz Israel* and then headed by his only son, Rabbi Zvi Yehudah Kook. Of the 'higher *Yeshivot*', this *Yeshiva* was perhaps the only one radically Zionist in orientation, for here a fervent nationalist ideology was fostered and Independence Day was celebrated with a uniquely pious and festive solemnity. In his address at the Independence Day celebration, Rabbi Zvi Yehudah agitatedly confided to his students that, while crowds had rushed into the streets to dance on the day of Partition in 1947, he had sat and mourned at what he termed the fulfilment of the prophecy of Joel (4:2): 'And My Land they have divided'. As *Davar* reporter, Danny Rubenstein, was later to describe it:

> His veteran students, who had learned Torah from him for years and were used to taking part in the traditional Independence Day celebration at the *Yeshiva*, say that for nineteen years Rav Zvi Yehudah had not told of his weeping . . . on the day of partition. And now, in May 1967, he continued . . . in a loud shout of anguish: Where is our Schechem (Nablus)? Where is our Jericho? Where is our (river) Jordan?
>
> Two weeks later, the students of the *Yeshiva* were already mobilized . . . They [shortly thereafter] passed through Schechem and Jericho bearing with them an overpowering experience – perhaps prophecy, perhaps 'a heavenly voice' that had come from the mouth of their rabbi.[7]

In the days and weeks following, Israel mobilized, negotiated, prepared. U Thant evacuated United Nations troops from Sinai and Gaza with an alacrity that may well have surprised even Nasser. The former ally, de Gaulle, turned indifferent, even hostile. The Western world urged patience and at the UN compromises and arrangements were proposed that were based on the assumption (or perhaps, hope) of Israel's absolute vulnerability. In Israel, public parks were quietly, indeed secretly, prepared as consecrated ground for the eventuality of mass burials. The Holocaust, in growing public consciousness since the Eichmann trial, arose in every mind as a memory and renewed possibility. Muki Tzur, reminiscing in a book of 'Soldiers' Talk', described it:

> We tend to forget those days before the war . . . but those were the days in which we came very close to that Jewish destiny from which we fled . . . Suddenly everybody began talking of Munich, of the Holocaust, of the Jewish people that had been abandoned to its fate.[8]

On 3 June, the Sabbath before the outbreak of the war, I attended the synagogue of *Bet Hillel*, of the Hebrew University. Most of the seats were empty, the members mobilized. The section of the Torah read that day included the *Tochecha*, the dreaded punishments to be meted out to Israel for betraying the covenant. The congregation sat through these half-whispered Torah passages depressed, almost in a daze.

At 10 o'clock on the morning of 5 June, Michael Elkins reported from Jerusalem that the Egyptian air force had been destroyed and that Israel had won the war. Both CBS and the BBC, not attuned to the miraculous, held up the story for several hours. Perhaps they lost a scoop; perhaps Hussein lost the information that might have saved him Jerusalem and the West Bank.[9] He could, of course, learn nothing from the Israeli media, which reported only vaguely on sporadic bombardments. By evening, while Jerusalem was being shelled, the news spread through the country: 'We're winning'. The speed and scope of the victory created an atmosphere and a feeling in the public that was, as Eliezer Schweid well described it, on 'the threshhold' of a religious sentiment.[10] Unlike the War of Independence of 1948, notes Schweid, this campaign was unexpectedly short and the achievements were greater than the expectations. Others commented that the insistence of Jordan's King Hussein to participate in the war, thus 'assuring' the liberation of Jerusalem, could be understood only in the Biblical idiom: God had 'hardened his heart'.

The return of the Jewish people, through its army, to the heartland of *Eretz Israel* and to Old Jerusalem was experienced as startling by many who had thought that it, and its most 'traditional' landmark, the *Kotel Ha-Ma'aravi* (Western Wall), meant nothing to them. In the words of one soldier:

> When we [in our unit] were riding to Jerusalem, some people were standing next to [Kibbutz] Huldah and shouting: 'The *Kotel* . . . the *Kotel* . . . the *Kotel*!' These words, nothing else . . . For all of us in the bus . . . that was enough. I have no religious inclinations, no one can suspect me of that. But that was something that touched all of us, that meant more than anything else.[11]

In the days of the battle for Jerusalem and its conquest, the focus of Zionism seemed to move, from the coast and the fabled Jezreel Valley to the mountains of Judea: from Tel Aviv, the 'all-Jewish city' to Jerusalem, the 'sanctuary of the King', and its only remaining concrete symbol. Andre Neher[12] has remarked on the dialectic of paratroopers, who had never given a thought to the *Kotel*, passing through the Meah Shearim quarter (an ultra-religious enclave in Jerusalem) on their way to its conquest. In Meah Shearim, despite the *Kotel*'s inaccessibility, it had remained a living presence, but the people there had neither the actual aspiration nor the physical strength or training to fight for it. This strength only the paratroopers had; they were the ones who made the *Kotel* again available for the faithful, and when they reached the Wall they were startled to find themselves crying, perhaps with tears long stored up in the Ultra-Orthodox sections of Jerusalem. The bond between *haredim* (Ultra-religious) and 'freethinking' warriors, expressed even in physical embraces, was not destined to outlive those short weeks. But when it appeared, it appeared as exhilarating, miraculous, messianic.

At the same time, there is testimony that the days of fighting brought a new generation, grown to adulthood since the War of Independence, into confrontation with the paradoxes that mark even a 'miraculously successful' war. Together with the joy of the *kibbutznik* from Sha'ar Ha'amakim, 'glad to go to the house of the Lord', there was death – and killing. A solider relates:

> During the battle we killed an Egyptian officer . . . among his papers, I see a picture of two little children, smiling at the seashore, and a letter in a feminine handwriting . . . I thought: What is the feeling of a family in the kibbutz when a son is killed? And here I killed the father of two children . . . Of course, these were soldiers who were fighting us . . . But nevertheless.[13]

The paradox and the tension is well stated in one Orthodox soldier's description of a shattering existential moment.

> A fellow with a transistor next to his ear shouts: 'Quiet! Quiet! Let's hear the news'. Suddenly his eyes brighten. '*Chevre! Chevre!* [Hey, chaps!] The old city of Jerusalem is in our hands.' I stand in a daze; it is hard for me to believe the news . . . Suddenly, shouts. 'Airplanes!' . . . from the direction of the setting sun a Mig appears . . . A cloud of smoke arises in front of us. I lie flat, cover my head with my helmet, and a flashing thought passes through my mind: Now? [To die] now? Jerusalem! No! No![14]

But soldiers reported on moral dilemmas and confrontations as well as existential paradoxes. One soldier relates: 'The moment I was in Gaza, and I saw that we were winning the war and were about to become an army of conquest, I sat my men down and told one of them . . . to read the story of Achan [who took booty from Jericho] in the Book of Joshua. If anything influenced my men on how to act as a conquering army, it was this chapter'.[15] Soldiers perceived that religion, despised by many of them and alien to most, may in its symbols and gestures hold a key to the paradoxes, provide a language for moral deliberation, provide a cultural context even for the pain of bereavement. Reena Barzilai, of Kibbutz Ha'Ogen (*Hashomer Hatzair* – affiliated to Mapam) writes on the evening the war ended:

> Six hundred and seventy nine emissaries / O Master of the Universe, to You, / To the kingdom of the King of all kings / To your holy land we despatched. . . . Wounded, ragged they will appear before You, / To intercede for us before the throne of glory. / And in our name present credentials that / With lead were inscribed on their bodies.[16]

On the morning of *Shavuot* (Pentecost), 14 June, the public at large was given access to the Western Wall and 200 000 came to it, or rather, stormed it on that day. Beginning at two and three o'clock in the morning Jews thronged the road leading to the *Kotel*, to be there on time for *Shacharit* (morning) prayers, which began simultaneously in scores of *minyanim*[17] at 4 a.m. Arab citizens kept indoors out of sight. The encounter with that problem, with that people, lay in the future and few Jews thought of them or were distracted by them that morning. It was experienced as a rare moment. Those who met at the Wall congratulated one another and exchanged tearful wishes of *Mazal Tov* ('congratulations'). From Independence Day until *Shavuot*, it seemed, the exile had finally ended. How could there be less than undreamed-of joy?

But that, even in those days, was not the whole story. During that very week, religious and non-religious Jews paid many visits to newly-bereaved families. Religious Zionists tended to exchange the traditional formulation of comfort, 'May you be comforted among the mourners of Zion and Jerusalem' with a new one: 'May you be consoled in the consolation of Zion'. Apparently, those who did so felt, as Harold Fisch wrote,[18] that the mourning of Zion was at an end. Whether that was the case – and, if so, what it meant – was to become the subject of long and heart-searching discussions.

SINCE *SHAVUOT* 1967: THEOLOGIES OF RESPONSE

'Secular' as well as 'religious' Jews experienced 'something' during the Six-Day War and testified to it, but only those who have a stake in – and ongoing concern with – religious meaning have to theologize. Moreover, testimony can rest on feeling alone, while systematic religious response requires an on-going 'habit of the heart'[19] and, ultimately, some integrating theory.

The theological or narrative-religious responses to the Six-Day War were, after the initial experience, extremely varied. They flowed, to a large extent, from habits of the heart and from orientations that touched on three fundamental, inter-locked issues:

(a) How shall one view the relationship between history and Torah?
(b) What is the spiritual significance of the present *vis-à-vis* the (sacred) past and the (Messianic) future?
(c) How shall one relate to Zionism, which is a Jewish movement *in* history, and very committed to the significance of the present?

History and Torah

What the relationship should be between historical events and the actual 'life of Judaism' is very problematic in the Jewish tradition; in modern Jewry, it is doubly so.

The tradition 'takes history very seriously'; it sees the hand of God in the Exodus, in the conquest of Canaan and even in the destruction of the Temple. Yet Israel is repeatedly warned not to be deceived by false prophets who promise salvation without authorization, and not to be shattered by historical tribulations; the essential thing is to be steadfast with God, which means to obey His commandments. We are told to see God's great hand in history but not to take this history seriously in epochs of divine eclipse – and to wait patiently for the Messiah. Thus, the *hope* of Judaism is the Messianic days, but the actual *life* of Judaism is the Torah and its commandments. Because history is serious – but subservient to Torah – theology cannot be divorced from history; but it may with impunity be severed from particular historical realities, that have been 'neutralized', as it were. Shalom Rosenberg has pointed out that the Sages gave *Channukah*[20] *halakhic*[21] permanence as the Independence Celebration of the Macabbean state even though that state had already been destroyed.[22] In a similar vein, the iconoclastic theologian, Isaiah Leibowitz, who insists that 'This bloody mess which is called History only reflects the wickedness and idiocy of man' and who has consistently urged the immediate and unilateral relinquishing of 'the territories', admitted after the war that:

> One thing will remain with us from all this. The twenty-eighth of *Iyar* [Hebrew calendar]. The day on which we took Jerusalem. I'm not sure that we will keep the city, but the day will remain.[23]

Yet, when the Messiah does come, obviously history, theology and reality can no longer be kept apart. And what if this tremendous series of events, coming after the beginning of Return and in the wake of the Holocaust, is the redemption? In that case, is 'returning to the routine of Jewish life' by, say, fasting on the seventeenth of Tammuz (to mark the ancient Babylonian breach of the walls of Jerusalem) not ingratitude and rebellion where, in other times, it would be pristine loyalty to Torah and *Halakha*?[24]

In the contemporary era, the problem of 'History-and-Torah' is confounded by the historical crisis of Judaism, characterized by the widespread abandonment of the age-old 'actual life of Judaism' – the regimen of the *mitzvot*.[25] Zionism, as anti-Zionist traditionalists have pointed out as emphatically as the Zionists themselves, is built on the premise that Jews need not be observant in order to be loyal Jews. They must simply return to their own land and take their place on the stage of history. Pietists have called this False Messianism; most Zionists have (perhaps romantically) termed it realism. But what should the realists do when they seem to be in the presence of miracles? How should the pietists react when the secularists seem to be 'returning to Judaism' because history appears to have vindicated Jewish tradition for them? Should the stubborn upholders of the tradition call this authentic redemption – or false prophecy?

Furthermore, in the age of crisis, can even religious Jews state categorically what 'the life of the commandments' is – and what constitutes living it – for everyone? Isn't the 'secular' Jew instructing his men in the *biblical* story of Achan – so that they will not loot – in fact teaching them Torah? Is the *kibbutznik* engaged in the conquest of Jerusalem and declaring his gladness at ascending 'to the house of the Lord' perhaps *praying* even while occupied with the *mitzvah* of Jewish self-defence? Conversely, in the present historical situation, do we know that the 'obvious' *halakhic* content of Judaism is, in toto, still commanded? Now that 'the old city of Jerusalem is in our hands', are we to rebuild the Temple and offer sacrifices – and tear down the Mosque of Omar? And assuming for sundry reasons, that it does not or cannot mean that, how about sacrificing the Passover offering which can be made without rebuilding the Temple? Why does no one do that?[26] Are, then, the prayers of 'the religious' for the restoration of the Temple service not 'serious'? Or are they serious only for 'when the Messiah comes'? Or shall we now, by force of will, welcome the opportunity to restore our days as of old', and plan actively for that which Messianic times, about to commence, will demand of us?

Between Sacred Past and Messianic Future

Nahum Arieli has posited[27] that what distinguishes secular Zionism from traditionalism is that the latter strives to live its Judaism within the sacred past, looking towards an anticipated redeemed future. In this scheme of things, the present is devoid of significance. One lives, as it were, alongside of it, trying to ignore it, leaving its functioning gladly to the gentiles, building bridges from past to future which span and contemptuously look down on it. On the other hand, the secular Zionist rebels against the past and seeks collective self-realization in the present. The future, which is the immediate continuation of the present, depends on what we do now. Arieli sees in classic religious Zionism a third option – that of remaining loyal to the sacred past and working to channel its contents into a relevant and responsible present. This third way is opposed equally by the ultra-Orthodox and by consistent secularists. We may suggest that the greatest test of religious Zionism comes when the Messiah, who is 'believed in' – if only because the anticipation of his coming is part of the sacred past – may be plausibly expected *in the present*. The 'real' traditionalists, who 'know' that He cannot possibly come on the wings of heretical Zionism, for whom 'the Jewish state' is simply another 'present-ness' to be negotiated and overcome, do not have this problem. Neither are those secularists who have no loyalty to the Messianic faith troubled. The 'crisis of Messianism', in Werblowsky's[28] pithy phrase, is a religious–Zionist one. Because of their commitment to the present, traditional Messianism is an embarrassment to religious Zionists. Yet, because of their commitment to the past, they cannot abandon the hope and expectation.

Zionism and History

The question of the relationship to past, future and present may, of course be linked to Zionism in a simple and straightforward manner: those who are Zionists have 'sold out' to the present; 'true' Jews, who maintain their indifference and hostility to the present, cannot be Zionists. This is the *Haredi* (Ultra-Orthodox) position.

In fact, this is an oversimplification. One can be a Zionist and remain loyal to tradition in one of two ways. First, one may be a

purely 'political Zionist' who will have no truck with new normative
'Jewish culture' where such culture contravenes or supersedes the
tradition. Such political Zionism is viewed by the religious adherent
as 'merely' a solution to 'the problem of the Jews', who wish neither
to be undermined by the culture of the gentiles nor to be slaughtered
by them; it is simply another strategy for dealing with the present,
providing a better plane on which to survive for the life of Torah
and to wait for the Messiah. A second option is to look upon Zionism
as a consummation of traditional Judaism, as 'the beginning of our
Redemption'. In this view, Zionism not only does not require the
abrogation of the traditional Torah but is Providentially charged to
restore errant Jews to the domain of the Torah – through the historical
dynamic it initiates.

Thus, in the case of 'dry' political Zionism, nothing that happens
has religious meaning for its religious partisan; God continues to be
'absent' outside the realm of Torah practice. In the case of theological–
Messianic Zionism, everything means something and the urge to
interpret and 'understand' becomes particularly great in 'great
moments'. Secular-minded Zionists are likely to fear the Messianic
ones as irresponsible and to pity the Orthodox political ones for their
halakhic 'fixations'. And between two types of religious Zionists,
especially if they are consistent, we may expect to find lively polemics.

In all religious responses to the Six-Day War, we may thus expect
to find positions and 'understandings', not only on the religious
significance of history, but on the theological importance to be
assigned to the present. Likewise, we may expect discrete views of
Zionism, as either understanding and responding to the theological
significance of the historical hour, or as *misunderstanding* it or
misrepresenting its insignificance. Finally, we may expect religious
discourse to assume and emphasize some connections between the
historical hope of Judaism – its Messianic dimension – and the
existential life of Judaism – in the Torah and its commandments.

SIX THEOLOGICAL POSITIONS

We shall briefly discuss six theological responses to the Six-Day War:
(a) Active Messianism; (b) The Celebration of Salvation as Historical
Vindication; (c) Gratitude at God's Miracles; (d) Zionist Moral
Halakhism; (e) Zionist Negation of Religious Historical Significance,
and (f) Anti-Zionist Negation of Present Historical Meaning.

Position One: Active Messianism

The young men who participated in the Independence Day celebration at the *Mercaz Harav Yeshiva* felt strongly, during the war and after it, that they were living in Messianic times, that the aniticipated future was – now. They and their teachers had carefully studied rabbinic texts which explained that the actual Messianic redemption is characterized by developments that they themselves had been witnessing: the Ingathering of the Exiles, political sovereignty, making the desert bloom and the conquest of the land. The Six-Day War was thus a radical movement forward towards total redemption. In the words of Rabbi O. Hadya, the events of the war and the victory were 'an astounding divine miracle . . . the end of days has already come . . . now through conquest *Eretz Israel* has been redeemed from oppression, from the *sitra achra* [Satan's camp]. It has entered the realm of sanctity'.[29] To this, of course, there is an *halakhic* corollary: 'If, God forbid, we should return even a tiny strip of land we would thereby give control to the evil forces, to the *sitra achra*'.[30]

God, therefore, is acting to redeem us *now*, and if we fail to understand this and thus act to sabotage the redemption, we shall only prolong the painful 'birthpangs of the Messiah'. Thus, Ephraim Yair, writing shortly after the war, declares that God has had to give us portions of our land three times in the storm of war (in the War of Independence, the Sinai Campaign and the Six-Day War) because we keep on returning them. If we return the land again, we shall therefore not be promoting peace but forcing upon God another move to restore our land to us – i.e., another war. The paradoxical result is that only an uncompromising position will bring peace to the area and the world.[31]

A similarly deterministic position, albeit milder in tone, is that which sees a kind of biblical redemption in the events of our time: the Holocaust and the return to Israel are analogous to the slavery in Egypt and the Exodus. For example, Spero applies Buber's concept of 'the leading God' who took Israel out of Egypt, to the circumstances of our days:

> when today, in fact, a Jewish population of three million inhabit the land in its biblical boundaries including Jerusalem and constitute the sovereign state of Israel, then the message of the events comes into . . . sharper focus. The God of Israel is *leading* His people back to the land . . . The invitation has turned into a summons.[32]

The *mitzvah* is clear: to go up to the land and settle it; to follow the leading God.

The disciples of Rabbi Zvi Yehudah Kook have also translated the present – allegedly redemptive – events into *halakhic* categories. They frequently cite Nachmanides's ruling that 'we are commanded to enter the land, to conquer its cities and to settle our tribes there' as well as the prohibition he formulates: not to return any part of it to gentiles and not to leave it lying waste. Porat deduces from this even the *mitzvah* of working the land, for 'he who leaves his land a wasteland . . . and uncultivated, transgresses against a negative commandment'.[33] Thus, the Zionist ethos of *kibbush hashemama* (conquest of the wasteland) is given *halakhic* sanction within the theology of a present 'age of Redemption'. The 'future-that-is-now' is firmly anchored in the norms of the sacred past.

Position Two: Salvation as Historical Vindication

Unlike the first position, which is publicly visible as an ideological group, the *Gush Emunim* (Bloc of the Faithful), who lead religious settlement on the West Bank, the second position represents simply an orientation, a religious mood. It is the mood of those who believe that the stirring events of the Six-Day War must be seen as religiously significant, and who view the Zionist enterprise as not indifferent to the covenant between God and Israel, though they refuse to draw deterministically redemptive conclusions from this. In this conception, a clear distinction should be drawn between God's *salvation* (*yeshuah*) and His *redemption* (*geulah*), between events like Purim[34] and events like the Exodus, though it is hoped that we will be worthy of seeing the present salvation as 'the beginning of our Redemption'. What characterizes this approach is, on the one hand, a 'realistic' view of history with its dangers, tragedies and complexities and, on the other, a belief that God is still with His people, Israel, and guards them. Israel is a singular people and is witness to God in history. Zionism, though a consequence of crisis and riddled with problems, testifies to the way Judaism can bear witness in the present, and it sets a stage for God's expression of His sovereignty over men and nations.

The scholar-statesman, Yaakov Herzog, articulated this position in another way. Addressing representatives of religious *kibbutzim* in 1968, he related how, after the Six-Day War, he travelled to Rome to discuss the future of Jerusalem with church officials. Upon his return home, the Greek Patriarch Benedictus of Jerusalem summoned him, to remind him that he too had the status of a pope and that Israel should treat with him, a friend, when discussing Jerusalem with the Christian world. Herzog relates that, as the Patriarch was speaking, he recalled the antecedents of the Greek Patriarchate. It was established, Herzog notes, in 451, solemnly to declare that the city belonged to the Church, that it had been taken from the Jewish people in perpetuity. Thus, for Jews, the initiation of the line of Patriarchs was an historical hour of trauma and tragedy. He continues:

> And I thought to myself that if, at that time, a Jew had come into a synagogue in Rome, or Crete, or Alexandria, and said to another: 'Have you heard? They want to seal the doom of Jerusalem, to cut us off forever from this city. They have appointed a Patriarch', and the other had replied: 'Despair not, my friends, because 1500 years hence a Jewish official of the Government of Israel will visit the descendant of the Patriarch now appointed and the ninety-fifth descendant will say: The city is yours; it is united under Providence. You have found the road. All I ask is that you recognize my rights as well' . . . those who heard such a statement would have thought the speaker a madman.[35]

What is the *halakhah* of this historical hour of salvation? It is to keep faith with God as He has kept faith with Israel, to use the opportunities accorded by the hour with moral intelligence and to hope that this may indeed be the beginning of redemption. Though one cannot know that it is, one can act with responsibility, dignity and a sense of religious wonder.[36]

Position Three: Gratitude for God's Miracles

The belief that God had 'shown His mighty hand', that the Six-Day War had a clearly miraculous dimension, appears to be close to the previous position, which celebrates God's salvation. Yet in this orientation the emphasis is more likely to be pedagogic than theological: Jews should now 'see the light' and 'return'. The 'there-were-miracles' position tends to generate the wonder-of-dependence rather than the confidence-of-covenant. The miracle may thus be viewed as divine aid to survive the present for the sake of the still distant future rather than as an indication of the religious significance of the present. Consequently, very varied groups of people – from Habad Hasidim, scholarly and simple residents of Meah Shearim and secular Jews – have joined religious Zionists in expressing the conviction that 'we have witnessed miracles'. Likewise, Jews who previously did not generally blend religious and national sentiments declared that 'we can depend only on God' (and not on 'seemingly friendly' nations).[37] An interesting listing of the miracles performed for Israel is given by Rabbi S. Y. Levin, editor of the renowned Talmudic Encyclopedia and respected sage. He mentions the victory of Israel, the swiftness of the campaign which saved many casualties; the decision of Jordanian King Hussein to join the war which made the liberation of Jerusalem possible; the hesitancy of Prime Minister Eshkol before the war which had 'many positive results'; Israel's fighting alone, without the participation of other nations, so that it could be an agent for the fulfilment of the verse, 'And the Lord alone shall be exalted'; the unity of the Jewish people in Israel and the Diaspora; and the awakening to eternal values.[38]

A significant *halakhic* aspect of this approach is to be found in the decision of the Chief Rabbinate to establish the day of the conquest of Jerusalem as a holiday – Jerusalem Day – to be marked by the recitation of the full *Hallel*[39] with the traditional blessing. This was more than the Chief Rabbinate had permitted for Independence Day. With regard to the latter, the ambivalence of the rabbinical establishment *vis-à-vis* the secular Zionist state could not be overcome. As Chief Rabbi Unterman expressed it:

> the victory in the Six-Day War – with all due respect and honour to our valiant soldiers . . . was a victory miraculous in every sense of the word . . . We cannot allow this miracle wrought by God to be unmarked by recitation of the full *Hallel* with the Blessing.

As for Independence Day, it is 'also a great thing worthy of public celebration . . . but this does not obligate the recitation of the full *Hallel* with the Blessing, or suspension of the *Sefirah*[40] restrictions, as in the case of Jerusalem Day, when we palpably saw a miracle occur'.[41]

Position Four: Zionist Moral *Halakhism*

This approach may be briefly stated as follows: We have been placed in an historical situation which constitutes a test of our ability and willingness to be a people of the Torah, representing and articulating the moral sensitivity and the moral norms which are the soul of the *halakhic* tradition. Members of this group therefore hold that the present historical hour of divine deliverance now awaits human sanctification through an understanding of Torah which is morally adequate to our unprecedented situation – of return to the land and collective Jewish responsibility in our state. (Since both this return and the life of the state were made possible by Zionism, Zionism is a political movement of great spiritual weight, requiring serious theological attention and religious care.)

The position of Active Messianism is denounced in this approach, for suggesting that holiness is inherent in Israel regardless of Israeli actions, for intimating that the holiness of the land lies in some inherent ('magical') qualities, rather than in the Torah's charge that here Jews are to live a holy life as a people.

The Six-Day War gave Israel not only the exhilaration of God's salvation, but the responsibility *and the capacity* to seek compromise and peace. Judaism declares that the real warrior is one who turns his enemy into a friend,[42] who is sensitive to the rights also of the other and who does not view Messianism as a narrow political conception, assuring territorial gains and military victories; Redemption must be left to God – He has entrusted to us the Torah, whose ways are the ways of pleasantness and peace. In the words of Aviezer Ravitsky:

peace, human dignity and justice – are these but 'western' values? Our conviction was, and remains, that these humanitarian values are also our own, and even fundamentally those of the Torah . . .

The taking [in the Six-Day War] of East Jerusalem and of territories that once were part of Israel triggered a profound joy among the religious youth . . . But in a short time, that joy slid into a sort of blind and intransigent passion that implicitly was isolated from other Jewish values . . . Of what did the prophets come to speak with the kings? Of 'Greater Israel'? Certainly not. They supported justice and righteousness.[43]

Position Five: Zionist Negation of Religious Historical Significance

In this view, it is posited that events have no religious meaning: *only the Torah and its commandments constitute Judaism*. Indeed, our historical situation does make demands, but they are rational and moral; secular people can understand these requirements as well as religious ones.

This position, stated most consistently by Isaiah Leibowitz, juxtaposes the *halakhah* and history. God *demands* adherence to the Torah

but He *gives* nothing but religious human stature to those who accept
the yoke of the Torah. Belief in salvational events is a delusion and,
politically, it leads to reckless and foolish behaviour. Zionism, an
historical movement of Jews who were 'fed up with living among the
gentiles', has nothing to do with salvation; indeed, the religious and
secular Jews who make up this movement cannot possibly, without
utterly corrupting the term, have a common conception of salvation.
Thus, Leibowitz defines all Jewishly meaningful terms in a *halakhic*
context:

> Never were holidays of remembrance or thanksgiving instituted in
> commemoration of victories and conquests. Even the
> Hasmoneans[44] – who are so often mentioned today in the current
> context – are cited in the sources and in the tradition solely for
> their *battle to preserve the Torah* . . . Furthermore, the whole
> concept of 'bravery' in Judaism is not confined to physical might.
> 'One should arise like the lion', the opening words of the *Shulchan
> Arukh*,[45] are directed not towards the soldier but towards one
> arising to worship God.[46]

Though this sounds like an *Agudist*[47] (anti-Zionist) position, it is here
a radically political–Zionist one. Physical and military bravery on
behalf of Israel is important for Israelis wish to have their own state.
But this is not a religious wish or need; it is a human one, shared by
pietists and atheists alike. What these different types of Jews disagree
about is 'the life of *mitzvot*'; in this disagreement, which may yet
lead to civil war, the Six-Day War is irrelevant.

Position Six: Anti-Zionist Negation of Present Historical Significance

This position may be stated as follows: There is no positive meaning
in the Six-Day War, and the very notion that there might be is
ludicrous. Zionism is a heresy and the *Galut* (exile) continues, in
Eretz Israel perhaps more than elsewhere, because of the pernicious
Zionists. Zionism is the worst heresy imaginable; moreover, it is a
cosmic catastrophe, impeding the redemption and strengthening
satanic forces in the world. Not only is it not a legitimate response
to the Holocaust, but it is, in fact, the very cause of it, for it
spearheads a rebellion against God and impudently seeks to 'force
the end'. The Six-Day War, as other seeming achievements or
victories of Israel, are nothing but satanic lures, tempting the faithful
(consisting only of Satmar *Hasidim* and *Neturei Karta*)[48] and leading

the State of Israel to well-deserved perdition. The truly faithful do well, therefore, not even to pray at the Western Wall, which was conquered by the hated Zionists.

This position has been most lucidly and radically expressed by Rabbi Joel Teitlebaum, leader of the Satmar *Hasidic* group.[49] While the extreme negative and demonic features of this theology are rejected by the more moderate *Agudat Yisrael*, the latter agree that neither Israel nor the Six-Day War have positive religious meaning. Whereas the *Neturei Karta* sees these (the state and the war) with a hating negation, those to the left of them in the Ultra-Orthodox community are characterized by indifference and varying degrees of contempt for the claims and enthusiasms of the Zionists.

TWENTY YEARS LATER

The map of Israel was considerably changed by the Six-Day War – ideologically and politically, as well as geographically. Religiously, there has been a shift to the political right; the *kipah serugah*,[50] due to the influence and high visibility of the Active Messianic position, has been increasingly identified with hawkish and maximalist orientations. At the same time, the exhilaration and the sense of new vistas has quite evaporated, and the sense of unity to which many testified in 1967 has been replaced by tension and profound distrust. What, then, remains of the positions that crystallized after the war?

The Active Messianic position, as is well known, became the platform of *Gush Emunim*, formally established to 'save the Redemption', as it were, after the setbacks of the Yom Kippur War. *Gush Emunim* mobilized much religious idealism and won considerable sympathy for its renaissance of 'values' in the individualistic and even hedonistic society of contemporary Israel. Many saw in them the true heirs of the *halutzim* (the early Jewish pioneers) the only 'real' Zionists left. But *Gush Emunim* also contributed to the alienation of many Israelis from religion. Its identification of Judaism (at least in the public eye) with policies of an aggressive and self-aggrandizing Messianism made adherence to humanistic values look like a secular virtue. Moreover, the discovery of a Jewish terrorist 'underground', sprouting from within the settlements and *yeshivot* of *Gush Emunim*, brought to public awareness that the politics of Messianism could engender violence and brutality as well as 'clean-cut' religious idealism. The 'underground' has, indeed, led to a soul-searching in *Gush Emunim* itself and may eventually occasion a split in that movement.

The theological position that hopes for Providential Presence in history without ever taking it for granted may, despite its ambiguities, again become the mainstream stance of religious Zionism, especially in interaction with the position of Moral *Halakhism*. If it returns to these positions, religious Zionism can maintain a hold both on historical Messianism and on the Zionist present, made holy through *halakhic* deliberation, critical loyalty and stubborn hope.

As for Position Three – based on the memory of miracles – one may learn from the experience of Elijah that miracles have little staying-power. After the fire and after the storm, comes the still small voice. If this is forgotten, even great miracles may leave no more than an ideological residue of ostrich-like confidence that anything we desire will come to pass no matter what we do. There may then be (and already is!) a kind of *haredi* nationalistic maximalism which finds expression in slogans on car stickers: *Yisrael: B'tach BaShem* (Israel: Put your trust in God), and which is comfortable with the idea that 'the whole world is against us'.

The Moral *Halakhism* of Position Four is represented today by *Oz V'Shalom* and *Netivot Shalom*.[51]. If these groups have less influence than they deserve,[52] it may be because the general (and religious) public cannot clearly distinguish their views from those of the secular-minded Peace Now movement, which denies the authority of the sacred tradition and is uninterested in Jewish Messianism as such. We suggest that those representing this position require dialogue with other religious Jews whose Zionist concerns have theological dimensions, including moderates in *Gush Emunim*.

Position Five, represented by Professor Leibowitz, has accurately predicted many of the negative features of redemptive politics in Israel. And yet, situated so idiosyncratically between *Agudat Yisrael* and the leftist non-Zionist Progressive Movement for Peace, it has lost touch with most religious Zionists and others who *do* ascribe spiritual significance to a state for which they may have to give their lives and who *do* look towards the day when 'the bloody mess of history' becomes, if not the Kingdom of God, at least – something else and better.

Position Six, at least in its moderate *Agudist* formulations, has gained in influence and strength, and our analysis suggests at least one reason for this. The *Haredim* have never allowed anyone to draw them into theological discussion. To use Arieli's conception, they knew themselves to be citizens of the past and future and they looked upon loyalists of the present as enemies, knaves and/or fools. This was not understood by the religious Zionists, who took the present seriously; they considered the *Haredim* as 'really very religious Jews', albeit quaint. Therefore, they remained 'open' to them, vulnerable to their influence.

When present events and, most particularly, the Six-Day War, appeared to Zionists to be the Messianic future itself, a theological confirmation of the (secular) Zionist ethos, the *Haredim* had only to wait for the enthusiasm to wane and for the hope to fade. Then they could convincingly argue that the enthusiasm was merely another false Messianism – that salvation lay in the past and in the distant future. And with that began the flight, even in *Mizrachi* (religious–Zionist) circles, from the challenges of the Zionist present into the citadels of Ultra-Orthodoxy, where there were no fighter planes to be manned, no moral problems of statehood to be tackled, no Zionist vision to be realized. *Gush Emunim*, in insisting that the redemption was already here, sounded much less realistic than *Agudat Yisrael*.

The enthusiasm and excitement of the weeks between Independence Day and *Shavuot* 1967 were appropriate to that time and in that place, despite the pain and bereavement of war. Those who said *El Male Rachamim*[53] also recited the *Hallel*, and justifiably so. But the experience of these twenty years indicates that what is authentic testimony in the flashes of light we call God's Presence may not be confused, certainly not in our concretely historical Jewish state, with theology and the life we call the service of God. Good testimony may be bad theology. A living Jewish faith in Israel as elsewhere, requires both – and the ability to distinguish between them.

Notes

1. Ephraim Yair, *'Yamim gedolim be-Yisrael'* (Great Days of Israel), *Amudim* (Journal of the Religious *Kibbutz* Movement) 256 (June 1967) (Sivan 5727) 301.
2. *Siach Lohamim* ('Soldiers' Talk'), published by Young Members of the *Kibbutz* Movement (Tel Aviv, Tishri 5728) 241 (translation mine). For an English edition of *Siach Lohamim*, see Henry Near (trans) *The Seventh Day: Soldiers Talk About the Six Day War* (Harmondsworth, 1970).

3. Emil L. Fackenheim, 'Jewish Faith and the Holocaust; A Fragment', *Commentary*, 46 (2) (August 1968) 86.
4. Hanan Porat, *'Ki Ayin B'Ayin Yir'u B'Shuv HaShem Tzion'* ('With Their Own Eyes They Will See God's Return to Zion') *Petachim*, 2 (32), Nissan 5735, 9–10 (Hebrew).
5. Milton Himmelfarb, 'In the Light of Israel's Victory', *Commentary*, 44 (4) (October 1967) 61.
6. A *yeshiva* is an institution of religious study where sacred literature, particularly the Talmud, is studied, often from early youth.
7. Danny Rubenstein, *Mi LaShem Elai: Gush Emunim* ('On the Lord's Side: *Gush Emunim')* (Tel Aviv, 1982) 22 (Hebrew).
8. *Siach Lohamim* (Muki Tzur, 'On One of Those Nights') 7. This and a number of citations from *Siach Lohamim* and several other sources in the first section of this chapter are discussed in my previous article, 'Moments of the Heart', *Judaism*, 17 (2) (Spring 1968) 211–24.
9. On the basis of a telephone conversation between Mr Elkins and myself, May 1987. Not only did both networks hold up the story, but the BBC broadcast, when it was finally given, reminded listeners that 'the truth is often the first casualty of any war'.
10. Eliezer Schweid, *'Yemei Shiva'* ('Days of Return') *Petachim*, 1 (1), Tishrai 5725, 20. Schweid states that 'In the war, the wall of estrangement [of secular youth from the Jewish tradition] seems to have burst'.
11. *Siach Lohamim*, 232.
12. Andre Neher, *'Chizuk Hazehut Hayehudit Al Yedei Ha'avarat Morashto shel Hayehudi Namoderni'* ('Strengthening Jewish Identity Through the Transmission of the Modern Jew's Heritage') *Bat'futzot HaGolah*, 3 (42) (Fall 1967) (5728) 16–21 (Hebrew).
13. *Siach Lohamim*, 40.
14. *Amudim* (257–258) (July–August 1967) (Tammuz-Az 5727) 363.
15. *Siach Lohamim*, 21–2.
16. Rena Barzilai, '679 Ambassadors' – first published in *The Week in the Kibbutz Ha'Artzi* (September 1967) and frequently reprinted.
17. A *minyan* is a quorum of ten males required for communal prayer.
18. Harold Fisch, 'Jerusalem, Jerusalem', *Judaism*, 17 (2) (Spring 1968) 265.
19. On 'habits of the heart' as a cultural phenomenon, see Robert N. Bellah *et al.*, *Habits of the Heart: Individualism and Commitment in American Life* (Berkeley, 1985) where, following de Tocqueville, they are defined as 'notions, opinions and ideas that "shape mental habits" and "the sum of moral and intellectual dispositions of men in society"'.
20. Festival of Light commemorating the successful Maccabean revolt against the Greeks (168–143 BC).
21. *Halakha* is the body of Jewish religious law.
22. Professor Shalom Rosenberg, of the Hebrew University, in conversation with the writer.
23. Isaiah Leibowitz, *Ha'Aretz* (30 June 1967) (Hebrew).
24. For an interesting discussion, see Tzuriel Admonit, *'Ha'evkeh . . . V'al Ma Evkeh?'* ('Shall I weep . . . and About What?') in Admonit's collected writings, *Betoch Hazerem V'negdo* ('Within the Stream and Against It' (Tel Aviv, 5737) 428–30 (Hebrew).

25. A *mitzvah* (plural *mitzvot*) is a religious obligation with the connotation of fulfilling simultaneously both a legal and a moral duty.

26. See Ya'akov Levinger, '*Chiddush Ha'Avodah B'zman Hazeh*' ('On Renewing the Sacrificial Service in This Era') *De'ot* (Journal of Religious Academicians) 34 and 35 (Fall and Winter 5728). See also, R. J. Zvi Werblowsky, 'The Temple and the Sacrifice', the *Jerusalem Post* (25 August 1967).

27. Nahum Arieli, '*Ha'Ide-a Hatzionit Hadadit – Hatif'eret V'Hakishalon*', ('The Idea of Religious Zionism – The Glory and the Failure') *Kivvunim*, 29 (Autumn 1985) 25–46.

28. See R. J. Zvi Werblowsky, 'Crises of Messianism', *Judaism*, 7 (2) (1958) 106–20.

29. Cited in Uriel Tal, 'The Land and the State of Israel in Israeli Religious Life', *Proceedings of the Rabbinical Assembly*, 76th Annual Convention, XXXVIII (1976) 10.

30. Tal, 'The Land', 10.

31. Ephraim Yair, *Amudim*, 256 (June 1967) (Sivan 5727). Yair, though, does concede parenthetically that it may be necessary to relinquish certain heavily-populated territories – but this, he stresses, is a pragmatic necessity and does not undermine the correctness of the theological position.

32. Shubert Spero, 'The Religious Meaning of the State of Israel', *Forum*, 24 (1) 74. While this position is not necessarily identical or politically in agreement with other forms of Active Messianism (specifically, *Gush Emunim*) it has been placed in this category for its basic orientation – that history is being 'changed' by the God of History at present, and that those who understand this will find various events, including the Holocaust, comprehensible as part of a redemptive process which demands the response of recognition and appropriate action.

33. Hanan Porat, *Hatzofe* (daily newspaper of the National Religious Party) 2 February 1973.

34. Festival commemorating the saving of Jews from annihilation in ancient Shoshan (Persia).

35. Yaacov Herzog, 'The Meaning of Israel's Resurgence', in *A People That Dwells Alone: Speeches and Writings* (London, 1975) 56–7.

36. On the distinction between salvation and redemption, and the requirements of the salvational situation, see also my discussion, 'The *Mitzvot*, the Messiah and the Territories', *Tradition*, 10 (3) (Spring 1969) 12–40.

37. Cited in Yona Cohen, '*Milchemet Sheshet Hayamim*' ('The Six-Day War') in *Shana B'Shana*, Yearbook of Haichal Shlomo (Jerusalem, 5728) 300–1.

38. Cited in S. Zalman Abramov, *Perpetual Dilemma: Jewish Religion in the Jewish State* (Rutherford, 1976) 247.

39. *Hallel* is a prayer recited on celebratory days; on such days which are also marked by tragedy only half the prayer is recited, but in this case, due to the momentousness of the occasion, the Chief Rabbi of Israel declared that the full prayers should be said.

40. During the period between Passover and *Shavuot* (49 days) all celebra-

tions are forbidden, except traditionally on the 33rd day and now, in Israel, on the 43rd day (Jerusalem Day).

41. Abramov, *Perpetual Dilemma*, 247.
42. See, for example, Ephraim E. Urbach, '*Aizehu Gibbor? Mi She'ose Son'o Ohavo*' ('Who is a Warrior? He Who Makes His Enemy Into a Friend') *Petachim*, 13 (5) (Iyar 5730) 5–8.
43. 'Peace as a Jewish Value: A Talk With Aviezer Ravitsky', *Oz V'Shalom*, English Bulletin 7–8 (Jerusalem, Fall 1986) 28–9.
44. The clan of the Maccabees and their successors, who fought against Hellenization and later, Roman oppression, determined to die rather than yield.
45. A code of Jewish behaviour, based on the Talmud, by Joseph Caro, published 1565.
46. Isaiah Leibowitz, 'The Spiritual and Religious Meaning of Victory and Might', *Tradition*, 10 (3) 7.
47. Agudat Yisrael – political and religious movement which views the Torah as interpreted by traditional commentators as the only legitimate code of laws binding on the Jews and on Israeli society.
48. Two strictly Orthodox anti-Zionist sects.
49. For a detailed discussion, see Norman Lamm, 'The Ideology of the Neturei Karta', *Tradition*, 13 (1) 38–53.
50. 'Knitted skullcaps' worn by religious Zionists, who have been traditionally in the mainstream of Israeli politics and less militant than the Ultra-Orthodox.
51. Two religious peace movements.
52. In the opinion of the writer, who is a member of *Oz V'Shalom*.
53. 'God full of mercy' – prayer of mourning.

14 Economic Developments Since 1967
Haim Barkai

Twenty years – almost a generation – have passed since the string of unexpected events which unfolded in 1967: the Arab attempt to strangle Israel; the war; and, eventually, the advent of Israel's control over the whole of what was, until 1948, Mandatory Palestine. The interval of two decades, and the geographic extension of political control had an inevitable demographic implication. Table 14.1 shows that Israel's population grew by 63 per cent over this period. Yet figures refer to population subject to Israeli jurisdiction and thus do not include the Arab population in Judea and Samaria or the Gaza Strip, and therefore reflect an underestimate of the significance of demographic developments. The *control* criteria offers an economically more relevant description of this factor. Israel's population was about 2.7 million just before the outbreak of the 1967 War. In its immediate aftermath the population under Israel's control was about 3.7 million. By the middle of 1987, it was already 5.75 million. This is a 55 per cent increase within 20 years.[1]

Jewish population grew at a somewhat lower rate during the twenty-year period to mid-1987 – from about 2.36 to about 3.57 million, by about 52 per cent. This implies an annual rate of increase of more than 2 per cent, a very high rate by the standards of industrialized societies. It was, of course, sustained by *Aliyah* (immigration) – which meant an influx of about 500 000 Jews. The net immigration balance was inevitably lower – 400 000 only. Most of the population growth among Jews reflected a 'self-sustained' natural rate of increase, which at its present annual rate of 1.5–1.6 per cent is very high by the current standards of developed economies. At the current corresponding high net reproduction rate (though lower than a decade ago) this means that the Jewish population will approach 4.8 million by 2010, even if the migration balance is zero.[2]

THE CREDIT SCORE

Population growth is indeed one of the features associated with economic growth. But on its own this does not mean that growth – in the sense of rising productivity and welfare – has taken place. These *sine qua non* features of the process are reflected and measured by economic variables *per se* derived from social accounting data. Looking retrospectively from the vantage point of 1987 the overall performance in terms of production and living standard measures are impressive. Israel's GNP in 1987 was about 2.65 times greater than that of 1967, and *per capita* product, which is a relevant aggregate measure for productivity, grew by 60 per cent over these two decades. These figures imply average annual rates of growth of 5.0 and 2.4 per cent respectively for the total and *per capita* measures of production.[3]

Welfare measures also suggest impressive performance. One of these is, of course, the employment record. Excluding 1986, in which unemployment temporarily shot up (Table 14.1), the record indicates that 'full employment' was the rule, one of the dominant economic and social features of the country in this period.

In spite of the rapid increase of its labour force, over-full employment suggested by unemployment rates of about 3–4 per cent, was the rule between 1968 and 1974, and also in some of the later years. During the last decade, unemployment rates hardly touched the 5 per cent level – that is, in the very period in which such higher rates were the rule rather than the exception in industrialized economies.

The welfare measures *per se* – consumption and *per capita* consumption – show an outstanding improvement. Total private consumption expenditures grew about threefold, and the *per capita* figure, which is perhaps the best indicator of trends in living standards, grew by 80 per cent over the two decades. This implies an average annual rate of 3 per cent for these twenty years which puts Israel's rise in living standards in the highest brackets among the world 'league' tables. On their own the overall figures suggest that the rapid rise in living standards was universal, though presumably unevenly spread between income brackets.

To overcome the social strains usually associated with rapid growth, which in a country having an unusually high ratio of 'new immigrants' might be even more severe, a social policy aimed at reduction of differences is obviously desirable. The entries in Table 14.1, line 5c, referring to overall expenditure on social services, health, education

Table 14.1   Selected economic indicators, Israel (1966–86)

	1966	1967	1972	1977	1986
1 Population:					
(a) Total	100	104[a]	121	137	163
(b) Jewish	100	102	117	131	152
2 Gross domestic product	100	102	180	213	264
3 Private consumption expenditure	100	102	153	197	298
4 Gross investment	100	78	226	195	183
5 The public sector:					
(a) Total consumption expenditure	100	138	222	285	280[b]
(b) Defence: Total	100	177	315	402	484
Domestic	100	153	317	428	469
(c) Expenditure on social services[c]	–	–	122	210	268
6 Import surplus[d]	100	115	183	274	285
7 Real net foreign debt[d]	100	100	230	478	738
8 Consumer price index	100	101	149	714	1,097,287
9 Unemployment rate (per cent)	7.4	10.4	3.6	3.9	7.2
10 Real wages	100	99	109	123	147[c]
Per capita					
11 (a) Gross domestic product	100	99	149	155	160
(b) Private consumption expenditure	100	99	127	143	180
(c) Government civilian consumption expenditure	100		121	134	122[d]

Sources:

Line 1   Central Bureau of Statistics (CBS), *Statistical Abstract of Israel* (1986) Table II–1, 26.

Lines 2–5a   CBS, *Statistical Abstract of Israel* (1986) Table VI–1, 170–1.

Line 5b   According to E. Berglas, *Defense and the Economy: The Israeli Experience* (Jerusalem: The Maurice Falk Institute for Economic Research in Israel, 1983) DP 83.01, Table A–1, 51–2 and H. Barkai, 'Israel's Attempt at Economic Stabilization', *Jerusalem Quarterly*, 43 (Summer, 1987) 3–20.

Line 5c   From data base in J. Kop, J. Blanket and D. Sharon, 'Social Service Structure and Forecast' (Jerusalem: Jerusalem Centre for Social Policy Research, 1987).

Line 6   N. Halevi, 'Perspectives of the Balance of Payment', in J. Ben Porath (ed.), *The Israeli Economy Maturing Through Crises* (Cambridge, Mass., 1986) Table 17.1, 243 and H. Barkai, 'Israel's Attempt', Table 1.

Line 7   CBS, *Statistical Abstract of Israel* (1986) Table VII–4, 202.

Line 8   CBS, *Statistical Abstract of Israel* (1986) Table X–2, 251.

Line 9   CBS, *Statistical Abstract of Israel* (1986) Table XII–2C, and the same Table in *Abstracts* of other years.

Line 10   National Insurance Institute Series from wage data base, prepared by Gira Silberman.

Line 11a–b CBS, *Statistical Abstract of Israel* (1986) Table II–1, 26.

Line 11c   Berglas, *Defense and the Economy*, Table A—1, 1, 55 and H. Barkai, 'Israel's Attempt', Table 1.

Notes:

a Population data for 1967 reflect the reunification of Jerusalem which involved a substantial increase in size of Israel's Arab population. The 1986 entries on the basis of the 1967 population data are 157 and 149 for total and Jewish population respectively.

b The entry for 1986 reflects a substantial (15–20 per cent) but temporary cut in the wages of civil servants. It therefore reflects only a temporary lower cost of government services and not a cut in the supply of services.

c Base year for entries in this line is 1970 = 100.

d Constant 1972 dollar prices – current dollar values of import surplus and of foreign debt deflated by US GNP implicit price index.

e The 1986 entry reflects the substantial but temporary cut in wages and salaries designed as part and parcel of the '1985 economic stabilization policy'. By 1987, the cut was restored to the 1984 wage level (which in terms of the entries in line 10 was about 154).

and transfer payments (particularly child benefits and old age pensions) present the implementation of such a policy in quantitative terms. It was designed to spread real incomes more evenly, both in the short and long run. An increase by about 2.7 times between 1970 and 1986 (significantly greater than the growth of GNP over this period), indeed speaks for itself.

There is perhaps no better indication of the rapidly rising pattern of living standards in all income brackets than the data on household use of durables and on housing density. Whereas in 1967, a density of one person or less per room could be afforded by only 30 per cent of households, the same density was afforded by about 60 per cent of Israeli households in 1986. On the other end of the scale, only 1.4 and 1 per cent respectively of households had a density of 2 and 3 persons per room in 1986 – the corresponding rates for 1967 were 14.1 and 10.1 per cent. Similarly, while in 1967 only 32 per cent of households had a washing machine, 83 per cent an electric refrigerator, 32 per cent a telephone and 9 per cent a car, the corresponding figures for 1987 were 85, 99, 75 and more than 40 per cent respectively. A similar pattern applies to all other durables. Thus, within these twenty years, Israel made the final dash into the social and economic milieu of a consumer-oriented society complete with the trappings of a welfare state, characteristic of the post-war group of industralized countries in the West.

JUDEA, SAMARIA AND THE GAZA STRIP

The rapid rise in production, living standards and welfare during these two decades spilt over into Judea and Samaria and the Gaza Strip. Indeed, the conventional social accounting measures indicate that economic growth in these areas was even more rapid than in Israel. Economic performance, in the first decade particularly, was nothing less than outstanding. By 1979 domestic product in the West Bank was 2.76 times higher, and in the Gaza Strip 2.4 times higher, than in 1968. The corresponding figures for 1986 (estimated on the basis of 1985 data) are 3.4 and 2.43 for the two areas. This implies an unusual growth rate of 7 per cent and 5 per cent respectively over almost two decades. The corresponding figures for the first 11 years to 1979 were, of course, higher – 9.5 and 8.2 per cent respectively. In view of the substantial fraction of national income which originates as wages in payment for labour employed in Israel and also in the

Arab oil countries – mainly Kuwait and the Emirates along the eastern littoral of the Persian Gulf – income data are a better indicator of economic performance and welfare in these area. In the nineteen years for which the relevant data are available, disposable income in the Gaza Strip grew by 3.4 times, at a somewhat higher rate than GNP, while in the West Bank it grew at a slightly lower rate – 3.2 times over the twenty years. Thus, whatever aggregate measure is adopted, the figures suggest an impressive performance, whether the standard of comparison is growth rates in these territories from 1948 to 1967, in other Arab countries, or in the industrialized and pre-industrialized groupings of the world economy.[4]

However, rapid population growth of about 2.5 per cent annually (for the 1980s) in Judea and Samaria and of about 3 per cent for the Gaza Strip imply, of course, lower *per capita* growth rates of income. Nevertheless at an annual average of 5.4 per cent for the first area and 4.6 per cent for the second, the rates are amongst the highest in the world 'League Tables'. The rates for the first of these two decades, 8.2 and 7.2 per cent, were significantly higher. This implies substantial slowdown in the growth of *per capita* income since 1979. In the case of the Gaza Strip it meant that since, say, 1980, *per capita* income had reached a virtual plateau.

The welfare implications of these overall real growth rates are expressed by aggregate and specific measures of living standards. *Per capita* private consumption expenditures in Judea and Samaria was, in 1987, about 2.4 times as high as in 1968; the corresponding figure for the Gaza Strip was lower – 2.2 times 'only'. These overall figures are supported by data on the possession of durable goods. Thus only about 14 per cent of households in Judea and Samaria and 5.7 per cent in the Gaza Strip had electrical refrigerators in 1972; the corresponding figures for 1985 are 66 and 78 per cent respectively. Similar improvements in housing amenities in terms of number of rooms in dwellings and density did occur over the same period.[5]

The direct and strong economic linkage between Israel and the Areas (Judea, Samaria and the Gaza Strip) is underlined by the structure of their foreign trade. About 60 per cent of the latter's exports is destined for Israel, with Jordan (and other Arab countries) absorbing about 35 per cent. About 80 to 90 per cent of the Areas' imports come from Israel. This, though, includes also goods imported through Israel's sea and airports.

'ECONOMIC BURDEN' OF THE AREAS

The foreign trade and balance of payments data also offer some insight into another dimension of this linkage – the so-called 'Economic Burden' issue. Balance of payments data from 1970 to 1986 indeed reveal a persistent export surplus of Israel with Judea, Samaria and the Gaza Strip averaging about $150 million annually. This would imply that if the Areas did not have the financial resources to pay for this excess of exports, then Israel is granting aid, and/or giving credits of about $150 million year in and year out. Note, however, that even if this were so, the size of this real 'burden' would be small. In terms of the $20–25 billion GNP of Israel's economy it would have amounted to one half of 1 per cent.

Yet this is not at all the case. While the Areas do not have a positive balance of trade with other areas to the extent of an annual rate of $150 million (which could be used to pay Israel for its export surplus with them), there are substantial unilateral transfers to the Areas: UNRWA funds of about $40 million; 'payments' by the government of Jordan to teachers and civil servants who, according to Jordanian law, are still Jordanian government employees; contributions of the Arab oil countries; and PLO funds transferred clandestinely. These funds are evidently a source of foreign exchange for the Israeli economy and appear on the credit side of its current account.

For obvious reasons we do not have full coverage on the size of transfers, and there are lacunae on trade data which distort somewhat the estimates; nevertheless the available data underline the fact that the Areas have not imposed an economic burden on the Israeli economy in the most obvious sense of this term. This conclusion is supported also by fiscal data which show that the 'budget' of the Areas has been close to balance through these twenty years. Israel's contribution to the Areas' budget has never been greater than the annual contributions of Israeli employers to the National Insurance Institute on behalf of employees from the Areas. These funds are not transferred to the authorities in these Areas (as the residents of the Areas are not eligible for old age pensions which these funds are to finance).[6]

The long-run perspective suggests, however, a less sanguine conclusion. From a more subtle point of view, for which measures of trade and payment flows are not relevant, the close linkage with the economies of the Areas did impose a long-term burden on the system.

The impact of this is due to the pulling into Israel's economic system of a great number of employees from the West Bank and Gaza Strip. These mostly unskilled or low-skilled workers, flowing into specific trades – particularly the construction industry, catering, and textiles – generated a strong downward pressure on wages of unskilled labour in these occupations and in the system as a whole. Thus, labour productivity in these industries particularly rose much slower than in other areas due to their higher labour-intensive features. The net result was a significant slowing down of the trend to mechanize these activities, hence a lag in the growth of productivity, which made these industries more and more 'low-wage' activities. This inevitably reduced the pulling power and the employment of Jewish labour in building and manufacturing, with concomitant social tensions familiar to European countries employing a great deal of '*Gastarbeiter*'.

THE DEBIT SIDE

The credit side during these two decades, in terms of production and living standards for the Israeli economy and for the territories under Israel's control, is indeed impressive. Yet the twenty years' vantage point also reveals entries in the debit ledger. Some of these are nowadays a major source of concern. The most serious of these is the decline in *Aliyah*, which in the century of Zionist rebuilding of the country was its main engine of growth. Annual (gross) immigration figures of 10 000–15 000 in the 1980s are a drop in the ocean when compared to the mass immigration years of the late 1940s and early 1950s. Indeed, they are hardly 30 per cent of the average figures for the 1960–73 period. This collapse in levels of immigration has obvious political implications. It has, however, also far-reaching economic consequences. The effect on aggregate demand (and thus on the level of economic activity) is only one of its facets. One of the more significant long-run effects of a lower inflow is the change in the age structure of the population. In consequence, there is a decline in the relative size of the labour force, and hence in the proportion of gainfully employed.

Immigration levels are undoubtedly dependent on politics, and thus on exogenous factors; the foreign policy of the Soviet Union is an obvious case in point. Yet the state of the economy and society, and thus the social and political milieu, does affect Israel's 'pulling' power. This 'gravitational' force has great relevance for potential immigrants from countries in which there are no political barriers to emigration. The relevance of this was quite obvious in the immediate aftermath of the Six-Day War through to 1973. Since most of world Jewry lives in countries in which emigration is free, the dearth of *Aliyah* from the West underlies the erosion in Israel's pulling power. As such, it is undoubtedly an unfortunate shadow on Israel's horizon at this point of time.

Another problem is the huge foreign debt of about $20 billion. Table 14.1 shows that this debt has grown by more than seven times over the twenty-year period, from a relatively affordable level of 25 per cent of GNP to a dangerously critical level of 80–85 per cent of GNP. This is of course directly linked to the huge rise in the (real) import surplus – by almost three times over these two decades (Table 14.1, line 6) which on its own is a major cause of worry. Though lower than the all-time high of a $5 billion import surplus in 1984, the 1986 import surplus of about $4 billion, and the even higher level in the first quarter of 1987 are unsustainable in the long run. These features are evidently the obverse image of an inherent flaw in the Israeli economy reflecting the economic and social policies pursued by Israeli governments through the last decade. These allowed consumption expenditures – private and public – to outrun production by a wide margin (Table 14.1, lines 2, 3 and 5).

THE GOOD YEARS: 1967–73

Table 14.1 underlines the uneven pace of Israel's economic development through the two decades since the Six-Day War. Reference to economic criteria allows a clear-cut distinction between two periods – the six years between the Six-Day and the Yom Kippur Wars, and the thirteen years from, say, 1974 onwards.

The first period is one of substantial immigration, with average annual rates exceeding 40 000, and of all-time high growth rates: GNP grew at average annual rates exceeding 10 per cent through to September 1973. This outstanding performance was achieved by a growing demand in the rapidly expanding markets at home and abroad. Immigration and rising incomes generated a tremendous demand for housing, and thus a corresponding expansion in the construction industry. The capture by Israel of the Old City of Jerusalem and of Judea and Samaria and the post-war euphoria amongst Jews all over the world generated a major expansion of foreign tourism. Farming and manufacturing, which were in the doldrums during the 1965–7 slowdown, peaking in an unemployment rate of 10 per cent just before the war, responded immediately to the pull of expanding markets. Foreign demand for farming and manufacturing exports followed the expansion of world markets in the environment of full employment in the industrial countries, in turn sustained by the US 'Vietnam' inflation. A successful 17 per cent devaluation *vis-à-vis* the dollar and the currencies of most West European countries in the wake of and identical with the devaluation of sterling in November 1967, strengthened the expansionary impact of growing foreign markets on the export industries. By maintaining the effect of real devaluation, stable prices (through 1969) offered similarly increased advantage to domestic producers of import-competing industries.

The subsequent boom in demand for farm products did increase agricultural output. At the same time, it reduced the opposition of Israeli farming interests to the opening of Israeli markets to farm products originating in Judea and Samaria. It smoothed the entry of Judea, Samaria and the Gaza Strip into what may be described as a full customs union with Israel. The booming demand in Israeli markets and the policy of 'open bridges' initiated in July 1967, which allowed trade with Jordan and its 'hinterland' stretching to Kuwait and the Persian Gulf littoral, boosted agricultural production in these areas. It was helped by the rapid adoption of Israel's modern agricultural technology by the West Bank farmers; this raised productivity and thus lowered costs. The market effects and the sky high revenues of the 'Oil States', which created a tremendous demand for trained labour, set the stage for rapid growth in Judea and Samaria.

Yet the main force in these years behind the rapid revving up of the Israeli economic engine was due to comings and goings in the manufacturing industry. The major thrust for growth was not in traditional industries such as textiles, leather, chemicals and diamonds, although these branches benefited substantially from rising demand. It was the 'high tech' industries, in their infancy before the Six-Day War, which really got going. Electronics, optics and aviation were the leading sectors; they pulled ahead owing to the tremendous demand by the defence sector, in turn generated by the politically motivated French embargo on the delivery of Mirage planes and other main weapon systems imposed by de Gaulle in 1967. This embargo, which prevented the delivery of an order of planes designed according to Israeli specifications, and partially paid for, signalled to all and sundry that 'self-reliance', in the production of the most up-to-date weapons systems, was the order of the day.

This industrial and technological breakthrough would not have proceeded as far as it did had a major increase in the defence budget, imposed on Israel by the adamant refusal of the Arabs even to consider peace, not been forthcoming. The Arab League's Khartoum policy of 'no recognition, no negotiations, no peace' was initiated by Nasser in the face of defeat and was the opening move in the 'War of Attrition' along the Suez Canal and in the Jordan Valley. This could be started and maintained only by a major Arab armaments effort. The wherewithal for this effort was provided first and foremost by the Soviet Union, which embarked on a crash programme to rebuild Egyptian and Syrian armies and arsenals. From the mid-1960s onwards, Arab oil money, though still modest in size when compared with the standards of the middle and late 1970s, was also a growing source of funding for Arab military budgets, particularly those of Iraq, Saudi Arabia and Jordan.

These developments forced Israel into a reassessment of its priorities, and inevitably led to a major upgrading of its defence effort. The defence budget grew by leaps and bounds; in 1972 it was (in real terms) more than three times as high as it was in 1966 (Table 14.1, line 5b). The all-time high average annual growth rate over these six years of defence expenditure of 21 per cent per annum, could be sustained, if at all, only due to the corresponding rapid growth of GNP at rates exceeding 10 per cent. Even so, this meant a very substantial increase in the defence burden – from about 6 per cent of GNP in 1966 – which allowed Israel to fight and win the Six-Day War – to 12.5 per cent in 1972.

Over the same span of time total government expenditure rose relatively less than did defence expenditures – by 'only' 2.2 times. This means that government civilian consumption expenditures and public sector investment grew more slowly than the growth of national product. The same did not apply, however, to another dimension of government involvement in the workings of the economy transfer payments. As usual in periods of rapid growth, growing affluence was not evenly distributed.

These developments were coterminous with an extremely important social process – the coming of age of the second generation of Israeli born and bred children of the mass immigration of the 1950s. This social grouping was – much more than their parents' generation – aware of its potential political power, and requested openly an income distribution more favourable to the lower income brackets. The government responded to these claims by the implementation of a major social policy expressed quantitatively in an increase of 88 per cent in cash benefits in the period 1970–2 (Table 14.1, line 5c).

One of the most prominent features of the period 1966–72 has therefore been the 'growth of government'. An increase in government consumption expenditure from about 18 per cent of GNP in 1966 to 22 per cent in 1972 and in transfer payments from, say, 4 per cent to 8 per cent of GNP, is one dimension of this all-embracing process. The obverse image of this tremendous rise in government spending through to 1972 is the corresponding rise in (gross) taxes from about 30 per cent of GNP in 1966 to 40 per cent of GNP in 1972. Furthermore, the rapid expansion of defence-related industries meant inevitably a much greater involvement of government in the promotion of specific lines of industrial activity and in the management of some of the biggest firms in manufacturing industries.

This major expansion of government demand did not however, 'crowd out' the private sector. On the contrary, private-sector investment grew to an all-time high level in 1972. Investment was about 125 per cent higher than in 1966 and more than 90 per cent higher than in the previous peak – the boom year of 1964. This major surge in investment was associated with even greater expansion of investment in dwellings, thus raising substantially the share of investment in housing in the total.[7] Private consumption expenditure similarly followed a rising pattern, though at a much lower rate than investment and at a significantly lower rate than GNP. Its 53 per cent growth during these six years was still expressed in a 21 per cent rise in *per capita* consumption, a comparatively high annual average rate of 4 per cent. However, if one considers spending on housing amenities, which are part of the standard of living and the rate of which can be deduced from investment in housing, it would appear that the standard of living in these three years rose at an even higher rate than the *per capita* consumption data indicate. The investment figures in housing suggest that living standards which are to reflect housing amenities, too, rose in these years at an even higher rate than suggested by the *per capita* consumption data. All in all, by 1972, *per capita* consumption had reached a level rapidly approaching West European standards.

Note, however, that in spite of the rapid rise in private consumption expenditures the latter grew at a *lower* pace than national product and real disposable income, not only between 1966 and 1972 but also through the entire post-1967 decade. This means that households and firms were saving substantial fractions of income through 1977. Government was indeed running a deficit which was, however, through this period smaller than private savings. This means that the level of net saving for the economy as a whole was positive. Rising living standards were accordingly sustained within the limits imposed by the rise in production. Indeed, the economy was even financing a substantial fraction of its investment from its own sources.[8]

Yet owing to the substantial and rising budget deficits, domestic

Table 14.2   Selected economic indicators, Judea, Samaria and Gaza Strip, 1966–86.

	1967[a]	1977	1986[b]
1 Population:			
(a) Total	100	116	141
(b) Judea and Samaria	100	117	140
(c) Gaza Area	100	118	142
	1968	*1979*	*1986*[b]
2 GNP:			
(a) Judea and Samaria	100	276	342
(b) Gaza Area	100	240	243
3 Disposable income:			
(a) Judea and Samaria	100	263	318
(b) Gaza Area	100	317	345
4 Private consumption expenditure:			
(a) Judea and Samaria	100	221	292
(b) Gaza Area	100	272	304
Per capita			
5 Disposable income:			
(a) Judea and Samaria	100	239	279
(b) Gaza Area	100	252	252
6 Private consumption expenditure:			
(a) Judea and Samaria	100	239	241
(b) Gaza Area	100	217	226

Sources:
Line 1   CBS, *Statistical Abstract of Israel* (1986) Table XXVII–1, 683, and unpublished estimate for 1986.
Lines 2–6   CBS, *Statistical Abstract of Israel* (1986) Table XVII–5, 6, and 8, 687–90.

Notes:
a Base: Population Census, September 1967.
b Entries are based on preliminary data for 1986.

savings were insufficient to finance the major investment effort. By 1970, as the economy reached full employment in late 1969, in the face of an ever-rising influx of labour from the 'territories' and of the increase in the labour force in the wake of the high levels of immigration, demand pressures were abundantly apparent. These were first absorbed by a rising import surplus which by 1972 was 60 per cent higher than in 1967 (Table 14.2) and inevitably, somewhat later, by rising prices. The latter were also affected by cost factors reflecting inflationary pressures on the world economy and the effects of the effective and formal devaluations of 1970 and 1971. Inflation was surfacing again, and the short period of comparatively stable prices – during the three years through to 1969 – led to a take-off of inflation. A 6 per cent rise of the price level in 1970 accelerated to an annual rate of 20 per cent in the three first quarters of 1973 – i.e., before the Yom Kippur War. This was a high rate even in terms of the inflationary experience of the economy as far back as 1940.

THE YOM KIPPUR WAR SHOCK WAVES

The immediate economic impact of the 1973 war was felt in price rises. The October OPEC price coup and the continuous rise in the prices of primary commodities in world markets pushed Israeli prices upwards. This cost–push effect was common to all the industrialized countries; yet, in view of its high import intensity, the cost–push effect was particularly strong. With inflation already running at an annual rate of 20 per cent, this external cost–push effect was very effective in accelerating the inflationary process. Inflation leapt to an annual rate of 40 per cent in 1974 and 1975. Although the strict disinflationary policies of the Rabin government succeeded in turning the tide towards an annual rate of 25 per cent in the first half of 1977, the price level by the middle of that year was still more than four times higher than the average for 1972, and this meant that within the ten years terminating in 1977, prices rose by more than seven times.

The inflationary tide did undoubtedly complicate matters, but the strategic implications of the OPEC price revolution on Israel's economy went much beyond their impact on other oil-importing countries. The immediate burden imposed by the so called 'energy crisis' was, as was the case for other countries, the increased real cost of oil imports. Israel's balance of payments thus suffered a heavy blow.

30–40 per cent of the deterioration of the current account in the immediate aftermath of the war can be attributed to the OPEC price coup, which in effect boiled down to a 'tax' imposed by OPEC on oil importers. In the case of Israel, which has virtually no domestic primary energy resources, it was particularly burdensome. From 1974 onwards, it amounted to a negative terms of trade effect virtually equivalent in size to a 3 per cent annual (foreign) disposition on GNP. By the end of the decade, and in the wake of the second (temporary this time) OPEC price rise, this so-called 'tax' reached a level of 7 per cent of GNP (on the basis of 1972 oil import prices).[9]

Yet though the direct burden imposed by what amounted to an annual 'OPEC tax' was substantial indeed, this was far from representing the full economic significance for Israel of the OPEC price revolution. The case of Israel was unique amongst energy importers due to an additional indirect secondary burden – the result of the mammoth rise in oil revenues of the Arab members of OPEC. A small fraction of the growing oil revenues were, from the middle 1960s onwards, contributed to the military budgets of Egypt, Jordan and Syria. These funds were still relatively small – not much more than, say, 100 million dollars annually. The oil price explosion meant, however, that through the 1970s and the early 1980s the sky was the limit for Arab oil revenues – these at one time were running at annual rates of more than $100 billion. The funding of the confrontation states' military budgets and of the military budgets of the oil exporters themselves (like Iraq and Saudi Arabia) rose correspondingly. By the middle of the 1970s these were running at levels of billions of dollars. Oil money upset the delicate military equilibrium and plunged the Middle East into a major arms race. Levels of military establishment and of hardware more appropriate to the larger European members of NATO became the rule in the confrontation states, particularly in Egypt, Syria and also in Iraq and Saudi Arabia.

Israel had no option but to follow suit. In the immediate aftermath of the Yom Kippur War, it was forced therefore to build up its armed forces – personnel and weapon systems – to levels undreamed of not only in 1966, but even in 1972. The mounting burden of the defence effort was revealed in the size of the ratio of domestic defence expenditures – from 6 per cent of GNP in 1966 to 14 per cent in 1972. It climbed further, reaching an all-time high ratio of about 17 per cent in 1974–5. This, of course, meant an all-time high in absolute terms – real domestic defence expenditures were by that time 80 per cent higher than in 1972, and almost six times higher than in 1966.[10]

Furthermore, this defence effort had to be implemented within an economic environment in which growth was slowing down to negligible rates.

The corresponding rising demand pressures in the full employment economy inevitably accelerated inflation – the surface expression of economic crisis. Though the cost–push effect of the first OPEC price rise was undoubtedly relevant, its real root was the collapse of the extensive Israeli boom of the late 1960s and early 1970s and the slowdown of the world economy sometime before (but particularly after) 1973. At that time, these developments and the major defence build-up required a corresponding belt-tightening – a highly restrictive economic policy. Yet the post-war mood of 1973 – which reflected the traumatic experience both of the surprise attack and of the conflict of the war itself – generated internal political strife.

Under such circumstances, governments are reluctant to admit the necessity and inevitability of imposing 'economic hardships' on the public. This was also the attitude of the Israeli government, although deterioration of the terms of trade, the slowdown in export markets and the corresponding collapse of Israel's growth rate did not offer any other way out. An attempt to reduce living standards was essential, in spite of a major increase in American aid which paid for part – but for a part only – of the increased defence outlays. An attempt to follow such a line by the tightening of fiscal policy was finally implemented in 1975. It indeed improved the balance of payments and did lower the inflation rate. It ended, however, with a political landslide – the defeat of the Labour Alignment in the 1977 elections, a change of government and the coming to power of an inexperienced Likud government after more than a generation in opposition.

The OPEC tax, the inefficiencies generated by accelerating inflation, the 80 per cent rise in domestic defence expenditures within two years (involving also an extension of reserve service and the restrictive fiscal policy of 1975), pulled the GNP growth rate of 10 per cent during the eighteen years prior to 1967 to 5 per cent in 1974, and to even lower rates through to 1977. Even a 5 per cent growth rate was never achieved again in the 1977–87 decade and the mean *per capita* growth of GNP was down to close to zero from 1977 onwards (Table 14.1).

The 'new economic policy', initiated with great fanfares in October 1977, was expected to revive flagging growth by reducing the involvement of government in the economy. The latter was identified as a target in its own right by the new 'central-right' government. The 'liberal' policies were implemented by a relaxation of currency controls. However, in spite of high-minded protestations to this effect, the new government implemented a reduction neither in public sector expenditures nor in the tax burden.[11] The pattern followed through the 1977–87 decade was rather in the opposite direction. Government involvement in the economy rose rather than fell.

The relaxation of exchange controls in the wake of the 1977 devaluation, carried into effect without supporting restrictive policies, turned out to be a fiasco. The anticipated inflow of huge long-term private capital – which was to 're-kindle' investment and growth – did not materialize. 'Hot money' indeed poured in (initially), but it fuelled inflation. The hoped-for major upturn of investment in industry and return to the previous growth pattern was never fulfilled.

Inspection of Table 14.1 shows that from 1975 the average annual growth rate of GNP was about 2.5 per cent. This means that *per capita* product hardly budged from the level reached by the middle of the 1970s. This figure also suggests that productivity was in the doldrums over the entire period. Nevertheless, through 1984 when the Likud government was replaced by a National Unity government, and beyond, living standards rose significantly – by about 26 per cent in terms of *per capita* consumption (Table 14.1). This means an average annual rate of 2.4 per cent – high in terms of international standards, and particularly high in view of the global economic slowdown for most of this period. The extensive social policies initiated in the early 1970s and implemented continuously through to 1987, meant that the rising pattern of living standards was fairly universal and applied to the whole spectrum of income brackets.

Yet this divergence between significantly rising living standards and stagnating production underlines an inherent contradiction. Its resolution was effected by a rise of about 50 per cent in the real import surplus between 1972 and 1977 and by a further, though much smaller, rise in the coming decade. This, however, had to be financed. It was done by the building up of the external debt to a dangerous level of about 85 per cent of GNP (in the mid-1980s) and by a major increase in United States aid. Yet the pressures generated by demand in the fully employed economy could not be contained by this import surplus alone.

THE ROAD TO 3-DIGIT INFLATION AND BACK

These pressures burst the seams by generating a pervading and rapidly accelerating inflation – the hallmark of the Israeli economy through to 1985. The take-off of inflation began in the early 1970s. By 1973 before the outbreak of the October War, prices were rising at an annual rate of 20 per cent. The first OPEC price rise pushed inflation at one go to an annual rate of 40 per cent, where it was contained in 1975–6 by a restrictive fiscal policy. The October 1977 New Economic Policy involving as it did a substantial devaluation, rekindled the upward trend of prices. Although the economy was operating at the time within the full employment range, no absolutely essential supporting restrictive fiscal policy was designed as part and parcel of the programme.

Though restrictive monetary steps were implemented, they were relaxed just as an inflow of 'hot money' necessitated further constraints. The linkage of financial assets to prices and to foreign exchange meant that the very high nominal devaluation of October 1977 had far-reaching consequences for monetary expansion. These, and the relaxation of currency controls (which allowed a smooth inflow of money from abroad), soon generated a significant pressure on prices. By 1978, inflation was running at an annual rate of 50 per cent. The second oil price shock, which came in 1978 and 1979, led to further acceleration of prices. By late 1979 inflation passed the 3-digit threshold – the 1980 annual rate was already 131 per cent.

These developments led to an ever-increasing linkage of prices, wages, financial assets and, finally, of virtually all money – indeed, to the emergence of an all-enhancing linked system. The 1980s through to 1985 saw, therefore, the emergence of inertial inflation, its corresponding damaging effect on the *modus operandi* of the economy due to the attempt of all and sundry to 'beat' inflation, and the inevitable erosion of the fabric of the social system.

The deceleration of inflation in the world economy from 1981 onwards gave Israel more leeway for its attempt to grapple with its much higher, out of line, variation. The opportunity was, however, missed. The government did not succeed in reducing its demand. The hoped-for substantial reduction in defence outlays after the completion of the withdrawal from Sinai did not materialize. The cost of the Lebanon War of 1982 imposed a new burden on the economy and had a negative effect on production. With a 400 per cent rate of inflation in 1984, and the huge 5 billion dollar import surplus, the economy was virtually hanging by a thread over the cliff of hyperinflation.

The inconclusive election campaign which forced upon the political system the establishment of a National Unity government in late 1984, put the economy (and the withdrawal from Lebanon) at the top of the agenda. Following an unsuccessful attempt to contain inflation by means of an incomes policy, a comprehensive economic stabilization policy was implemented in July 1985. The declared targets of this policy were twofold: to reduce inflation rapidly to low single-digit rates and, concomitantly, to reduce the import surplus from the still unsustainable $4 billion level. Accordingly it involved higher taxes and reduced subsidies (aimed at reducing the budget deficit) and substantial devaluation and the pegging of the dollar exchange rate at the higher level. The latter was intended as a sign of stability, thus operating as a device for the lowering of inflationary expectations. Finally, an incomes policy, which involved a temporary cut of 20 per cent and more of real wages, was an inevitable component of the package.

The attempt to reduce inflation was successful and the 500 per cent annual rate of inflation which had prevailed in the second quarter of 1985 (before the programme's implementation) was, within several months, down to an annual rate of less than 40 per cent. By the middle of 1986 through to the middle of 1987 inflation, supported by the continuous pegging of the exchange rate, decelerated to an annual rate of 20 per cent – the rate at which it had been running in the first three quarters of 1973.

The very restrictive monetary policy and the pegged exchange rate which together acted as a brake on inflationary expectations – and thus of the inertial momentum of inflation – succeeded in eliminating the budget deficit. Yet the rebound of real wages towards the end of 1986, lower uncertainty about employment, and the huge accumulation of liquid assets which were now at the disposal of households led through 1986 to a substantial increase in (aggregate) demand and, inevitably, in imports. The second and crucial target of the policy – a significant improvement in the import surplus – was accordingly not achieved. By the middle of 1987, two years after the implementation of the programme, the import surplus was still at a level which could not be maintained in the long run without further increase in American aid, which had already been running at more than $3 billion annually. This is seemingly not in the offing, nor a promising option for society and the economy, even if it were forthcoming.

One promising feature, though, is the government budget. The government did slightly reduce its real demand for resources, and substantially its direct subsidies. The former was mainly carried into effect by a meaningful reduction in the defence budget. Yet with a budget involving domestic demand of 24 per cent of GNP in 1986, and of about 26 per cent of GNP for transfers and subsidies, the government in 1986 was still forced to tax to the extent of 52 per cent of this aggregate to avoid a renewal of demand pressures and inflation. The impact of these necessary high tax rates on incentives, and the corresponding tight monetary policy, essential for maintaining price stability, led to the maintenance of very high interest rates. These two factors – the erosion of incentives and high real interest rates – are adverse to the much required 'dash for growth'. Whether a revision of the size and involvement of government in the economy is in the offing is anybody's guess. The formula of high employment and big government is a (political) fact of life in 1987 as it was in 1977, at the advent of the 'political turnabout' (the Likud coming to power) which opened a new era in Israel's politics.

Notes

1. Though jurisdictions differ, the whole area in which free mobility of goods, capital and (with some restrictions) effectively also of labour are maintained is evidently a single economic entity. It can be conceived as a full customs union.
2. Population and fertility data are according to CBS, *Statistical Abstract of Israel* (1986) Tables II–1, XXVII–1, 2, 13 and similar Tables in *Abstracts* of previous years.
3. Table 14.1, lines 2 and 11a. Preliminary data for 1987, not entered in Table 14.1, indicate that the 1966–86 entries are a very good proxy for the 1967–87 figure.
4. By the middle of the 1980s the ratio of net factor payments from abroad to GNP were 24 and 43 per cent for the West Bank and the Gaza Strip, respectively. National product and income data of Judea and Samaria and the Gaza Strip can be seen in CBS, *Statistical Abstract of Israel* (1986) Tables XXVII–6, 7, and 8, 688–90. The base year for social accounting data in these territories is inevitably 1968.
5. 1972 is the first year for which such data are available. The low entries for this year suggest negligible figures for 1967. For comprehensive data of household ownership of durables, see CBS, *Statistical Abstract of Israel* (1986) Table XXVII–15, 697. See also Table XXVII–14 for data on housing density and dwellings.

6. The statements on the trade and balance of payments of the Areas are based on: R. Meron, *The Economics of Judea, Samaria and the Gaza Strip, 1970–1980* (Jerusalem, 1982) (Hebrew). See particularly 54–62, and Tables 1.7 through 5.3; and on detailed balance of payments estimates for 1984–6 in *Bank of Israel Annual Report* (1986) Table 7–13, 1980.
7. See Yoram Mayshar 'Investment Patterns in Israel' (Jerusalem: The Maurice Falk Institute for Economic Research in Israel, 1984) DP 84.07, Fig. 2, 35.
8. See Mayshar, 'Investment Patterns', Table A–1, 37–8.
9. See Haim Barkai, 'The Energy Sector in the 1960s and 1970s', in Y. Ben Porath (ed.), *The Israeli Economy: Maturity Through Crises* (Cambridge, Mass., 1980) 270–1.
10. Though in 1982 the ratio of defence expenditures to GNP was somewhat lower – about 16 per cent – the all-time high hitherto, in absolute terms, was reached at this point in time and was, of course, associated with the Lebanon War.
11. Bank of Israel, *Annual Report* (1984) (Hebrew) Table E6, 100.

15 The Arab Citizens: Israelis or Palestinians?
Atallah Mansour

The 1948 civil war in Palestine turned the Jewish *yishuv* into an independent state, but the Palestinian Arabs became three groups: one of refugees, another of Jordanian citizens and a third an Arab minority in Israel. The last of these groups, some 150 000 strong in 1949 and 650 000 in 1987, is our concern in this chapter.

The first thing that ought to be known about this minority is that it consisted, mainly, of farmers and poor villagers who decided to risk staying in their homes under Jewish rule in an attempt to rescue their lands and save their families from the humiliating fate of refugees in foreign countries. These Arabs, Muslims and Christians, were no different ethnically from their Palestinian brothers who became refugees or Jordanians. It is geography that denied them Jordanian passports. The Jews conquered their land. They did not become refugees because they took the risk of remaining and the Jews did not massacre them or drive them away.

BEFORE 1967: MILITARY GOVERNMENT AND UNDERDEVELOPMENT

The new Jewish rulers, dominated by their recent trauma from the Second World War, placed their Arab subjects under a strict system of security supervision. Until 1966, these Arabs were unable to travel from one village to another. They lived, in some cases, under dusk-to-dawn curfews for more than ten years. They had to stay home at night, when they were unable to visit neighbours or travel. To visit a medical clinic or hospital in a nearby town they needed a written permit, for which they had to wait for days and sometimes for weeks. The military commander never lived in the Arab villages. He might come or he might not: at any rate the Arabs were not in a position to question his decision as to whether to issue the permit; he could always invoke the 'security of the state' as an excuse for not issuing it. Even the High Court of Justice refused in many cases during the 1950s to challenge the military government's actions.

In those days, to be an Arab in Israel was a harsh experience. The arbitrary decisions of the army officers could close areas to farmers for years and the failure of farmers to plough these lands could make it possible for another arm of the Israeli government to claim them as public lands, since they were not used by their owners. Other lands were confiscated for 'public interest', which meant new Jewish settlements. In the period between 1948 and 1966 the Arab citizens of Israel lost most of their privately-owned lands; Arab sources estimate the loss at around one million dunams of land, the government published no figures. Today, Arabs own about 600 000 dunams, around 4 to 5 per cent of cultivated land in Israel. Arab citizens were unable to move freely in their homeland, and when they could travel they were ordered to take this route and not the other, and return home before dark. Sometimes they were ordered to refrain from entering certain areas in a town. During that period I was a journalist for Israel's top-quality daily *Ha'aretz*, yet my travel pass prescribed that I could visit Tiberias but only 'up to the cemetery' and Safed 'not including Mount Canaan'. Most people faced even greater travel restrictions. Moreover, they were illiterate or lacking in vocational training for those jobs Israel needed. Their leadership was old-fashioned and unable to lead them in the new predicament. One obvious example is the mayor of Nazareth in 1958, the late Amin Jarjura, a graduate of Istanbul University and a personal friend of Israel's second president, Yitzhak Ben-Zvi. I asked him about the causes of the water-supply failure in Nazareth and he told me that the pipelines were laid with a population of 10 000 to 15 000 in mind, 'but now we have twenty thousand', he said. Why were these lines not replaced? The old mayor asked me if I could make a contribution for the necessary resources. I asked him about the government's attitude and if he had asked for a loan. Mr Jarjura was angry with me. 'Do you want me to enslave the town? And from where will I pay back such a loan? Should I sell my wife's jewellery?'

Today, some twenty-eight years later, no mayor of any Arab town or village will refuse any loan from any source, and every mayor knows that no-one will ask his wife to repay the loans of the local government. Mr Jarjura's episode sounds like a joke. But old-fashioned mayors and corrupt leaders contributed to the fact that Arabs in Israel failed to close the gap with the Jews.

DOUBLE DISCRIMINATION

On the economic side, Arabs were not integrated into Israel – except as a reserve force of cheap labour for difficult jobs in the deserted farms of their brothers, who became the refugees across the borders. The fact that Israel's budget – since, and indeed before, the State's inception – included significant amounts of foreign aid from Jewish communities abroad provided an easy excuse for the Israeli establishment to claim that those Jews in the United States, Britain, Western Europe and South Africa had donated their money to help their own brothers – the Jews, and not the Arabs or other Israeli citizens. These Jews, the Israeli leadership could claim, wished to help their brothers who had arrived as refugees from Nazi Europe or from the Arab–Muslim countries. Worse than that, this leadership was far from being in a conciliatory mood after the 1948 war. The fact that the neighbouring Arab states continued their hostile rhetoric against Israel made it easy for the Israeli establishment not to provide its small Arab minority with the chance to prove how loyal it was – or meant to be. To make sure that this minority was pacified, the Israeli government enacted special laws and regulations to enable the creation of Jewish settlements along Israel's new borders and in the midst of any group of Arab villages. Arab villages like Ikrit and Biram were destroyed. Refugees who moved to nearby towns during the war were not allowed to return to their homes.

The grim fate of these Arab citizens of Israel became more bleak because the country in its early years suffered from real economic hardships. Moreover, Israel's resources were to a large extent strained by defence and the absorption of new immigrants. Though the Arabs shared in the services available to all citizens and their standard of living gradually improved, they were the last group on Israel's priority list for care, and in periods of economic stringency accordingly suffered the worst. But only if we remember that their 'good brothers' across the borders declared them to be both traitors who had accepted Israeli citizenship and servants of the Zionists can we really appreciate the depths of the plight of this tiny, backward minority of the Palestinian people. In addition to being unable to move freely in Israel, the Arabs were prohibited from travelling to the bordering Arab states, which, with the rest of the Arab League countries, unanimously ostracized this minority as traitors.

Owing to restrictions by these Arab states, Muslim citizens of Israel could not, for thirty years, carry out one of their faith's main commandments – the pilgrimage (*Haj*) to Mecca. Christian Arab citizens were able to visit Bethlehem on Christmas Eve but only for 24 hours and only after walking through a tedious Via Dolorosa of Israeli–Jordanian bureaucracy and security checks. No Arab citizens of Israel, even today (April 1987) can visit an Arab state – except Egypt – to meet his brothers or schoolmates. The Arab states treat members of the Arab minority in Israel as Israeli citizens.

But in Israel, the Arabs were not treated as such except on one level, that of civil rights. The Arab minority could vote in elections to the Knesset, and for a few municipal councils in the mixed towns such as Jaffa, Haifa, Acre, Ramle, Lydda or Nazareth and some of the big villages. Arabs were allowed (and were indeed sometimes forced) to vote. In theory, they could stand as candidates for elections. But under the prevailing conditions of military government, these rights were nominal at best. A candidate in an opposition list could not travel freely and his supporters could become suspect for mere non-conformism, especially because of the attitude of Mapai, the ruling party of Israel for almost thirty years (1948–77). Voters cannot be truly said to have been free to vote as they wished if they were endangered after being seen in an opposition party meeting, or if caught reading or distributing an oppositional newspaper. Only the brave, who were willing to suffer and pay a price for expressing their opposition, did so.

THE SHIFTING ARAB VOTE

The vast majority of Arab votes in Israel between 1949 and 1966 went to Mapai and its allies in what later became the Labour Alignment. In the early elections this majority was around 75 per cent, and it soared to more than 82 per cent in 1959, but it then dwindled over the years. In 1965, Mapai (its main list and its affiliated Arab lists) won just around 50 per cent of the Arab vote.

To illustrate this process of change, I have compiled a table of the Arab voting record in Israel's general election campaigns from official sources (Table 15.1). I found that too detailed a breakdown might serve no purpose since Israeli voters – Jews and Arabs alike – tended to vote for some twenty lists in an average election. I have therefore combined these lists into three blocs: the Labour bloc, the Right bloc (Likud and the religious parties) and the opposition Left bloc. I included all of the Arab lists as well as Shinui (since they are partners

Table 15.1   Four early Knesset election results

Year	Labour bloc	Right bloc	Opposition Left bloc
1949	72.9	4.6	22.2
1951	72.6	10.9	16.3
1955	78.1	3.5	15.6
1959	82.5	4.9	11.2

to Labour in the current National Unity coalition), as well Ezer Weizman's Yahad in the Labour bloc. This bloc, in the early elections, also included the Sephardi Party (of the late Beckhor Shitrit) who in a later campaign of the 1950s joined Mapai – Labour's main party.

The Right bloc includes the religious parties, although for most of the early period the National Religious Party (Mafdal) was a partner to Labour in government coalitions. But since this party has increasingly become a partner for the Likud, after joining the Likud-led coalition in 1977, I added them to the Right bloc along with the more militant and smaller religious parties. The third bloc is that of the Left opposition lists – the Communists, Progressive List for Peace, and Civil Rights Movement.

The vast majority of Arabs voting for the Labour bloc in these early years of the State of Israel is quite easy to explain. This was the 'government' and as such won most Arab votes. Even the opposition Left bloc was losing support with the loss in influence it suffered with the failure of the Israeli flirtation with the USSR (Table 15.2).

Table 15.2   Last three Knesset election results

Year	Labour	Right	Opposition Left
1977	36.9	13.9	49.0
1981	43.0	12.0	43.0
1984	36.0	10.0	50.5

These results reflect an obvious change from the earlier elections in that both Labour and Right blocs together have no simple majority of the Arab votes. The Arab voters now feel free to announce their dissatisfaction with government policy and the way they are treated. In addition, these results show that Israel's Right failed to lure Arab voters. Even the fact that it came to power in 1977 did not make it more attractive to them. On the contrary, it seems to be losing some of the support which it won while in opposition.

A more significant lesson may be drawn from these figures: the Arab voters have been drifting more and more to the left. The 1977 elections saw the sensational appearance of the Democratic Movement for Change on the Israeli scene, and the Likud's coming to power. But the Arab voters for the first time moved left, denying the Zionist parties a clear majority of their votes. That year Rakah, Israel's New Communist List – the Arab-dominated pro-Moscow group that split in 1965 from Maki (the Israeli Communist Party) – launched its campaign as the Democratic Front for Peace and Equality (DFPE). Though doing little to win support, it benefited from the general feeling in Israel, among Jews and Arabs alike, that Labour was corrupt and that change was in the air. The Communists added one Jewish non-Communist (Black Panther) to their list who hardly attracted a few dozen votes. But they also added an Arab who was not a party member, the late Hanna Mois, Mayor of Rama and first chairman of the National Committee of Heads of Arab Local Councils. Mr Mois's inclusion was not effected with the agreement of the Arab mayors, but nonetheless gave to the DFPE list a kind of general representativity. The DFPE won around 50 per cent of the Arab vote in the first campaign under its new name.

The Communists, who had begun their record by appealing to the most pro-Israeli group of Arabs (as well as Jews) in 1949, and had won some 22 per cent of the Arab votes, moved to an increasingly strong oppositional stand following the USSR's successes in the Arab states. The Arab voters moved on parallel lines. Soviet Russia supplied arms to Egypt and later on to other Arab states and adopted more pro-Arab policies, and the voters were willing to cast more votes for Maki–Rakah–DPFE.

The best proof of the connection between Moscow's policies and election ballots in Arab towns and villages in the Galilee can be seen in the Israeli elections of 1959. A few months before these elections, the late Egyptian leader, Jamal Abdul-Nasser, clashed with the Soviet leader Khrushchev over influence in Iraq. The Israeli Communists, as always, sided with the USSR – and paid the price in the worst decline yet in their support from Arab voters: Maki lost around 30 per cent of its total vote and its share of the Arab vote dropped from 15.6 per cent in 1955 to 11.2 per cent in 1959, while Mapam doubled its support from Arab voters from 7.3 per cent in 1955 to 14.4 per cent in 1959, and the Labour bloc peaked in its share of Arab vote at 82.5 per cent.

PROGRESS UNDER LEVI ESHKOL

The military government was abolished in December 1966. Its regulations had been imposed on all Arabs in Israel since the 1948 war but enforced more strictly in some areas and more so in the early years. By the 1960s, all Arabs in Israel could feel a certain relaxation of these rules, especially during elections campaigns. Certain areas were opened for civilian movement, other areas were opened to those who could obtain an annual permit. Arab citizens in Israel could travel around in search of employment – and this was the main issue at the time. Many thousands of Arabs in the relatively small work force were unemployed. Arab society, being conservative, kept its women from working in faraway places. Being rural and strictly religious, it knew very little of family planning. One man was usually and typically the sole provider for a family of ten, and since he too came from such a background he could not be expected to have attained any higher education. The circle of poverty and need dominated the scene, even without the factor of military rule; its regulations could only exacerbate the suffering.

The economic slowdown of the mid-1960s made life harsh for many in Israel, including most Arabs. The abolition of the military government and the first government public works to absorb the unemployed came as a great relief. Very many ever since have believed that the late Levi Eshkol was the first Israeli Prime Minister to think of Israeli Arabs as potential partners to Jews in Israel. (Ben-Gurion, for his part, refrained from visiting Arab villages or meeting his own party's Arab Knesset members.)

Under Eshkol, it was felt that the Arabs would integrate as citizens in Israel. More and more local councils were elected, water supplies introduced, connecting roads paved. The Histadrut had opened its gates to Arabs in 1959, but they were given the full rights of membership only in this later period under Eshkol (in 1965). Most Arabs in Israel felt more and more Israeli. The failure of the attempt at Egyptian–Syrian unity in the United Arab Republic (1962) and the pan-Arab movement led by Egypt's Jamal Abdul-Nasser made many Arabs in Israel stop listening to Cairo Radio and tune in to the Voice of Israel.

THE IMPACT OF THE 1967 WAR

It was at this point that Israel's Arab minority faced an upsurge of fear from war. Many Palestinian refugees became guerilla fighters and began attacks across Jordan's borders. There followed the Israeli counter-attacks against Jordan and Syria. These attacks and counter-attacks escalated and brought the 1967 explosion on 6 June 1967. The results of this swift war have clearly shaped the Middle Eastern map ever since. What was the influence of the war on Israel, and especially on its Arab population?

The first clear effect was one of overwhelming insult. The old wound which seemed to have healed was open again and bleeding. Jewish neighbours and customers or workmates began talking about cowardly dirty Arabs and the arrogant jokes left no place for misunderstanding – Arabs, all Arabs, were objects of disdain. I remember two separate incidents concerning personal friends. A garage owner was asked by his Jewish clients to do things properly, 'not Arab work'. In a second case, my neighbour was provoked by one of his Jewish aides who repeated in detail how he had beaten Arab soldiers and how Arab women had kissed his feet, asking for mercy. My neighbour was so angry that his aide lost his teeth and he lost his job.

Many Israeli Jews felt free and unconstrained by the lessons of Jewish history and its moral bonds. They felt themselves superior to normal human beings. Only an Arab like myself who lived in Israel during 1967, before and after the war, and who met many Jews from different walks of life, can really see how this war, though so short, could transform people so completely. Only a few strong characters stood firm and were puzzled to see the shift in public opinion. I know some of these real heroes as well.

ENCOUNTER WITH WEST BANK ARABS: A NEW POINT OF COMPARISON

Against this background, one could easily come to the conclusion that the 1967 war was a real setback to Arab–Jewish relations inside Israel. However, the fact that this war lifted the siege under which Israel (and its Arab minority) had lived since 1948, and that Arabs from Nazareth or Tira could now meet their brothers and sisters in Jerusalem or Nablus came as a great relief. Another major positive aspect was the fact that Israeli Arabs, for the first time, had a yardstick with which to measure their social and economic achievements. Now they could tell for sure that their brothers in Jordan were far better off in terms of academic education, commerce and integration within the government bureaucracy. The figures for students and university graduates in the Gaza Strip and West Bank were clearly in favour of Jordan (which had no university at the time!) and Egypt when compared with the Arabs in Israel. The West Bank merchants were far more affluent than their Arab brothers in Nazareth or Haifa. But the most striking discrepancy lay in the question of access to official posts. The highest Arab in Israeli government service was a probation officer. The highest judge was a magistrate, and there was only one. There were no Arab ministers or Supreme Court justices, nor a District Court judge or a head of department in the Ministry of Education. The Muslim Affairs Department in the Ministry of Religious Affairs was, and still is, run by a Jew. No industry of any significance existed in the Arab sector. The very few clear points in favour of Israel in social services to labour – genuine trade unions and National Insurance support – did not have a strong appeal for the rich middle classes which dominate Arab society. In a few cases, for example, I could hear some landlords on the West Bank accuse Israel of creating the trade unions, to grab their farmers and force landowners to sell the land.

Other points in Israel's favour were the free press and political parties, but these were not manifest clearly in 1967 since only in the past few years has there appeared the first Arab political party, The Progressive Movement – the predecessor of the Progressive List for Peace (PLP) – which managed to win two seats in the 1984 Knesset elections, and only in 1983 did *al-Sinnara*, the first independent Arab weekly, start publishing in Nazareth, along with other weeklies. Before that, only a government-subsidized daily and a Communist weekly were published in Arabic.

Israel's establishment at first hoped, after the 1967 war, that the members of the Arab minority in Israel would influence their brothers across the 'Green Line'. However, the Israeli objective in seeing such influence wielded was never defined, and Israel never asked the West Bank leaders for anything beyond putting pressure on the King of Jordan to negotiate peace with it. But, to my understanding, all paths leading to peace with Jordan were tightly blocked with Israel's resolution to 'unite' Jerusalem and annex the Holy Places to Israel. (I wrote that in *Ha'aretz* in August 1967.) Israel's people and leadership were not, however, in a mood to listen at the time. They lived in the state of total euphoria of 'slaves who came to rule' – as the late Moshe Dayan used to describe those who used to mistreat Arabs in the occupied territories.

Still, the post-1967 encounter between Arabs on either side of the 'Green Line' resulted in the lifting of Israel's Arab citizens from the bottom of the Israeli social scale. Former manual labourers on building sites in many cases became sub-contractors. Many former farm workers began to act as suppliers of cheap labour to their previous masters. Junior employees in firms were now despatched to the occupied territories to promote sales. Arab employees of Israeli political parties and trade unions won major promotions to work with their brothers across the 'Green Line'. An Arab lawyer was appointed as a District Court judge, a Knesset member became the deputy minister of health; another was made deputy minister of communications, a third deputy speaker of the Knesset. This inflation in the number of Arab deputies indeed assumed a farcical colouring when an Arab became deputy head of the Arab Department of the Histadrut. Half a dozen Arabs became advisers to ministers. One of them became deputy to the prime minister's adviser on Arab affairs.

ISLAM AND 'PALESTINIANIZATION'

On the other hand, some real problems were solved. Within a few months of the Six-Day War, no unemployment of any kind existed in Israel. Even on the sentimental, nationalist level, the old problems were solved. The Palestinian *fedayeen* activities inside the occupied territories or launched from Jordan or Lebanon proved to Israeli Jews that a war of a kind was still going on, and that the Six-Day War triumph was not final and total. To the Arabs in Israel, these Palestinian *fedayeen* were not seen as entirely right or wrong. They were seen as brothers, and their refugee camps as no longer unreal: Israel's Arabs now saw at first hand the misery of life in such places as Balata, outside Nablus, or al-Shati near Gaza. They could not blame their brothers for keeping their issue alive by committing atrocities, such as placing bombs in theatres or hijacking civilian planes. Some Israeli Arabs publicly criticized their brothers, while others condoned these actions.

Only 350 young Israeli Arabs joined the PLO between 1967 and 1973. 50 others joined between 1973 and 1976. Knowing quite a few of these Israeli Arabs who decided to cross the lines, I know that many of them did not choose freely. In many cases, these young people were faced with two equally bad alternatives – either to hand over their brothers to an Israeli jail when approached, or join them in underground activities. Such incidents created some tension between Arabs from Israel and the West Bank and Gaza Strip. This tension was eased only in 1971, when PLO activities became minimal inside Israel and the occupied territories.

But on one level, the cultural one, the influence of the West Bank never ceased. This was manifest especially on the religious front within Muslim society.[1] The Israeli Muslims were, on the whole, far from being fluent in religious doctrine or practice, and for historic reasons they were lacking in leadership as well. But immediately after June 1967 they discovered that their brothers to the faith in Jordan (and beyond Jordan in over forty states) were willing and able to offer them moral and material support. Today, twenty years later, this process is clear. Hundreds of new mosques, perhaps over 1000, were built. Many clubs, football teams, economic and educational institutes were established. The influence of this movement is manifest in the tall minarets towering over all Muslim villages in Israel. It also appears in the low voter turnout in some villages, especially in the 'Triangle', where it dropped to no more than 50 per cent in 1984. There fundamentalist Muslims order their followers not to take part in the Israeli elections since none of the candidates are real Muslims. Islam, as they understand it, prohibits believers to give political legitimacy to non-believers in this way. The presence of Muslim candidates for Labour, the Likud, Mapam or the DFPE, did not change matters for them. The percentage of Arab voters in Knesset elections thus fell from one campaign to the next in a consistent manner – from around 90 per cent in 1950 to 68 per cent in 1981. In the last elections (in 1984) the percentage of Arab voters increased for the first time in more than twenty years to 72 per cent. The obvious and only reason is that, for the first time, a party participated which placed a Muslim as the first on its list – Mohamed Miari of the Progressive List for Peace. Mr Miari is far from being a fundamentalist Muslim, but for some of these elements the fact that he was a Muslim by birth was sufficient – and the heavy support he mustered in Muslim villages proves this. The rumour has been spreading since 1984 that other parties may follow the PLP example. The small Christian minority (around 100 000 out of the 700 000 Arabs in Israel) which used to get more than its share of Knesset seats may lose its last, that of Tawfik Tubi of the DFPE.

Another process which was triggered by the Six-Day War was that of the 'Palestinianization' of Israel's Arabs. This process came as a natural outcome of the renewed encounter between those Arabs living in and beyond the 'Green Line', on the one hand, and the decline of the Arab states and pan-Arab ideology, especially after Nasser's death and King Hussein's massacres of the Palestinians in 1970's Black September on the other. The Palestinians in the occupied territories and those inside Israel became more and more dependent on the newspapers published in East Jerusalem, and these three dailies were Palestinian.

How Palestinian are these Palestinians, the Arab minority of Israel? No doubt they all want a solution to the Palestinian problem, a homeland for the refugees, an end to the suffering. I doubt if many are dreaming of a Palestinian victory over Israel as the means to put an end to the state of exile forced on the Palestinians. But most expect some kind of pressure from the USSR or the USA or the international community generally to force Israel to negotiate a peace agreement with the Palestinians. Do they insist that the PLO is the sole representative of the Palestinians? The answer is yes, and this is no wonder. Most countries have recognized the PLO, and the Palestinians have no other recognized body to unite them. The Arab minority in Israel, unlike the Arabs in the West Bank and Gaza Strip, did not receive massive financial support from PLO funds – but the Palestine National Council in April 1971 allotted three seats to ex-Arab citizens of Israel, poets Mahmoud Darwish and Habib Kahwaji and attorney Sabri Jiryis. The three left Israel in the late 1960s and joined the PLO in Beirut after a long confrontation with the Israeli government. Darwish was active in the Communist Party and from a visit to Moscow he deserted to Cairo and later on to Beirut. Jiryis and Kahwaji were among the founders of al-Ard, a pan-Arab nationalist group that supported Nasser's aspirations to unite the Arab states in the Middle East and North Africa. Today Darwish, the most famous of the three, is living in exile in Paris. Kahwaji lives in Damascus and helps Hafez al-Asad of Syria to dominate the Palestinians through a Palestine National Salvation Front attempting to substitute for the PLO. Jiryis is running a PLO magazine in Cyprus.

TWENTY YEARS LATER – STILL A SEPARATE COMMUNITY

But the platform of most Israeli Arabs is rather to pursue a struggle for equality within Israel. The problems are immense, both on the national and personal levels. The national ones are too obvious – the Palestinians are denied the right of self-determination in any part of their homeland. Those who live in Israel are Israeli citizens and on the whole have no aspiration to change this status. But the fact that their brothers across the 'Green Line' are denied the right of self-determination, or even those civil rights enjoyed by the minority within Israel, does not enhance their situation or relations with the Jewish majority inside Israel, not to mention the suffering and hardships of their brothers in the Arab states. But also on the civil rights front, these Israeli citizens are far from achieving their rights. Most of the government posts of middle and higher rank are closed to them (the appointment of a first Arab diplomat as Consul in Atlanta after thirty-nine long years was described by Israeli officials as a revolutionary step). No Arab judge has been promoted to the Supreme Court. No Arab has become a deputy minister in the past ten years. No government official won a post of any significance beyond managing a local branch in an Arab town. On the contrary, it can be demonstrated that fewer Arabs have been hired to work for the government agencies or the Histadrut or any of the latter's economic enterprises. Few Arabs were hired by Israeli universities (many more were hired on West Bank campuses), although some mutual economic projects were begun for Israeli citizens and their brothers on the West Bank, especially in the tourist industry.

But the societies in the West Bank and of Israel's Arab minority have not merged back into one people as before 1948. Twenty years of separate rule and definitely different sets of vested interests have kept the two communities apart. The Arab citizens of Israel were deeply moved by the Six-Day War, but they still stand firm in the same state of affairs as before this war. The earthquake did not cure their wounds, nor kill them.

Notes

1. Over 74 per cent of the Israeli Arabs, some 480 000, are Muslims. The others consist of 100 000 Christians and 70 000 Druze.

Part IV

In the Jewish World

16 Failing God: American Jews and the Six-Day War
Leonard Fein

It has long been generally acknowledged that the Six-Day War was a watershed event in American Jewish history. Indeed, it is rare that an event is felt to be historic at the very time of its unfolding, yet that is how it was in those fateful days of 1967. My purpose here is to describe in some detail the context that made of it a watershed, and then to explore the unsettling elements of its ongoing aftermath.

A generation or so ago, it was generally assumed that American Jewry was rapidly approaching its end. Not that there would soon be no more Jews, but that the vast majority would fade away, whether through active assimilation – or, more likely, through indifference and apathy – leaving behind only a small band of cultists. By now, however, it is apparent that though all may not be well with American Jews, they are hardly at death's door. The Jews endure – and more: beyond the unpredicted persistence of Jewish commitment, there has been a dramatic resurgence of interest in matters – ideas, problems, possibilities – Jewish.

In the transformation of a community suffering from atrophy into a community of Judaic energy and ambition, the Six-Day War was an important element. Yet it is a mistake to assert, as some observers have, that 1967 marks the turning point for America's Jews. The larger truth is that trends and events prior to the war provided the context that made the war itself so signal an event. The impact of the Six-Day War cannot be adequately understood without an appreciation of just where America's Jews found (lost?) themselves on the eve of the drama.

HOW IT WAS: JEWISH CONFUSIONS

Back in the early 1960s, the Levy's rye bread company of New York launched an advertising campaign at whose heart was the assertion,

'You don't have to be Jewish to love Levy's real Jewish rye'. The campaign was testimony to how far Jews had come in this land, to how much they had made it their own, to the ease they had here attained. It was also, however, a remarkable clue to the persistent American Jewish dilemma. For if you did not have to be Jewish to love Levy's real Jewish rye, the implicit follow-up question could not long be repressed: What *do* you have to be Jewish to be able to do? That is, what could a Jew do and feel and know and think and say and be that another could not? And if the answer was 'nothing' – then why stay Jewish?

Inertia? Perhaps, in a world where there were no costs attached to being Jewish, one might as well have stayed as left. Although the costs had diminished, none would deny that there were still costs. Why suffer the costs if there was no substance behind them, if the only thing that set the Jews apart was that they called themselves Jews? If we ate the same rye bread – or junk food — and drank the same wine and, for all practical purposes, prayed the same prayers (or worshipped the same idols) – why not share the same table, the same bed, the same dreams?

A distinctive culture? But a living culture is based on actual, not merely remembered, experience. How long could Isaiah significantly connect Jew to Jew, significantly separate Jew from other, in a world where Charlton Heston's presence was more immediately compelling to Jew and non-Jew alike – or, for that matter, in a land where Isaiah's language is part of the common rhetoric?

Religious belief? Try fitting the same suit of theological conviction on the members of Los Angeles' Hillcrest Country Club, Williamsburgh's Satmar *Hasidim*, and the Central Conference of American Rabbis, the professional association of Reform rabbis. No Jew who accepted God doubted that there was only the one God. We agreed on His (unpronounceable) name – but there the agreement ended.

Language? Hebrew school in this country was mainly remembered as the place where Hebrew wasn't learned. The proportion of Israeli Jews who spoke English was (and remains) many times greater than the proportion of American Jews who spoke Hebrew – or, for that matter, even read it. And Yiddish, for most, was the language the grandparents spoke when they didn't want the children to understand.

Interests? Defending against anti-Semitism, ensuring Israel's safety and welfare, pressing for the rights of persecuted Jews everywhere, insisting on the separation of church and state in America – all these were ways of protecting the Jews. If Jews were safe, then they could practise their Judaism. But if they did not know what the Judaism they were safe to practice was, they were unable to make use of the opportunity the successful defence of their interests had earned them. Would that not sooner or later dawn on them? Would it really suffice to mobilize vast numbers of Jews to protect interests that mattered only to a tiny few? It might be necessary for the Jews to come together as a political action committee – but that could not be sufficient, that could not be the whole of Judaism.

Zionism? Zionist theoreticians might twist to find a way of encompassing a sedentary American Jewry within the fold, but Jews knew better. Here they sat, sometimes remembered Zion, but did not weep. And did not make *Aliyah*. Lovers of Zion, perhaps, but surely not Zionists.

HOW IT WAS: AMERICAN SEDUCTIONS

For very many Jews, as late as the mid-1960s, it was the logic of such facts that drained their Jewish motives. The temptations of America, a land of so many available parts, were immediately at hand; as against them, Judaism appeared to offer only guilt as its motive: Stay Jewish, for if you do not, our people will die.

Before 1963 or so, the threatened demise of the Jews lacked not only aesthetic, but also bite. The common (but not universal) response was a yawn. So what? Judaism is about Europe, or about the Lower East Side, or about general and non-distinctive ethical stuff. Judaism was then; this is now. Or Judaism is about God, and God is either dead or (same thing) irrelevant or too confusing.

At the same time, the America the Jews had encountered was as much a faith as a place. The God who shed His grace on America did not exclude its Jews; they shared the American bounty in full measure. Their ideological confusions hardly impeded their success, and the sweet smell of that success doused their traditional apprehensions, balmed their confusions.

But on Friday, 22 November 1963, America-as-faith began to come undone. The killing of John F. Kennedy marks the beginning of America's most traumatic twentieth-century decade, more wrenching still than the Great Depression, a decade of assassinations (Robert Kennedy, Martin Luther King, Medgar Evers, Malcolm X), burning cities, political corruption – and, above all, Vietnam, where, in the name of democracy, this 'last, best hope of mankind' sought to napalm its way to victory.

(No, it was not quite that simple. The Lyndon Johnson of the deceptions was also the Lyndon Johnson of the Great Society, the president who virtually led a joint session of the United States Congress in the singing of 'We Shall Overcome'; the Henry Kissinger whose lies, big and little, distorted public debate for eight years was also the Kissinger of the Mid-East shuttle, brilliant and indefatigable; the petty and corrupt Richard Nixon, he who dishonoured his office, was the Nixon who recognized China and pursued détente. The point is not that the period from 1963 to 1973 was in its entirety a disaster, but that its disastrous components were a direct challenge to the notion of America-as-faith.)

Most starkly, it appeared that God's grace had been withdrawn. America did not, after all, have all the answers, and some of the answers we thought it had were plainly wrong. Nor could Americans any longer simply assume that the heady progress they had known was their inevitable destiny.

And once the old faith was tarnished, once question marks began replacing exclamation marks, other flaws became apparent: Why, indeed, had this country closed its doors to the Jews in the hour of their most urgent need? And not just 'this country', but the very president in whom the Jews had most enthusiastically believed, Franklin Roosevelt himself? (Most Jews first became aware of the failure, and of Roosevelt's own inadequacy, through Arthur D. Morse's *When Six Million Died*, published in 1968.)

In 1968, in New York City, the old and comfortable alliance between blacks and Jews was shattered. The context, a battle over community control of the public schools, culminating in a prolonged strike by school teachers, accompanied by vicious accusations of racism and bigotry, was doubly disturbing: not only did the long history of fervent Jewish participation in the civil rights struggles of this century mean – apparently – nothing, but the public schools, long seen as the principal vehicle for Jewish upward mobility, were suddenly endangered.

Even the universities were in trouble. At a time when barely three of every ten Americans of college age were attending college, nearly nine of every ten Jews of college age were enrolled. And now in these sheltering groves the galoots were cursing the Jews and burning their research papers. And to add terrifying insult to painful injury, the galoots were the Jews' own children, the first generation (so they had imagined) of complex-free Jews, born with no memory of the desert, heirs therefore to America.

Spuring their inheritance, they turned their backs on America, on the laboratory, on success, on mobility, on their parents, on 'plastics'. They turned to drugs and to communes, they turned to things their parents did not know and did not want to know. They spoke of 'consciousness-expansion', toyed with Zen, lectured us on our own narrowness, and demanded that we subsidize their rebellion.

What sort of promised land was this, a land that set its children against their parents? This was to have been the Land of Enlightenment. One could accept an occasional throwback, since no one was so naive as to suppose that all the darkness was already gone. All that was required was a decent trend line. Was it possible, was it even thinkable, that there was no such trend, that the American promise, too, was a chimera, as the Jewish promise mostly seemed to have been, that the promise was merely a form of self-advertisement, a local booster's fantasy? How terribly frightening, disorientating, here, on the verge at last of a permanent mooring, to be cast adrift again.

A TIME TO REMEMBER

Call it miracle, call it coincidence: Just when the American house came to seem cursed rather than blessed – or, more precisely, just when it came to be seen as a mixed blessing – there transpired an event so awesome, so spectacularly precise in its dimensions, in its structure, even in its timing, as to offer the Jews new hope, new faith.

So much has happened since those days in May 1967 that it is now exceedingly difficult to recapture the sense of how it was back then. But the unexaggerated fact is that around the world, the growing crisis that followed President Nasser's closing of the Straits of Tiran to Israeli shipping had the feel of a medieval morality play, Good against Evil, and back then there was no doubt whatsoever, anywhere in the free world, that Israel was Good. Such an assertion today, in the wake of everything that has since transpired, seems implausible, if not downright absurd. But that is how it was in the days of Leon Uris's *Exodus* and the Arab *fedayeen*, as the terrorists were then known. (Nor had it yet occurred to the media to call them 'guerrillas', much less 'freedom-fighters', rather than terrorists.)

In Tel Aviv, new cemeteries were prepared to receive the anticipated victims of the war that loomed; 20 000 graves were dug. In Minneapolis, Jews frenziedly sought to locate the gas masks that Israel had urgently requested to counter the poison gas it was feared Egypt planned to use. In Miami and Wichita and Spokane, people in the hundreds, then thousands, non-Jews as well as Jews, volunteered to go to Israel to help defend the country, gave millions, then tens of millions, ultimately hundreds of millions of dollars to help prevent what everyone feared: another Auschwitz.

The fear was precise, and 'Another Auschwitz' was its name. Back then, no one yet knew how resourceful and how tough and how skilled at war the Israelis had become. So when some Arab leaders boasted that the Jews would be driven into the sea, the Jews of America felt terror, as Jews.

Nowadays, people tend to remember the war itself, those remarkable six days in which Egypt's air force was destroyed while still on the ground, and the Golan Heights were scaled in hand-to-hand combat, and Jerusalem, the city with the wall in its heart, was reunited. The swiftness of it all, and the surprise of Israel's victory – a victory that soon enough came to be widely resented, as the world tried and failed to adjust to the notion of the Jew as victor, a victory whose fruits would soon enough turn bitter to the Israelis themselves as they tried and failed to find surcease in its aftermath – would alone have been sufficient to impress themselves upon the American Jewish consciousness. But it was, in the end, less the stunning victory than the weeks of terror that preceded it that made the month from the closing of the Straits to the silencing of the guns so memorable an experience.

Perhaps, then, the experience could serve as a reminder to a people newly adrift of the power of ancient moorings? Perhaps, in search of a new faith, one had only to revert to the old? If, after decades of numbness, Jewish nerve endings were still so alive, the availability for fear and trembling, hence also for awe and wonder, so immediate – perhaps then here was a place to drop anchor? Perhaps God Himself had remembered His ancient promise, had finally remembered the Jews, His people?

THE NEW RELIGION

I use religious language here because for very many Jews, the experience of the Six-Day War had religious significance. Specifically, it was after the Six-Day War that Israel came to occupy the centre of the Jewish religious consciousness and consensus. In a very precise way, Israel had now become the faith of the American Jew. Suddenly, the fact of Jewishness had become considerably more salient to America's Jews: just when the faith in America was tarnished, the faith in Israel was enhanced.

And this at a time when America itself was undergoing a critical transformation, having to do directly with the notion of the melting pot.

In 1963, on the eve of the saga I have here been sketching, Norman Podhoretz, then the newish editor of *Commentary*, wrote a widely-praised article entitled 'My Negro Problem – and Ours'. In that article, revealing with startling candour a widespread elite sentiment of the day, Podhoretz asks why negroes should wish to survive as a distinct group:

> I think I know why the Jews once wished to survive (though I am less certain as to why we still do): they not only believed that God had given them no choice, but they were tied to a memory of past glory and a dream of imminent redemption. What does the American Negro have that might correspond to this? His past is a stigma, his color is a stigma, and his vision of the future is hope of erasing the stigma by making color irrelevant. I share this hope, but I cannot see how it will ever be realized unless color does in fact disappear: and that means not integration, it means assimilation, it means – let the brutal word come out – miscegenation. (*Commentary*, February 1963.)

So if a group is ideologically connected (memories of glory, dreams of redemption), perhaps it is warranted in its desire to preserve its identity; otherwise, let it dissolve. In 1963, it was not easy to imagine another way. The American experience did not readily allow the formal recognition of the group. In diverse decisions, the Supreme Court had endorsed that denial, insisted that the system could recognize only the individual, not the group. And progressive Americans were nervous in the extreme in the face of claims to ethnic or racial self-determination, having witnessed far too often the dark places where assertions of kinship and blood might lead.

In 1963, the possibility that a group might take its place in the American sun was not plausible, not unless the group were a quaint, exotic outcropping – the Amish, for example – that chose to dwell apart. In 1963, for some of the same reasons, a leading Jewish editor and intellectual, later to become a fervent advocate of Jewish assertiveness, could put his speculations on why the Jews 'once wished to survive' in the past tense. And why not, after all? If the group, as group, had no logic behind it, no theory under it and if, at the same time, the religion were in disarray, if none could say what it was that connected Jews to one another as they were not connected to all others, why the desire to survive? Time, instead, to move along, to move beyond anachronistic instinct.

Still, whether understanding their reasons or not, most Jews did and do want to remain, somehow, Jews. Traditionally, American Jews had understood that their best shot at group survival was to emphasize their religious – as distinguished from their ethnic – partnership. The nation, after all, at best ambivalent towards ethnicity, was relatively cordial towards religious diversity. The legal system, too, did not acknowledge ethnicity, but offered special protection to religion. Religion was respectable, ethnicity scruffy. So most Jews found it easier to stake their claims on America in religious terms. And as a religion, Jews were accepted as full partners in America's tripartite – Protestant, Catholic, Jew – arrangement, whereas as an ethnic group we were only one among very many.

This emphasis was wholly artificial, even a distortion; Judaism cannot be separated from Jewishness. Unlike other ethnic groups, Jews are connected not only by their history and interests, but also by their ideology; there is, after all, an 'ism' in the Jewish experience. Jews may no longer know quite what that 'ism' means or where it points, but the fact of it distinguishes the Jews from, say, the Irish: 'Irishism' is not part of the language or even the intention of the Irish. But unlike other religions, Judaism has a history that is not merely ecclesiastical; the history of the Jews is not principally the history of their religious doctrine and development – even though one may become a Jew through a formal act of conversion. It is, instead, the history of a people – of, if you will, what Mordecai M. Kaplan called 'an evolving religious civilization'.

But the Jews, sensitive to America's biases, themselves confused regarding the contemporary meaning of peoplehood, sought to emphasize their status as a religion, to downplay their status as an ethnic group. They did this not because of their religious fervour or certainty – in fact, there was little fervour, still less certainty – but because it seemed better to suit the American circumstance.

Then came the final instalment of the miracle: In 1967, the distinction between faith and ethnicity collapsed. The reunification of Jerusalem could hardly be classified as only a piece of national history; Israel's toughest and most secularized generals approached the Wall as pilgrims, the whole House of Israel – that is, the Jewish people - wept in transcendent gladness. As Jerusalem was reunited, so were (briefly, as it turns out) the ethnic and religious elements of the Jewish understanding. It would no longer be possible for American Jews to deny their ethnic commitment.

And just as it ceased to be possible, it ceased to be necessary. Overnight, prodded by blacks, America had changed its mind about ethnicity. The system that twenty-five years ago was blind to groups today wrestles with affirmative action and quotas, with a growing number of people who seek status, recognition and protection not as individuals, nor even as partners in religion, but as members of racial and ethnic groups, of age-defined and sex-defined and sexual-preference-defined groups. Ethnicity has become a fact to celebrate, not a condition to escape.

(On the eve of the Six-Day War, at the height of the panic, a Jewish community in the north-east debated how to respond to the Arab threat. One proposal was to delegate the most auspicious leaders of the community to travel to Washington, there to intercede with the authorities on Israel's behalf. A second proposal was to call a mass rally in the city's major public park. The first proposal was easily adopted; the second was debated for some hours, the opposition centring on the 'unseemliness' of such an assertive public act. Was it not too divisive an assertion of group interest? In the end, the compromise that was adopted was to hold the rally, but not to publicize it. Today, there'd be no question about holding a rally, except that the park is most likely booked for such rallies months in advance.)

Twenty-five years ago, observing Jewish confusions, one might have wondered, as some did, why the Jews would want to survive. Today, the naive utopian universalism that regarded the Jews as a transient anachronism, that promised a homogeneous America, that taught many Jews (along with others) to deprecate their own heritage, lies by the wayside, victim to a decade of trauma – and of pluralism's maturation.

THE AFTERMATH

I have gone to such lengths to describe the specific context within which the Six-Day War took place because unless that context is fully appreciated the current response of American Jews to Israel cannot be fully appreciated.

In the beginning, American Jews were no less swept up and away by the war than their kinfolk in Israel. How delicious it was so suddenly to be transformed from a people of anaemic accountants and orthodontists to a people of muscular heroes. And how satisfying it was to learn that the curse had been lifted, that the Jews were now charmed, that scorn had become admiration and that Jewish life did, after all, have a centre. Israel was the standing room only hit show of our Jewish time; the audiences flocked to see and applaud, and American Jews from comfortable distance, were the ticket-takers, the ushers, even the stagehands.

The magic moment lasted for seven years, and passed.

It had to pass, and the obvious disappointment America's Jews have experienced as it has become clear that Israel is not magic but mundane, and hence fallible, is only a part of the reason.

The pre-1967 Israel was a lonely country on the other side of the world. The Israel of 1987 is a major actor on the world stage, and its adventures and misadventures are nightly chronicled on the television news shows, greet us from our newspapers as we drink our morning coffee. In an earlier time, every rose that bloomed in the Negev and every toddler that bloomed in the Galilee was confirmation that Jews had entered a new and redemptive era. A thorn here, a weed there, no matter. Jews either did not know, or saw these as annoyances that could and would easily be defeated. Now, however, Israel twists and turns to free itself of the thorn bush, and it is no longer so easy to refuse to see its inevitable flaws. Dealing with those flaws has become a major and divisive item on the agenda of American Jewry.

There are those who blame the messenger: bashing the press has become a predictable response to unpleasant news regarding Israel. Lamentably, the press offers enough distortion in its reporting to allow its critics plausible foundation for their allegations. Others, defenders of the faith, become apologists, tracing every example of Israeli miscreance to the original sin of Arab intransigence.

At the same time, there are those who, their fantasies collapsed, feel – and express – resentment towards the erstwhile object of their affection.

At the heart of these assorted reactions and distortions lies the principal legacy of the Six-Day War, the continuing Israeli occupation of the West Bank and Gaza. With each passing year and with each new episode of violence it becomes more difficult to rationalize one's way out of the curse of occupation. The stream of reports, the revisionist histories of the early years, cannot be dismissed as quirky iconoclasms; their growing bulk deflates the efforts at airy rationalization. And while most American Jews do not follow such publications, they inevitably affect the tone and content of public discourse, trickling down, as it were, to the popular level. Readers of the morning's *New York Times*, for example, are treated to a lengthy front-page report on the demographic implications of the occupation, a time-bomb that has been ticking for all the years since the occupation but has until now remained a somewhat esoteric bit of information.

The organized Jewish community remains stalwartly and steadfastly a defender of Israel. Its political and financial support remain at their traditionally remarkable high levels. There is little hard evidence of the kind of erosion, whether of support or merely of morale, that these considerations would suggest. Yet the impression grows that the community is no longer quite satisfied to organize Jewish life exclusively around the theme of Israel.

Sunshine soldiers? On one reading, perhaps. But there is another reading: A community that yesterday needed Israel in order to define itself has today begun the work of defining itself in its own terms. One cannot say how much the emergence of an incipient theory of American Judaism owes to disillusionment with Israel, how much to a growing recognition that something very special in Jewish history is happening here. Most likely, the growing understanding that the story of American Jewry represents a significant chapter in the saga of the Jewish people has had its origins in the need to find a more proximate underpinning for this community of nearly 6 million people than classic Zionism provided. No self-regarding Diaspora community could indefinitely get by if it accepted Zionist categories that relegated it to the periphery of Jewish history. Israeli writers like Amos Oz and Hillel Halkin and others might well and passionately argue that American Jews are merely a museum piece, bystanders (or, more politely, ushers, ticket-takers, stagehands, a claque) to the authentic Jewish drama of our time, the drama of Israel. For a time, most American Jews passively accepted that interpretation, those categories. But the increasing tedium of the Israeli drama, which is marked less by daily Entebbes than by conventional pettiness, finally required something more – more indigenous and, therefore, more authentic. Surely, after all, there are more interesting things for a community to argue about than the legitimacy of dissent, as the matter of public disagreement with Israeli policies has come to be called.

CODA

Ours is the first empowered generation of Jews in some 2000 years. Until now, Jews were mostly required to imagine how they would behave if only they were permitted to behave as they chose; their actual behaviour was constrained by the contraints imposed upon them from without. But now, in America as in Israel (obviously in very different ways), Jews are empowered. It is no longer sufficient to excuse our failings by blaming our circumstances. While we ought not, in so interdependent a world, exaggerate the autonomy of our communities, it is plain that our opportunity to be that which we have all along said we would be, if only we could, has been significantly enlarged. So the question that faces Jews, both in Israel and in the United States, is whether there was truth in Jewish self-advertising. When young people ask what it means ιο be a Jew, it is no longer what the prophets wrote that provides the most compelling evidence for the answers; it is how Jews today behave.

It is out of that awareness that a new relationship may, if properly nurtured, grow. In the meanwhile, one witnesses an interaction both liberating and threatening: An American Jewish community slowly develops enough internal strength to be able to let go its fantasies, fantasies born as much out of its own desperate need as out of Israel's propaganda; Israel continues to take its admirers on a roller-coaster ride, from the heights of 'the beginning of the flowering of our Redemption' to the squalid depths of administrative detention. Perhaps all this would have happened even had the Six-Day War not happened. But that is, of course, an idle speculation.

In the aftermath of the Six-Day War, returning soldiers compiled a book of memoirs and essays entitled, *The Seventh Day*. The book attracted an admiring readership, for it appeared to confirm that Israelis are reluctant warriors, who kill only when they must, and even then kill gently, as it were. The book confirmed our image of Israel and, by extension, of the Jews.

It is now, as it was bound to be, the eighth day.

17 The Soviet Jewish Revolution

Zvi Gitelman

The Six-Day War was an unmistakable historical turning point for Israel and world Jewry. Israel survived a deadly serious threat to its very existence and expanded greatly the territories and population under its control. For world Jewry the Israeli victory was an affirmation of the viability of the Jewish state. Jews shared vicariously in the Israeli victory, and felt a sense of pride and vindication which affected their behaviour, not only towards Israel, but also *vis-à-vis* the populations among whom they live as minorities. While this was true also of Jews in the Soviet Union, who are the third largest Jewish population in the world, the war had a different impact on them because they were citizens of the state which supported the Arabs most strongly and was the largest supplier of the physical means by which Israeli Jewry might well have been destroyed. Their own country had directly contributed to a possible second Holocaust. Moreover, they were powerless to change their country's policy and could not even protest it. Many were acutely embarrassed by both these realities – that their country was strongly supporting the effort to eliminate the Jewish state, and that they were impotent to affect it. This was such a trauma for some that they were moved to reject the land of their birth and adopt Israel as their homeland, at first only in their minds, but soon physically as well. For those already convinced that Zionism was the solution to the 'Jewish problem', the war served to reinforce their beliefs; for many others, it awakened them to the precariousness of their situation as Jews, activated their latent discontents and forced them to examine the viability of their status as Jews in the USSR. Even those who did not identify with Israel and saw themselves, now and in the future, as unquestioningly loyal Soviet citizens, were made uncomfortable by the policy of their country during the war and, especially, the powerful anti-Zionist campaign which followed it. Thus, the alienation of some from the Soviet system was reinforced by the war, while for others it was engendered by it. This was to lead to a phenomenon unparalleled in Soviet history and unthinkable before the war: the emigration of hundreds of thousands of Jews, most of whom settled in Israel. The most prominent foe of Israel outside the Middle East, the country from which emigration was virtually unknown, the state in which no Zionist activity was permitted, became the single largest source of *Aliyah* for many years following the war. Moreover, on 10 June 1967 the Soviet Union, expressing its outrage at Israeli policy – really, at the Israeli humiliation of its clients — broke diplomatic relations with Israel, a step which was followed by Yugoslavia and all the countries of the Soviet Bloc, except Romania. This, too, was to have unforeseen consequences over a long term for the Soviet Union and for Soviet Jewry. Thus, while some of the effects and consequences of the war for Soviet Jewry were similar to those experienced by Jewish populations elsewhere, perhaps nowhere else was the war to have as revolutionary and long-lasting an effect as it did in the USSR. To understand why this is so, we must examine the situation of Soviet Jews before 1967, the Soviet Union's role in the events leading up to the war and its position during it, and the consequences of the war for Soviet policy and Soviet Jewry.

SOVIET JEWRY UP TO THE 1960s

In a country which underwent revolutionary transformation, the Jews experienced enormous cultural, economic and social change. In the decade following the Russian Revolution, the traditional Jewish way of life was largely destroyed. The authorities mounted strong campaigns against religion, Zionism, the Hebrew language, and Jewish political and cultural organizations. As a result, these were largely destroyed, with some remnants driven underground. While the long-range alternative to these was supposed to be assimilation into other cultures, the Bolsheviks sponsored an intermediate range substitute, a socialist Yiddish culture which would serve as a bridge between 'bourgeois–clerical' Jewish culture and the universal culture that was supposed to emerge from the mutual 'drawing together' and assimilation of nationalities. But the Yiddish schools, press, theatre, books, and even courts that the state organized and financed proved to be an unpopular alternative either to traditional Jewish culture, still holding the allegiance of the older generation, or to the developing Soviet socialist, industrial urban culture dominated by the Russian language, which attracted the great majority of the younger generation. Neither the Jewish agricultural colonies nor the Birobidzhan experiment solved Jewish economic problems. Nor did they halt the tendency toward acculturation and assimilation. For about twenty years after the revolution, Jews enjoyed great social mobility, unparalleled opportunities in education, culture, politics, the professions and the military – and, for the first time in Russian history, suffered no restrictions or disabilities beyond those imposed on the population as a whole. At the same time, the state actively fought anti-Semitism, which was considered to be only a 'survival of the capitalist past', and the 'Jewish problem' seemed to be on the way to solution. As Jews streamed from the *shtetlech* to the cities, learned Russian and mingled with non-Jews, interest in Jewish culture, in whatever form, fell off, intermarriage rates rose steeply, and Jewish identity seemed irrelevant to many.

The vision of acceptance and integration proved to be illusory. By the end of the 1930s the campaign against anti-Semitism was dead, Soviet Yiddish culture was on the wane, and the heavy hand of terror had stifled even the most innocuous expression of national sentiment or even interest. When, in 1939–40, the USSR annexed Eastern Poland, the Baltic States and parts of Romania, nearly 2 million largely unassimilated Jews of those areas became Soviet citizens. They brought Jewish knowledge, commitment, and practices to a country where these were waning or had disappeared altogether. They reconnected Soviet Jews to their cultural heritage and to developments in world Jewry. Many Zionists among them were imprisoned or exiled, but they managed to communicate their political ideas and convictions to some Soviet Jews.

The Holocaust, which took the lives of about 1.5 million Soviet Jews, dispelled many illusions of national equality and assimilation. Not only did the Nazis single out Jews for 'special handling', irrespective of their Jewish commitments, but segments of the Soviet population proved to the Jews that anti-Semitism survived well into the era of socialism. Jewish disillusionment was deepened by the loud silence which surrounded the Holocaust. Jewish suffering could hardly be mentioned after the war. Jews were accused of having 'fought the war in Tashkent', that is, far from the combat areas, despite the fact that half a million Jews had been in the armed services. To have lost so many Jews to the Nazis and then to be slapped in the face by their fellow citizens was a double blow that awoke many from their dreams of 'friendship of the peoples'.

Shortly after the war yet another blow was dealt to Soviet Jewry, this time from the very top of the system. Joseph Stalin, 'father of all the peoples', initiated a campaign against 'rootless cosmopolitans', which to a large extent, though not exclusively, was directed against the Jews, who were presumed not to have roots in the Soviet Union or any other country. Jews were suspected of disloyalty and were expelled or demoted in large numbers from their positions. The doors to higher education, once a main entrance to upward mobility, swung closed. Jews were eliminated from hierarchies where they were once prominent: the military, Party leadership, secret police, the ministries of foreign affairs and foreign trade, academia, research institutes, editorial boards, and the arts. The purge of Jews culminated in the 'Doctors' Plot' of 1953, in which prominent Jewish physicians were accused of murdering national leaders by deliberate malpractice. They were linked to the Joint Distribution Committee and Western intelligence agencies, emphasizing the supposed connection between Jews and the enemies of the USSR. Only the death of Stalin in March 1953 prevented what appeared to be a major move against the Jews, perhaps including mass deportation to Siberia.

Following Stalin's death, overt governmental anti-Semitism abated, though nothing was done to counter anti-Semitism in society. There was only a symbolic revival of Jewish cultural institutions. Khrushchev mounted a large-scale campaign against religion beginning in 1957, and the number of synagogues declined precipitously due to forcible closures by the authorities. The synagogue was said to be a nest of speculation and economic crimes, linking Jewry to another major campaign of the period, the drive against economic crime. Not only was the proportion of Jews accused of economic crimes higher than that warranted by their numbers in the population, but the proportion of Jews among those executed for such crimes was extraordinarily high. On the other hand, Jews found it possible to enter higher educational institutions once again. They remained excluded from sensitive governmental and Party posts, but science and technology seemed open. The last channel of upward mobility seemed to be in the scientific and technological areas, and Jews went in those directions in large numbers. Nevertheless, it was quite clear to Jews as well as others that they were no longer equal members of society but a tolerated marginal group, excluded from the mainstream and relegated to sectors where they could make a particular contribution.

Khrushchev introduced a major shift in Soviet foreign policy that would also indirectly affect Soviet Jews. Stalin saw the world as divided into two irreconcilable camps, the capitalist and socialist blocs. Khrushchev argued that this was overly simplistic. He identified a third camp of newly-independent states whose allegiances would have to be won in competition with the capitalists. The Arab Middle East was a prominent part of that 'Third World', and, beginning in 1955, the Soviet Union began to reach out actively in an attempt to cultivate the Arab states. One consequence of this policy was a deterioration in Soviet–Israeli relations and an acceleration of anti-Israel and anti-Zionist messages in Soviet media. Israel was identified with the 'capitalist' and 'imperialist' camp, and her claims to being a socialist country were ridiculed. But Jews were learning more about Israel as a result of contact with Israeli diplomats and visitors and with Jewish tourists from the West. Concerts by Israeli performers drew overflow audiences; visiting athletes were cheered on by people who eagerly sought out any visiting Israeli; Israeli participants in the 1957 Moscow Youth Festival were besieged by people, some of whom displayed remarkably detailed knowledge of Israel, while others simply wanted to contact part of that distant Jewish state.

In the mid- and late 1950s the return of Zionist prisoners from camps and exile also contributed to interest in Israel and knowledge of Zionist ideology. The Eichmann trial in 1961 reminded younger generations of the fate of the Jews during the Holocaust. But the single most effective force for the preservation of Jewish identity and the growth of national consciousness was social and governmental anti-Semitism. The Soviet authorities themselves have done more to preserve Jewish identity through the system of official nationality identification and policies that single out the Jews than any efforts by 'Zionist conspirators' and their allies.

Yosef Mendelevitch, later imprisoned for trying to leave the country illegally, describes how he felt as the only Jew in an elementary school class. He waited 'like a hunted animal' as the teacher went around the room asking students their nationality. '"Jew", I breathed with effort. The whole class burst into laughter. From that point I no longer grew up like an ordinary Soviet citizen and I did not like the Soviet Union'.[1] Alla Rusinek describes her dread each year when on the first day of school each child had to announce his or her name, nationality, and father's occupation. 'She asks my nationality and then it begins. The whole class suddenly becomes very quiet. Some look at me steadily. Others avoid my eyes. I have to say this word . . . which sounds so unpleasant. Why? There is really nothing wrong with its sound, *Yev–rei–ka* [Jew]. But I never hear the word except when people are cursing somebody . . . Every time I try to overcome my feelings, but each year the word comes out in a whisper: *Yev–rei–ka*'.[2] Some children learned early on that they were quite different from all the rest, and that difference was not in their favour. For others, the awakening came later – when denied entrance to a university for which they qualified, or for a job for which they had all the credentials, or a promotion, or a trip abroad. Twenty years earlier, they would have accepted their fate with resignation, but in the 1960s many were determined not to reconcile themselves to such treatment. During the campaign against 'rootless cosmopolitans' the best people could do, even highly placed ones, was to make themselves as inconspicuous as possible. In a time when terror had receded, some reacted by taking the chance and asserting themselves, rather than hiding.

About a decade before the Six-Day War several of the leading Zionist activists in the Baltic had begun to create a new mood of national affirmation by forming amateur musical and dance groups. Jews of several generations began to sing in a choir or meet in small groups to learn Hebrew or discuss topics of Jewish interest. Jews began to go out to the mass graves of those murdered by the Nazis in order to hold memorial meetings. At first attended by only a few dozen, from year to year the commemorations drew larger numbers. People of all ages thus remembered the fate of their fellow Jews and could not help but ponder their own. A different kind of gathering also became popular at about the same time. In the major cities where, at best, one synagogue remained open, young people began to congregate on the joyous holiday of *Simchat Torah*. They turned it into a social and national occasion, where large numbers of Jews could meet and socialize, exchange views, information, or simply telephone numbers. They did not come to pray, largely because they did not know how. They were coming together as a community of fate, not one of faith.

THE SOVIET PRESENTATION OF THE SIX-DAY WAR

The events of the Six-Day War were presented in a highly tendentious manner in the Soviet Union. A Soviet specialist on Israel later explained that Egypt's actions in the Sinai were 'defensive measures', and that Israel had planned her 'aggression' at least six months in advance. Nasser demanded the withdrawal of the UN troops, but 'one of the motives for this request was that the presence of UN troops . . . would give Israel military advantages in the event of an armed provocation against Syria'.[3] Closing of the Straits merely reaffirmed Egypt's 'undisputed sovereign rights to the Gulf of Aqaba'. Moreover, all Egypt wanted to do was to force a 'broad examination of the problems of Arab–Israeli relations at an international forum, and this, to some extent, undoubtedly lay at the back [*sic*] of the restraint displayed by the UAR leaders on the military–strategic level'. It was Israel that insisted on a military confrontation.[4] The absurdity of these arguments and the use of qualifiers ('to some extent') reflect the embarrassment of the Soviets in trying to explain the events as the outcome solely of 'Israel's aggression'.

Soviet authorities very quickly depicted Israel's 'aggression' as part of a larger 'imperialist' effort. The Central Committee of the Party, in one of the first such statements on the war, proclaimed that 'Israel's aggression is the result of a plot by the most reactionary forces of international imperialism, first and foremost the USA, directed against one of the detachments of the national-liberation movement'.[5] Israel's militancy was said to be motivated by the desire for territorial expansion and to protect the interests of the oil companies (!). Other Soviet commentators cited Israel's desire to topple 'progressive' regimes in Syria and Egypt and move other Arab states closer to the West.[6] The media relied mostly on the Arab press and radio – though they were always careful to point out the source of their reports – and on Soviet correspondents in Cairo and Damascus. Some Western observers assert that the Soviet press did not fully report Israel's victories,[7] but an examination of the Soviet press reveals that the attentive Soviet reader would have no trouble discerning the extent of the Israeli advance and of the Arab defeat. On 7 June, for example, the press reported that Israel had captured Gaza and quoted General Rabin announcing the capture of Jenin in Jordan and of several points in the Sinai.[8] The next day *Pravda* reported that the Egyptian army had 'retreated to a second line of defence', as Israeli tanks were on their way to the Suez Canal and Israeli troops had taken a series of 'inhabited places' in Jordan.[9] E. Primakov, *Pravda*'s chief correspondent in Cairo, reported that same day that Israeli aircraft had bombarded Helwan and industrial suburbs of Cairo and that Israeli warships could be seen around Alexandria.[10] *Izvestiia* that day quoted Reuters on the extent of the Israeli advance in the Sinai and mentioned that Israeli troops had taken 'Old Jerusalem', the Jordanian half of the divided city'.[11] Quite realistic reports were filed by Soviet correspondents about conditions in Cairo and Damascus. *Pravda* reported also the capture of El-Kuneitra and noted that it is

55 miles from Damascus, as well as stating that Israeli planes had bombed Damascus and Homs.[12] By 13 June an *Izvestiia* correspondent acknowledged that 'The Israeli army stands in the Suez Canal region, on the West Bank of the Jordan River, and is on Syrian territory'.[13]

One somewhat difficult task for the media was to explain the defeat of the 'progressive' and numerous Arab forces by the outnumbered Israelis. A major theme in the explanation was the surprise element, labelled '*blitzkrieg*' in order to arouse associations with the German attack on the USSR in 1941. It was admitted by some that the Israelis were well trained and well educated, though it was asserted that they had 'military men of Jewish nationality from Western armies' to assist them.[14] On the other hand, most of the Arab soldiers were poorly educated peasants. 'This was the big difference. On the one hand was a modern army of invaders under the black banner of colonialist enslavement, an army of fanatics just like Hitler's army was at the beginning . . . while on the other hand, we had an army of peasants and workers, upholding their just cause, peasants and workers who manned tanks and self-propelled guns, but who had not yet mastered them completely'.[15] It was not mentioned where those weapons had come from.

Of course, many Jews did not rely on Soviet sources alone for their information. Any Western or Israeli radio broadcast was listened to with great attentiveness. Alla Rusinek describes how a Jewish couple from Riga found two issues of *L'Express* in their Kiev hotel room, bribed a maid not to confiscate them, and brought them back to Riga where they were translated and circulated widely in *samizdat*.[16] The remarkably efficient system of informal transmission of information that many have noted in the USSR was working overtime among Soviet Jews, who were mining every conceivable source for information about the war. But even one who confined himself to the Soviet media would have had a fair idea of its outcome, if not a detailed one of its conduct, and certainly not a balanced one of its origins.

THE IMPACT OF THE SIX-DAY WAR ON SOVIET JEWRY

The war made a great impact on all Soviet Jews, though its effects were different among different groups. Ironically, it was the committed Zionists who were probably least changed by the war, since it merely reinforced their convictions both about Israel and about the Soviet Union. Hillel Butman, for example, in 1970 a defendant in the Leningrad airplane hijacking trial, had begun his Zionist activities some years before the war, and he does not even mention it in his memoir.[17] On the other hand, Ilya Ehrenburg, a respected member of the Soviet establishment and author of a famous article in 1948, which rejected Israel as a claimant on Soviet Jewish loyalties, saw the war as having a great potential impact on Soviet Jews. He said, in a private conversation, that it was a good thing that the Israelis were not 'exterminated' by the Arabs because 'There is still this unpleasant feeling that it's "natural" for Jews to be massacred. If, following in Hitler's footsteps, the Arabs had started massacring all the Jews in Israel, the infection would have spread: We would have had here a wave of anti-Semitism. Now, for once, the Jews have shown that *they* can also kick you hard in the teeth; so there is now a certain respect for the Jews as soldiers' (italics in original).[18] So even those wedded to the Soviet system could see that the events in the Middle East had a direct impact on their lives in the Soviet Union. As Mark Azbel notes 'The . . . war was the most exciting experience of a lifetime to thousands and thousands of Soviet Jews. None of us thought of anything but the war during that agonizing week. We hovered over our radios, hardly daring to breathe . . . Overnight we recognized how close was the fate of Israel to our hearts'.[19]

This realization was compounded by the recognition that their own country was aiding in the potential destruction of Israel. Mark Dymshitz, born into an assimilated Jewish family, married to a Russian, with children registered as Russians, had encountered anti-Semitism in his work as a pilot. But what turned him into an active Jew was that 'At the very time in which the Egyptian dictator was loudly declaring his aim of destroying Israel, here was my country, the Soviet Union, supporting and arming this would-be exterminator. This shook me. I was powerless to decry this one-sided Soviet stand from within. And then the thought came to me that if I cannot oppose Soviet policy . . . from the inside, I had better leave and go to where I could say what was in my heart, to Israel'.[20] A young librarian in Odessa came to a similar conclusion: 'I understood that I could have no future in the country in which I was born . . . I began to interest myself in everything connected with Israel and friends who felt as I discussed the possibility of leaving for Israel'.[21]

It is an exaggeration to claim that 'Most Jews were awakened as

Jews by the Six-Day War'[22] because, as we have seen, Jewish consciousness had long been stimulated, on one hand, by anti-Semitism and second-class status and, on the other, by positive feelings toward Israel and aspects of Jewish culture. What did happen was that in the month before the war many Soviet Jews realized how endangered the Jewish state was, and how much their own country had contributed to that danger. During and after the war their pride in being Jewish, and thus being associated with Israel, was increased tremendously. A sixteen-year-old girl at the time recalls that 'We were changed completely . . . I remember coming to class the morning after hearing on the BBC that the Israelis had reached Gaza. There were several Jewish students and we discussed it openly . . . as we had never before dared to do. We felt so exhilarated . . . I felt that I was born just then'. In a family that had 'never . . . exhibited any signs of their Jewishness', a party was made to celebrate the victory 'as if we had taken part in the war ourselves'.[23] Jewish dignity and self-confidence, eroded by years of impotence in the face of discrimination, were restored. Alla Rusinek notes that 'It is difficult to describe how Jewish backs were straightened after the War . . . And the more anti-Israeli articles appeared in the Soviet press, the surer we were that Israel and we were right'.[24] As Mark Azbel comments: 'What a different world it became when the most notable event in one's national consciousness was not the familiar tale of persecution and defeat, but a triumph that would live in history'.[25]

The war had an effect not only on Jewish self-perceptions, but on how non-Jews saw their Jewish neighbours. On the one hand, Soviet Jews were associated with Israel in the minds of Soviet non-Jews and respect for the Jews grew with Israel's victory. Nearly 60 per cent of several hundred Soviet Jewish emigrés questioned reported that non-Jews associated them with Israel.[26] Azbel no doubt exaggerates when he says that 'No pro-Israeli or pro-Jewish propaganda . . . could have done half as much to defeat popular anti-Semitism as this war',[27] but at least temporarily the Jews gained respect in the eyes of their neighbours.[28] In Central Asia, however, with its large Muslim population, hostility toward the Jews rose, as the local populations believed that the Israelis had engaged in an anti-Islamic war and had seized and desecrated holy places. Nearly 70 per cent of Central Asian Jewish emigrés questioned reported that non-Jews connected them with Israel.[29]

The events in the Middle East were given great prominence in the Soviet media, and one could hardly avoid the barrage of excoriation that was aimed at Israel. Meetings to protest Israeli occupation of Arab territory and alleged atrocities were held throughout the country. A review of the Soviet press reveals that no fewer than 260 meetings protesting Israel's 'occupation' were held in Soviet factories just in the week of 10 June, and there were undoubtedly many more such meetings that were not reported in the press. Hundreds of letters were sent to newspapers by groups and individuals protesting Israel's actions. Support was pledged to 'the Arab peoples', though its precise nature was not usually specified. One can easily imagine how Jews felt when participating in such meetings or even just reading and hearing about them.

These meetings were only the beginning of a massive propaganda campaign condemning Israel and Zionism. It is interesting that at this point Jews were not mobilized to express publicly their condemnation of Israel, unlike what became standard Soviet practice in later years. A prominent theme in the campaign was that the Israelis were committing atrocities in the territories they had captured. Prime Minister Alexei Kosygin said at the United Nations that 'atrocities and violence in the captured territories bring to mind the heinous crimes perpetrated by the Fascists during World War Two'.[30] Israelis were accused of murdering prisoners of war, expelling people from their homes, and publicly hanging women and children.[31] The Soviet satirical magazine, *Krokodil*, portrayed Moshe Dayan as a Nazi and labelled him 'Moshe Adolfovich Dayan'.[32]

In late July 1967 a massive anti-Zionist propaganda campaign was launched by the Soviet government and Party. William Korey suggests that its purpose was to identify a scapegoat which would explain why the USSR's clients suffered such a major defeat, and why the USSR itself had not succeeded, through diplomatic means, in forcing an Israeli withdrawal from captured territories. 'Tiny Israel' could not be the explanation for these failures, and so 'the enemy must rather be presented as a hidden, all-powerful, and perfidious international force, linked somehow with Israel'.[33] This was Zionism. There is no doubt that the USSR was deeply embarrassed by the outcome of the war. In some respects, it reacted childishly: it struck out irrationally at forces which had little to do with its defeat, it shifted blame for its own miscalculations on to others, and it conjured up some uncontrollable malevolent force as the cause of the catastrophe. Jonathan Frankel, on the other hand, suggests that the anti-Zionist campaign was a response to 'an essentially internal issue, a crisis even', namely mounting pressure by Soviet Jews for emigration to

Israel.[34] However, Frankel focuses primarily on the campaign in 1969–71, whereas Korey describes a campaign launched immediately after the 1967 war. The two approaches are quite compatible: what may have begun as a campaign designed to explain away the USSR's political defeat and the Arabs' military one in 1967, changed into an 'internal dialogue' of the Soviet government and the Jews. Zev Katz adds to these explanations the possibility that the Soviets wanted to dampen internal opposition to their Middle East policy, counter doubts about it among East and West European Communists, and demonstrate their support for the Arabs.[35] Whatever its motivations, the escalation of the campaign was unmistakable. Whereas in 1967, seven books attacking Israel were published, in 1969 the number rose to ten, and between 1970 and 1974, 134 such books were published, according to one count. In 1967 there were at least 110 articles in the press on Zionism and Soviet Jewry; in 1970, there were 332.[36]

One of the salient themes in the anti-Zionist propaganda was the equation of Israel with Nazi Germany, a theme which had been raised in Khrushchev's time but which was later dropped. As early as 5 July 1967, when Party Secretary Leonid Brezhnev addressed the graduates of a military academy, he said, 'The Israeli aggressors are behaving like the worst of bandits. In their atrocities against the Arab population it seems they want to copy the crimes of the Hitlerite invaders'.[37] A month later, a Ukrainian newspaper sounded what was to become a common theme: 'In essence, Zionism is a species of racism, a variety of Fascism'.[38] An analysis of political caricatures in the Soviet press concludes that in *Pravda*, Nazism was linked to Israel more often than to the Colonels' regime in Greece, the Vietnam war, or NATO. 'The parallel with the Nazis was focused almost exclusively on Israel, especially during the summer of 1967 and the winter of 1970. The names of Nazi concentration camps were mentioned solely in an Israeli context'.[39] One of the more virulent 'specialists' in Zionism, E. Evseev, linked Zionism to capitalism, fascism and Israel. Israel's military appetite was said to be whetted by 'the support of an unseen, immense and powerful empire of Zionist financiers and industrialists, which is on no map of the world but which exists and operates everywhere in the capitalist camp . . . In the practical application of Zionism to the affairs of the Near East, genocide, racism, perfidy, aggressiveness, annexation – all characteristic attributes of Fascism – are present.[40] Traditional anti-Semitic images of 'unseen, immense and powerful' empires were combined with the linkage between Zionism and Israel.

The identification of Israel and Zionism with Nazism may have been designed to render concrete, terrifying and repulsive an ideology and a country about which the great majority of the Soviet population had no inkling. If they looked on a map they would have to ask themselves how such a small state could be so successful in defeating so many enemies who were considerably larger. While few Soviet citizens could have any idea of Zionism, all knew only too well what Nazism and Fascism represented. By linking Zionism and Israel to the ideology and country which had caused the death of some 20 million Soviet people, and which had destroyed much of the country, Soviet propaganda was attempting to excite genuine passions among a population who might otherwise have remained quite indifferent to a regional war involving peoples with whom they had little contact and for whom they had little sympathy. Jews were disgusted and enraged by this identification of the Jewish state with those who had murdered 6 million Jews but this, of course, did not restrain the Soviets. While the theme may have aroused more anti-Israeli and anti-Zionist feeling among the population at large – there is no way to ascertain this empirically – it almost certainly reinforced a Jewish sense of alienation and embarrassment at living in a country which could adopt such a position. Thus, just as the events preceding the 1967 war and those of the war itself increased the alienation of many Jews from their Soviet native lands, so did the subsequent anti-Zionist campaign, one which seems to have backfired as far as the Jews were concerned.

AFTER THE TURNING POINT

The 1967 Middle East war triggered the beginnings of a new era in the history of Soviet Jewry, though possibly a short one. On the one hand, the war served as a catalyst activating interest in Israel and Jewishness that had been developing among some Soviet Jews. On the other, it jolted many out of indifference to their own Jewishness. It strengthened Zionists in their beliefs about the impossibility of Jewish life in the Diaspora and the desirability of living in a Jewish State. It convinced people that the State was viable. On these grounds, many began to apply for emigration to Israel, launching a mass movement that was to last for six years, when the emigration movement began to shift direction and head more for the United States and less to Israel. The period 1967–73 became one of unexpected mass *aliyah* from a country which had hitherto allowed only tiny numbers of Jews to go to Israel. It was also a period which saw the creation of a national network of Jewish activists, creating linkages and providing support across the republics, and generating an impressive Jewish *samizdat*, petitions and manifestos. Inspired and instructed in part by the dissident movement, Jews in the Baltics, Georgia, Russia, the Ukraine, Belorussia, Moldavia and Central Asia took part in Hebrew, and later religious, study groups, disseminated information about Israel, and delved into Jewish history and culture.

The effect of the war was compounded for one segment of the Soviet population by the Soviet invasion of Czechoslovakia, slightly over a year after the war. That forceful interference with a process of socialist reform, renewal and the attempt to fashion a 'socialism with a human face' convinced many in the USSR, a large number of Jews among them, that the Soviet system would not tolerate reform, not even in allied states. Many who had pinned their hopes on internal reform abandoned them and joined the growing numbers of Jews who were giving up on their native land and seeking to go to Israel.

As Jews began to emigrate, the number of Jews admitted into institutions of higher education began to decline. Jews also found it more difficult to gain employment or promotion. From the official Soviet point of view, this was only logical: if Jews were potential emigrés, and hence, 'traitors' to their country, why should the USSR educate them, promote them or put any faith in them? Following the war a qualitative change came about in the relationship between the regime and the Jews. It may not have been the result of a comprehensive policy, but it emerged from the actions and reactions of the two parties. It seemed as if the relationship was deteriorating to the point of a final divorce. Reconciliation between the regime and the Jews became impossible, as each side felt injured and betrayed by the other.

A second major consequence of the war, more easily reversed than the first, was the Soviet Union's rupture in relations with Israel. The absence of relations might have reduced the volume of potential immigration to Israel because it made it more difficult for Israel to refute the picture drawn of it in the Soviet media. Perhaps an Israeli presence might have resulted in a few more people deciding in the USSR to go to Israel rather than to the United States, but this possibility should not be exaggerated. What is more certain is that the 'drop-out' phenomenon, wherein Soviet emigrés leaving with a visa for Israel 'drop out' at the Vienna transit point and choose a destination other than Israel, might have been reduced considerably. The Soviets have not permitted direct flights from the USSR to Israel on the grounds that there are no diplomatic relations between the countries. Were such relations to exist, presumably the overwhelming majority of Soviet emigrés would fly directly to Israel where they might have lost their refugee status in the eyes of American law and could not enter the US any more easily than other Israeli citizens, or in any event their encounter with Israel might have induced them to stay in that country.

Finally, in the long run, the USSR's breaking off relations with Israel has constrained some of its roles in the Middle East. While it continued as a major arms supplier to the region, over the years it has found that its ability to play the role of negotiator, go-between and peace maker has been restrained by Israel's logical insistence that states which do not recognize her cannot be expected to play a neutral role in Middle East negotiations.

In addition to its effects on Soviet Jewry and the USSR's role in the Middle East, the war contributed to instability in Eastern Europe. Part of the Czechoslovak intelligentsia was dismayed by the alacrity with which their government followed the USSR in breaking relations with Israel, despite the fact that the sympathies of most of the Czechoslovak people seemed to be with Israel. In November 1967 at a Czechoslovak writers' congress some people pointed to the government's action as an example of its lack of sovereignty, toadying to the USSR, and unresponsiveness to the people. This was one of the expressions of dissent that led to the political crisis of late 1967 and brought the reformist group to power. In Poland, the consequences were different. Painfully aware that substantial segments of Polish society sympathized with Israel during the war, if only because Israel was fighting the clients of the USSR, Wladyslaw Gomulka warned that such sentiments would not be tolerated and if there were Jews whose loyalties were divided between Poland and Israel – and he asserted that there were – they had better leave the country. The 'Zionist' issue was then seized upon by Mieczyslaw Moczar and other political enemies of Gomulka, who tried to turn it against him by accusing his regime of being shot through with Zionists. Moczar and others demanded a purge of the Jews, which did take place, but their ultimate goal seemed to have been to replace Gomulka with their own group, and in this they failed. Ironically, Gomulka's speech in March 1968 – where he said that Jews in Poland who felt tied to Israel were 'going to leave our country sooner or later' – was reprinted in *Pravda*, triggering hope among some Soviet Jews that socialist countries other than Poland would allow emigration to Israel.

The war moved the Soviet Union closer to the Arabs, and after they broke relations with Israel, the Soviets found that their room for manoeuvre among the players in the Middle East was more restricted. They also found that the Arab–Israeli conflict became a major issue in their relations with the United States, so much so that in the next war, the October 1973 conflict, the two superpowers moved dangerously close to a military confrontation with each other.

The 1967 Arab–Israeli war proved to be a true turning point in several respects, and not only for Israel. In the Soviet Union it crystallized and made visible certain tendencies toward national affirmation and assertion that had been building up in the previous decade. Among some Jews, it brought a shock of recognition that their position in Soviet society was precarious and that, like it or not, they were affected by what went on in Israel. It changed the self-image, the behaviour and the tactics of many Jews in the Soviet Union. It accelerated the tendency toward *Aliyah*, though by the late 1970s that tendency had been transformed into one of *Yetziah*, emigration *from* the Soviet Union rather than *to* Israel. The war changed the USSR's position in the Middle East. The fact that the Soviet Union still has not re-established relations with Israel has influenced the course of the multisided process of attempting to resolve what is one of the thorniest international issues of the century.

Notes

1. Yosef Mendelevitch, *Mivtza Khatuna* (Jerusalem, 1985) 14.
2. Alla Rusinek, *Like a Song, Like a Dream* (New York, 1973) 20.
3. Galina Nikitina, *The State of Israel* (Moscow, 1973) 317.
4. Nikitina, *The State of Israel*, 318.
5. *Pravda*, 22 June 1967.
6. L. Sheidin, 'The Arab Peoples' Just Cause', *International Affairs*, 8 (1967) 40.
7. See *Jews in Eastern Europe*, III (7) (November 1967) 57.
8. 'Ozhestochennye boi', *Vechernaia Moskva* and 'Voennye deistviia prodolzhaiutsiia', *Zaria Vostoka* 7 June 1967.

9. 'Voennye deistviia na blizhnem vostoke', *Pravda*, 8 June 1967.
10. 'Boi prodolzhaetsiia', *Pravda*, 8 June 1967.
11. 'Soobshcheniia o voennykh deistviiakh', *Izvestiia*, 8 June 1967.
12. 'Siriia vedet oboronitel'nye boi', *Pravda*, 11 June 1967.
13. L. Koriavin, 'Na provode-Kair', *Izvestiia*, 13 June 1967.
14. Radio Peace and Progress in English for Asia (13 June 1967) quoted in Yaacov Ro'i, *From Encroachment to Involvement* (Jerusalem, 1974) 448.
15. Ro'i, *From Encroachment*, 449. Nikitina later added the arguments that the Israeli Communist Party had been suppressed, eliminating domestic opposition to the war, and that Israel had used especially brutal tactics, including napalm bombings.
16. Rusinek, *Live a Song*, 259.
17. Hillel Butman, *Leningrad–Yerushalayim, Vekhaniya Aruka Beineihen* (Tel Aviv, 1981).
18. Alexander Werth, *Russia: Hopes and Fears*, 218–19, quoted in William Korey, *The Soviet Cage* (New York, 1973) 124–51.
19. Mark Ya. Azbel, *Refusenik* (Boston, 1981) 214.
20. Interview, *Jerusalem Post*, 4 May 1979.
21. Raiza Palatnik, quoted in Leonard Schroeter, *The Last Exodus* (New York, 1974) 242.
22. Sylvia Rothchild, *A Special Legacy* (New York, 1985) 105.
23. Rothchild, *A Special Legacy*, 52.
24. Rusinek, *Live a Song*, 260.
25. Azbel, *Refusnik* 215.
26. Survey conducted by Zvi Gitelman, Israel (1985).
27. Azbel, *Refusnik*, 216.
28. The identification of Jews with Israel in the minds of other Soviets is illustrated in the following anecdote, widely circulated at the time. A Jew appears in court to complain against a Soviet officer who had attacked him. The accused explains his actions. 'The radio said the aggressors had taken Gaza. Then I heard that they had reached the Suez Canal. Then I turned around, and I saw the aggressor had already reached Moscow. I had to defend our country against the aggressor, so I hit this Jew'.
29. Survey by Gitelman (1985).
30. Quoted in Ro'i, *From Encroachment*, 452.
31. *Izvestiia*, 15 June 1967, quoted in *Jews in Eastern Europe* VIII (7) (November 1967) 77.
32. *Krokodil*, 19 (July 1967).
33. Korey, *The Soviet Cage*, 144.
34. Jonathan Frankel, 'The Anti-Zionist Press Campaigns in the USSR 1969–1971: An Internal Dialogue?' *Soviet Jewish Affairs* 3 (1972) 5.
35. Zev Katz, 'The Aftermath of the June War – Soviet Propaganda Offensive Against Israel and World Jewry', *Bulletin on Soviet Jewish Affairs* 1 (January 1968) 21–3.
36. Benjamin Pinkus, *Yehudai Russiya ubrit HaMoetsot* (Beersheva, 1986) 398–9.
37. *Pravda*, 6 July 1967.
38. *Pravda Ukrainy*, 5 August 1967.

39. Yeshayahu Nir, *The Israeli-Arabs Conflict in Soviet Caricatures 1967–1973* (Tel Aviv, 1976) 81.
40. E. Evseev, 'Lackeys Running Errands' *Komsomolskaia pravda* 4 October 1967, translated in *Bulletin on Soviet Jewish Affairs* 1 January 1968, 29–30.

18 Zionist Ideology in Time of Change
Nathan Rotenstreich

The exploration of the impact of the Six-Day War on Zionist ideology faces two preliminary considerations, one related to the war as such, the other to the presence or absence of Zionist ideology in the post-State of Israel era.

Concerning the Six-Day War, there is justification for asking the question as to why it is considered, both in popular consciousness and in historical awareness, as a pivotal event. The Suez campaign, as it is called – or the *Kadesh* campaign in Hebrew parlance – preceded the Six-Day War. But the former did not give rise to either a broad solidarity of the Jewish people with regard to the State of Israel, nor to a conception of its own position as a turning point in the development of the state and its relation to the Jewish people. Hence the question as to the particular position of the Six-Day War becomes even more pertinent when compared with the aftermath of the preceding war.

It is plausible to assume that, since the Sinai campaign was initiated by a decision of the State of Israel, along with a complicated tripartite agreement between Israel, Great Britain and France, this may have mitigated the tendency to view the war as fundamental from the point of view of the State of Israel and consequently from the point of view of a new interpretation of its position and direction. Indeed, the Sinai campaign did not give rise to new considerations with regard to the very position of the State of Israel and its political orientation.

IMPACT OF THE NEW JEWISH REALITY

The situation is different when we refer to the Six-Day War. That war was a response to a threat, and in this sense it was interpreted in a manner which drew out the points of affinity with the War of Independence of 1948–9. Moreover, wars of independence, looked at comparatively, are a widespread phenomenon, being a common stage in the struggle for national independence. In contrast, the Six-

Day War was a response to an attack on an existing political realm, the State of Israel. It brought to the fore the fact that the Arab world had not adjusted itself to the existence of a Jewish state. Hence it sharpened awareness as to the basic strategic concern of the State of Israel and, at the same time, of the position of the State of Israel within the scope of contemporary Jewish existence outside of it. The war emphasized the place of Israel as the focus of Jewish solidarity, which becomes – and indeed became – more prominent as the focus is threatened physically. Hence the enhancement of solidarity can be attributed to the Six-Day War and mainly to its outcome. The overwhelming victory, militarily speaking, of the State of Israel, has been understood as a new dimension of the reality of the Jewish people, which combines in itself the threat and the victorious response to it.

A second consideration related to Zionist ideology against the background of the Six-Day War arises from a negative angle – i.e., from an absence. There is no Zionist ideology which incorporates in its purview both the background to the existence of the State of Israel on the one hand, and on the other, the presence of Jews in the Western world living in countries in conditions of emancipation – i.e., in states based on human and civil rights.

One could argue that, in the development of the Zionist movement in the pre-state period, there was not – and perhaps could not be – a monolithic Zionist ideology. There were various trends, such as that which stressed the problem of the Jews as the main issue, or that which stressed the problem of the culture of Judaism; there was a trend which emphasized a synthesis between the political and socioeconomic aspects and that which rather placed the emphasis on the dominance of the political dimension of the Zionist aspiration, etc. But what happened following the establishment of the State of Israel, and concurrently with the new character of Jewish life in the Western world, was that there emerged no new ideological formulation which would have placed the reality of the State of Israel within the broad context of contemporary Jewish existence. There is no common awareness of the position of Israel, both as the realization of aspirations and as a point of departure for a new development. Rather, Zionist ideology maintained its classic formulation as it had developed against the background of Eastern and Central European realities prior to the Second World War. No 'old–new ideology' has been formulated, let alone integrated, in the present-day awareness of the Jewish people. The very shift towards solidarity is an indication of that ideological absence; solidarity became not a wellspring of an ideology but a substitute for it.

It is thus important to stress the limitations of any attempt to analyze the impact of the Six-Day War on a formulated or semi-formulated Zionist ideology. Yet because of the direction of the hostility of the Arab world and the victory of the State of Israel in the war, the sovereignty of the state became very prominent in the Jewish world. Appreciation of the fact of statehood, which was implicitly and explicitly present in the political realm, became an even more prominent component after the Six-Day War. The very existence of the sovereignty of the state could thus be understood as an explication of the achievement of Zionism. An achievement, as we learn from history, overshadows its problematic character and shifts the attention from the need for a new analysis to what can be described even as euphoria.

THE ARAB PROBLEM AND PARTITION

When we move to a more detailed analysis, we have to consider two basic facts of the background and content of Zionist ideology as a programme for establishing a Jewish collective existence in the modern era. Collective existence, as a rule, takes the shape of a state based in a population which lives its everyday life within the framework of the state and – deliberately or otherwise – attempts to shape it.

The first fact concerns relations with the Arabs. There is a widely accepted view that Zionism neglected the Arab problem and that it has had to pay the price for that lack of awareness and the lack of lessons drawn. One may wonder whether this assertion is correct since we find from the beginning of the new waves of settlement in the Land of Israel expressions of the lesson to be learned from the encounter of the Arab population in the land – as we can see in Professor Yosef Gorny's book – *Zionism and the Arabs – 1882–1948.*[1]

Yet it is possible to say that what developed within the history of Zionism is a distinction between awareness of the Arab problem on the one hand, and, on the other, attempts to solve it collectively, which is to say politically as well. This difference between the two aspects of the encounter is to be seen as an expression of a certain position, whether formulated explicitly or not: namely, that as long as Zionism, representing the Jewish people, was not realized in the political realm in a way that would express the collective existence of the Jewish people, it would be unable to come to grips with the Arab problem and formulate – let alone agree to – a reasonable solution to it. The hard core of the controversy between the Zionist mainstream and the *Brith Shalom* movement in the 1930s can be formulated as expressing this basic difference: the approach represented by *Brith Shalom* was to move in the direction of the solution of the Arab–Jewish problem, while the mainstream opinion considered a solution to the Arab–Jewish problem as dependent upon a new status for the Jewish people, to be expressed in a Jewish state. The second direction led, obviously, to a partial postponement of the solution.

The second issue, related to the first, is the fact that Zionism agreed to the partition of the Land of Israel and hence to the establishment of two states in Palestine west of the Jordan river. Zionism – the majority of Zionists – had already accepted this attitude and solution to the conflict in the 1930s when it was proposed by the British government, and agreed to it again after the Partition Resolution of the United Nations in 1947. The Arab world did not accept partition as a solution and attempted to annihilate the Jewish state before it came into existence and, as said before, at the time of the Six-Day War – that is to say after it came into existence.

What happened in the day-to-day realm and to some extent on the level of ideology after the Six-Day War can be characterised as an attempt by some Jews and Zionists to return to the situation which preceded the partition of the Land of Israel. The reality of removing Jordanian sovereignty over the West Bank, whether this sovereignty had been legal or not, was seen as the point of departure for overcoming Arab sovereignty altogether over that part of Palestine which had not become a part of the State of Israel after 1948. The historical conditions since 1967 have thus been practically and politically interpreted as opening up the vista for overcoming the historical reality first accepted by Zionism in the 1930s and which served as the horizon of its reality until the Six-Day War – the partition of the Land of Israel.

This change of approach may be formulated as follows. The earlier acceptance of the partition of the Land of Israel has to be seen as a manifestation of the basic Zionist awareness that Zionism can be realized only within the given historical context. This is so because Zionism is fundamentally an attempt to posit the Jewish reality within history as it is, and thus to overcome both the retreat from history to the ghetto as well as the dissolution of the Jews into societies and states existing in real history. The attempt to take advantage of the victory of the Six-Day War and the subsequent administration of the occupied territories is to be seen as an attempt to utilize historical circumstances in order to materialize what has been viewed as Messianic expectations, which have in turn been understood as focused on the sovereignty of the Jews over the territory of the Land of Israel. To be sure, there has been here an adjustment to reality too, beause the expectations in terms of territorial sovereignty have been limited to the Western part of the Land of Israel, forfeiting the trans-Jordanian dimension.

From the ideological point of view, it can therefore be said that the impact of the Six-Day War expressed itself in an attempt to bring together the historical dimension of Zionism with Messianic expectation, in which Messianic expectation has been interpreted as relating to territorial sovereignty. At the same time, the holiness of the Land of Israel has been interpreted as related to the space of this land and not intrinsically to the modes of life of human beings – i.e., of the Jewish population within the state.

ZIONISM AND MESSIANISM

From the point of view of historical research, the question is still open as to the relation or comparison of Messianic expectations to the fundamental trend of Zionism: namely, whether Zionism replaced Messianism or whether it is a particular interpretation of it. But what has occurred since the Six-Day War has been an attempt to materialize or realize Messianism within the boundaries of Zionism, interpreting the extension of the sovereignty of the State of Israel – to say the least – as a move towards the Messianic fulfilment. Sovereignty, from the negative point of view, is the overcoming of submission to the gentile world, and has been understood both as a realization of the Zionist expectation and as a realization of Messianism. Zionism, at least in some of its trends, was concerned with an attempt to establish an integrated society expressing itself in the political realm.

In the wake of the Six-Day War, the territorial and political aspects became increasingly isolated from the integrated approach to Jewish reality, as if the political component could be self-sufficient. The problem of ruling over the Arab population was thereby confronted without considering that the extension of sovereignty implied such

rule and the problems co-related with it. Instead of looking at
statehood as expressing human reality, statehood has been viewed
as occupying an independent or even self-enclosed status. This
ideological trend has been the most prominent since the Six-Day
War.

When we look at this development from a broader point of view,
two aspects have to be mentioned. In the first place, we can consider
Zionism in its classical shape as being characterised by a synthesis –
though such a synthesis is always volatile – between an utopian
aspiration and a pragmatic approach to day-to-day reality. This
synthesis led Zionism to many of its achievements. The utopian
expectation, inherent in the very return to the Land of Israel, did
not overshadow the various attempts to take advantage of the
processes of reality and the possibilities or opportunities which these
processes brought to the fore, and provided for the Zionist aspiration
the means whereby it could be realized in a piecemeal way. After
the Six-Day War, the utopian component became detached both
ideologically and practically from the pragmatic one – or, to put it in
a different way, the pragmatic component is no longer a significant
part of a synthesis between utopia and practicality. At the centre of
the dissolution of the synthesis lies the interpretation of statehood
and sovereignty, replacing the interpretation of the relations between
the populous and the political realm.

A second aspect concerns the relation of moral considerations to
pragmatic ones. The negation or the denial of the rights of the Jewish
people, which has been the major motivation of the Arab world in its
hostility to Israel, should not lead to a denial of moral considerations in
the Jewish encounter with the Arab world. The negation of the Jews,
either practically or ideologically, also became the focal point of
Arab nationalism, at least of the Palestinian variety. What Herzl
remarked about a people – that it exists as an entity because of a
common enemy – became paradoxically the focal point of Palestinian
nationalism – which is to say that the Palestinians consider themselves
as a national entity expressed in their rejection of Zionism and the
State of Israel. That awareness grew with the process of opposition
to Zionism and to the Jewish entity embodied in the State of Israel.

The lack of awareness of these aspects of both ideological points
of consideration and day-to-day reality became a negative feature of
Zionism after the Six-Day War. One could say that Zionism has been
swept up by day-to-day reality, without consideration being given to
principles and ideas. But being swept up by that reality means that

one is not in a position of guiding it and directing it towards one's goals.

ZIONISM AND THE CONTEMPORARY JEWISH CONDITION

Another major lacuna in Zionist ideology after the Six-Day War reflects its relations to two major historical events: the shift of Jewish life to the Western world and the existence of the State of Israel.

The conjunction of these two factors brought about a new reality within which Zionism must act and in relation to which a hitherto absent new Zionist ideology must be formulated. The position of the State of Israel and its continuous needs made the State a focus of Jewish solidarity, expressed through the proffering of support and help. This attitude replaced commitment to the State of Israel through day-to-day participation in its existence and its moulding by living within it. Solidarity became a substitute for concrete identification. This trend is continuously enhanced by the lack of an analytical and ideologial approach to the situation of Western Jewry which, of course, is not exposed to persecution; on the contrary, it lives its life in a sociopolitical framework of equality and mobility.

Historically, one could say that Zionism was an ideology seeking to replace the Jews' lack of emancipation with the to-be-achieved auto-emancipation. But once emancipation became a prevailing factor in Jewish existence in the Western democracies, and once Jews became partners in the existence and creativity of the societies in which they lived, the question was posed as to whether Zionism could develop a meaningful ideology that would integrate this new reality. What has, in fact, happened within the broad profile of Jewish reality and Zionism is that Zionism has become an organization and ceased to be an ideology; concurrently, it did not attempt to come to grips with the new situation. Hence the atmosphere of solidarity on the one hand and the lack of ideological analysis and commitment found within it on the other.

The Six-Day War became the focus of Jewish solidarity. Its aftermath did not change this prevailing trend in the contemporary Jewish world. Hence it is essential to ask whether there can be a new ideologial approach to the reality of contemporary Jewish life, an approach which is based on the Zionist presupposition of aiming at the establishment of a collective Jewish existence in the modern

world. That aim was earlier on formulated *vis-à-vis* the Eastern and
Central European Jewish communities as an attempt to provide Jews
with the opportunity to be fully-fledged citizens in a collective Jewish
existence against the background of the lack of such a possibility in
the societies and states in which they lived.

A major change in Jewish history occurred when the Jews in the
West became full citizens in their societies. This situation brought
about the disappearance of the prevailing Jewish commitment to
adhere to traditional Jewish modes of existence. To be a full citizen
also calls for participation in the creativity of the surrounding society.
This new situation brought about a disequilibrium between what have
been traditionally called 'Jewishness' or 'Judaism' (*yahadut*) and
'Humanity' (*enoshut*). The traditional Jewish components in the lives
of the Jews are being increasingly relegated to the status of relics,
and are not prevailing factors of their day-to-day reality. If there is
to be meaning to a Zionist ideology in the present-day situation, it
must come to grips with the fact that the simultaneous existence of
the Jews as individuals and the non-existence of a national Jewish
collectivity no longer pertains. This lack of continuity in Jewish reality
is not accidental – it is the other side of the coin of the immersion of
the Jews in modernity as exemplified in the Western world.

Paradoxically, the feeling of solidarity enhanced by the Six-Day
War and its aftermath did not become a catalyst to the formulation
of an 'old–new' Zionist ideology. It even became an obstacle in the
attempt to formulate an ideological approach, certain individual
voices notwithstanding. Jews pay a price for the position that the
State of Israel has become a focus of Jewish solidarity rather than a
major factor in a reorientation of contemporary Jewish awareness,
especially on the level of the lives of Jews as individuals living in a
Jewish collectivity.

An ideology is not just a sociocultural analysis. Inherent in it is
the direction for its own realization and the demand for realization.
Hence any ideology faces the problem of the motivation of those
who are to realize it. In the preceding period – i.e., before the
Holocaust and the establishment of the state – the pressure to which
Jews were exposed was considered to be the major factor leading
towards the process of Zionist realization. The historical fact is that
many, very many, Jews were exposed to pressure, but only a portion
of them translated this into a motivation for the realization of
Zionism. In the present-day situation there is no pressure stemming
from the outside world – or by and large there is no pressure of this

kind. Hence the motivation has to stem from the ideology itself, or
from the concern for the historical – i.e., collective – needs of the
Jewish people. Experience shows that an ideological motivation of
this sort is to be expected only from a minority.

Notes

1. Y. Gorny, *Zionism and the Arabs – 1882–1948. A Study of Ideology* (Oxford, 1987).

Name Index

Subject Index

Soviet Union – *continued*
  impact of war on foreign policy
    8, 45f
  involvement in peace process 8
  and Israel 8, 19f, 118, 134, 157
  and Israeli political parties 258
  and Palestinians 74
  response to Israeli victory 8, 134,
    286
  support for Arabs xvi, 8, 19, 42,
    46, 99, 117, 135, 285
  and Syria 8, 15, 19, ch. 9 *passim*
  and Third World 142f, 145, 163
  and United Nations 23, 134
  and United States 9, 115, 134
  and War of Independence xvi
Suez Canal 3, 9
Syria xvii
  in Lebanon 13
  after Lebanon war 14f
  military strength 43
  political developments 48f
  Soviet relations with 8, 15, 19,
    ch. 9 *passim*

Taba 17
Tami 186
Temple Mount 22
Terrorism 13, 60, 70, 262, 273
Third World
  attitudes to Israel 7, 152, 156f,
    159, 163f
  Israeli policy towards 155
  and Palestinians 125
  and Soviet Union 142f, 145, 163
Tulkarm 55
Turkey 115, 155

United Nations
  Arab policies in 4
  attitudes towards Israel xvi, xviii,
    ch. 10 *passim*
  Emergency Force 121
  Human Rights Commission 159
  legal responsibilities 3, 212
  as part of events leading to war
    133
  Partition Plan (1947) xviii, 31,
    74, 155, 199, 302

  in peace process 40
  Resolution 242 5, 118, 122, 138,
    156, 159
  Resolution 338 5
  Resolution 3236 (Zionism and
    Racism) 73, 156, 158
  after Six-Day War 23
  Soviet Union in 23, 134
  UNEF 133
  UNESCO 159
  United States and 4
  UNRWA 91, 101, 238
  WHO 159
United States
  Jewish Community of ch. 16
    passim
  and Lebanon War 13
  in Middle East 42, 46f, 99f, ch. 8
    passim
  peace initiatives 14, 15, 19, 46,
    118, 123
  relations with Arab regimes 9
  and Soviet Union 9, 115, 134
  support for Israel 9, 18f, 23, 46,
    156, 248
  in United Nations 4
United Arab Republic 259

Venice Declaration 11
Vietnam 120, 125f, 137, 241
  impact on US foreign policy ch. 8
    passim
Village Councils 66

Wadi Salib 174
Wailing Wall 213
War of Attrition 5, 42, 123
War of Independence xvi
West Bank chs 5, 6, 7 *passim*, xvii,
  economic situation of 236f, 244
  education in 58
  emotional importance of 44
  and Israeli economy 236
  in Israeli ideological debate 25f,
    chs 12, 13 *passim*
  Israeli rule of 6f, ch. 5 *passim*
  in Israeli security considerations
    59